i am free

PATRICIA INGLE

i am free

Mother and Son

Mother and Son

Published 2016
by Mother and Son
Templemartin
Bandon
Co. Cork
Email: info@motherandson.ie
Website: www.motherandson.ie

Copyright @ 2016 by Patricia Ingle

Printed by Lettertec in Cork, Ireland
First Printing 2016
ISBN: 978-1- 911180-26- 5
A CIP catalogue copy for this book
is available from the British Library

Book design by: Orlagh O'Brien

Dedicated to the people left in hospital,
through no fault of their own,
due to lack of funds and initiative

Foreword

This is a book to remind us to take nothing for granted and to capture each day, as it may be the last as we know it. Tricia's days as she knew them pre-injury are over, but the days ahead are full of hope and joy as she proudly signs off on her autobiography and plans the construction of her own purpose-built home in Limerick.

In my experience, the love, support, care, attention and faith of family will never, ever be beaten by the totality of all the world's best human rehabilitation institutions to bring about change for the better. The Ingle family's dedication to their beloved Tricia is, literally, where and how Tricia's emergence from 'locked-in' arose. It is their love and devotion to her which enables her to continue to flourish today against all odds, and proving wrong all those who prognosticated so gravely in the early days.

Tricia is an inspiration in the true sense of the word. She has brought out the best in everyone: medics, lawyers, therapists and all whom she has met on her extraordinary journey. She has shown us all what the human spirit is capable of. She has always been a pleasure to work with.

When I first met Tricia in the High Dependency Unit in the Mid-Western Regional Hospital, I couldn't imagine how she could bear to look to tomorrow, such was the dire situation she found herself in. But Tricia, I now know, was never going to allow herself to be beaten by her injury. She was determined, courageous and tenacious in her will to get home, get better and get going. I never imagined, when I first met Tricia, that she would someday walk, talk, breathe unaided, travel, attend concerts, go on shopping sprees, lecture in and attend at university, manage her own care regime and, most of all, get home from hospital for good. Tricia was incarcerated for some 1,069 days; but now she is indeed free.

Tricia proved me wrong. I thought I knew, when I first met her, what her future held, but she has shown me what real tenacity is. I am eager to see what she is going to do next!

The late great Muhammad Ali has recently been quoted at length. One such quotation I came across caused me to immediately think of Tricia:

"Impossible is just a big word thrown around by small men who find it easier to live in the world they've been given than to explore the power they have to change it. Impossible is not a fact. It's an opinion. Impossible is not a declaration. It's a dare. Impossible is potential. Impossible is temporary. Impossible is nothing."

Susie Elliott
Partner
Cantillons Solicitors
28th June, 2016

Prologue

2008 is a year my family will never forget. In the three years that followed, the 2008 calendar hung on the wall at home, the clocks were never changed, the seasons turning without anyone noticing. Time stood still for my parents and sisters, their lives continuing only through mine, our past a fading memory and our future a terrifying unknown entity.

*

I was finished with secondary school. It was so exciting leaving my schooldays behind (nothing unusual there!) and looking forward to what life had in store for me. A few months after I'd completed my Leaving Cert in Scoil Carmel in Limerick, I saw an advert for a job as pet-care adviser in Petmania, a new pet store opening in the town. Working with animals has always been my dream so I sent off an email to apply for the job. I was delighted to be called for interview. I'd been working with an electrical retailer since I'd left school and the manager gave me a glowing reference, saying I was computer literate, reliable and quick to pick things up. This sealed my chances and I was over the moon when I was asked to start work with the company in November 2007. I spent my first week on a training course in the Waterford branch and then joined the Limerick team in their brand-new store.

I loved having my own money and more importantly my own car, a delightful green VW Polo that I was really proud of. My passion for driving had begun at a very young age: in playschool where I spent more time driving tractors than colouring in pictures!

I was enjoying my first proper taste of independence – driving around, playing dance music and savouring the freedom my car gave me. Earning my own money and being in a position to buy things for myself was liberating. My world seemed limitless. I taught my older sister to drive (not without its squabbles!) and was happy to pay back some of my parents' kindness by providing a taxi service on their nights out.

My friends were a huge part of my life, my evenings and weekends mostly spent with them. I had already caught the travel bug and thoroughly enjoyed family trips to France and Florida, with a list of foreign destinations on my lengthy to-do list.

Looking back, I see how good my life was, how normal things were. Anything and everything held possibility and one day I hoped to realise my ambition to set up a dog-grooming business.

I had a wonderful dog, Cody. He was only little, a Patterdale terrier, black all over. How I adored him! Having a dog of my own was something I had dreamed about, something I had imagined – and pleaded to my parents for – until finally I got him.

But in a cruel twist of fate my little dog and so many other hopes, dreams and ambitions were cruelly taken from me.

*

Life is so different now. What's considered 'normal' has changed significantly for me (and my family), my physical achievements since 2008 a miracle in themselves, yet a long way from the plans I'd been making.

Through no fault of my own, my independence was harshly taken away from me when I contracted a rare disease and became extremely unwell. My father has become adept at managing the array of equipment required to keep me alive. But this has come at the huge cost of his permanent job in the ESB. Now he's at home every day and, together with Mam and my two sisters, he plays a vital part in my fulltime care. I'm sure it's far from the plans he'd been making for how he and Mam would enjoy life once their three daughters were grown up and independent, but he never complains and never shows resentment.

When I first became seriously ill, my parents were told my chances of survival were extremely limited. But, despite numerous grave diagnoses, they refused to give up on me. Mam in particular says she blocked out that piece of information and worried instead about how I'd react to my hair being shaved on one side of my head!

Thank God Mam was right – at least on one point – I did indeed survive. As for my reaction to having my hair shaved, it was significantly delayed. Mam needn't have worried. By the time I regained full consciousness approximately five months after the operation, looking in a mirror was the furthest thing from my mind.

I have survived neurosurgery and defied the odds stacked against me, emerging from a locked-in state of complete paralysis. I'm unable to eat by mouth and am fed instead through a tube into my stomach. I've been left with a shunt in my skull. It still runs from my brain to my stomach. I don't mind if people want to feel it. I also have a scar on the right-hand side of my abdomen. I have no idea why this is there, but again it doesn't bother me. I'm guessing it's from my operation and I'm happy to leave it at that. I don't really want (or need) to find out too much more.

But it's not all doom and gloom.

My determination is as strong now as it always was and I've worked really hard over the last few years to make slow and steady progress. Miraculously, I have managed to accomplish some of what my doctors considered impossible, a few examples being:

being alive,

breathing without assistance for any length of time,

having use of my limbs,

having facial expressions,

communicating,

speaking,

remembering,

concentrating,

understanding,

reading,

laughing,

showing emotion,

walking (admittedly with help),

cooking,

using my iPad,

watching TV,

playing trivia games,

travelling,

going to concerts,

shopping,

voting,

and finally, the most important of all in my opinion, living at home with my family.

But unfortunately there are endless impossibilities too, including the prospect of driving again. There are reasons why I shouldn't and, though it's extremely disappointing and frustrating, I have no option but to accept these harsh realities:

I find it hard to focus on road signs,

I don't have proper feeling in my hands so guiding a steering wheel would be very difficult,

I react fast to things but I'm nervous,

I have problems with balance,

I am ventilator-dependent for a lot of the day and fully ventilator-dependent at night while I sleep,

I am reliant on around-the-clock nursing care.

*

Little did I (or my family) know as I left my home in Ballinacurra Weston on September 1st 2008, feeling very ill and needing to see my doctor, that I would spend 1,069 days in hospital and have to employ an expert legal team to find out the truth as to what happened to me, argue on my behalf and fight for compensation so that I could be released from the confines of hospital to come home to the care of my family.

On the inside I'm the same Tricia I always was, the same Tricia described in this beautiful verse which was so kindly written for me by my brother-in-law's aunt, Caroline Henderman.

P - Patience beyond compare

A - Always so upbeat

T - Through your trials and worries

R - Ready to compete

I - Intensely brave and strong

C - Commencing a new chapter

I - I hope you get what you deserve

A - A happy ever after

And on the outside? Who am I?

Let me tell you my story …

Chapter 1

Patricia Ingle
1st September 2008
Ballinacurra, Weston, Limerick
Leaving home …

Neighbours watch as I'm carried into my father's car. I'm too ill to care.

What is wrong with me? I'm really scared. I've been unwell for a few weeks but I've never felt this bad before. I'm only 19 years old but I may as well be 90! My head feels as though it's going to explode. I've been vomiting for a few hours.

"Don't worry, Tricia. We'll get you the help you need."

Dad's scared too. He's doing his best to hide it but I sense his fear. He's not letting on to me how worried he is, but I overheard him talking to my mam and my sister Kiera as they tried to decide what to do. Should they call an ambulance again? Or would that be a waste? The hospital sent me home last time. But now, the pain is excruciating and I can't stop empty retching. This has been going on for hours. What is wrong with me?

Mam's on the phone to our GP's secretary, giving her an update and asking for advice.

"Tricia's condition is far worse this morning. What should we do? We're really worried about her."

*

I have been feeling unwell for a few weeks, ever since my throat started to hurt really badly at the end of July. My GP has certified me unfit for work on a number of occasions already, but I'm still no better. I'm worse in fact. The antibiotics he prescribed haven't had much of an effect. I also had blood tests to rule out glandular fever. Because my tonsils are inflamed and I have ongoing sore-throat symptoms, he has made an appointment for me with an Ear Nose and Throat specialist at the Mid-Western Regional Hospital in Limerick. The appointment is for this week – the first week in September.

Two weeks ago, around the 19th August, I started getting really bad headaches. I felt feverish and generally off form so I went to the GP's surgery again. My mother came with me and together we explained to a lady trainee doctor how badly I'd been feeling. I was already off work because of my throat and my dad was getting more and more concerned.

"It could be meningitis, Tricia. Is the light hurting?" he asked me almost every day.

But I hadn't noticed the light bothering me. And I didn't have a stiff neck or a rash, the common telltale signs for meningitis.

"Are you eating, Patricia?" the doctor asked.

"Yes, my appetite is okay, but my headaches are excruciating and making me feel really unwell."

"Can you describe these headaches?"

"They travel around my forehead and really hurt the front of my head. I'm hot and tired and generally off form." I also explained how I'd been feeling hot and cold since the night before. My throat was still hurting and I had a mouth ulcer.

After that visit, the GP diagnosed tonsillitis and summer flu and handed me a prescription for Augmentin Duo antibiotics, which I filled at the chemist next door to the surgery.

When we came home that morning, Dad went back to work and my mother told me to go to bed and relax. I duly did as I was told and took the tablets as prescribed. When Dad came home that evening, I was still in bed.

"Feeling any better, Tricia?" he asked, sticking his head around my bedroom door.

"I'm not sure. I can't get comfortable."

"And the headaches?"

"They're not as bad as they were," I told him, noticing the relief on his face when I relayed this to him.

*

The next morning, I became extremely unwell. I'd started vomiting during the night and it got progressively worse as morning approached. I was unable to move. Every time I lifted my head from the pillow, my headache intensified and I started to throw up again. The room spun around. I felt weak, dizzy and hot.

Mam was really concerned and called an ambulance. Dad had already left for work but my mother called him in a panic as I was deteriorating so quickly. He rushed home immediately.

I continued empty retching as I travelled in the ambulance to the Mid-Western Regional Hospital (MWRH). In the A&E department, I was put on a trolley.

"I need to get to a bathroom," I told a nurse. I knew I needed to get sick again.

"Stay on the trolley and I'll get you a dish."

A&E was busy when we arrived at 6.45 a.m. I had to wait quite some time to be examined. I wasn't given anything to ease my distress. My head hurt. I continued vomiting and I was sweating.

"We'll get a doctor to see you shortly," the nurse explained, wheeling my trolley into a cubicle and turning on a fan to keep me cool.

Mam and Dad sponged me down with a damp cloth, rinsing it over and over and placing it on my burning forehead.

Eventually, doctors came and examined me, taking my temperature and blood pressure. "Have you taken alcohol or recreational drugs?"

Not a surprising question, I suppose, considering my symptoms and my age. I shook my head.

Then they asked about my lifestyle.

"I live a normal healthy lifestyle, Doctor," I confirmed and went on to explain how much pain I was in and how bad I was feeling.

"We'll get you on an IV," he said, proceeding to organise a saline and antibiotic drip.

I also remember them taking a urine sample and telling me I had a bug.

"You should be okay in a few days. Stay in bed and take it easy. The symptoms should pass."

Leaving the MWRH shortly after midday, I was surprised to be discharged without a prescription.

I hadn't the strength to walk without help. Mam and Dad supported me as we walked to the car, holding me up between them. But at least the headaches and vomiting had eased somewhat. I went straight to bed when I went home and had a reasonably comfortable sleep that night.

Clinging to the doctor's assurance that I'd feel better in a few days, I was really disappointed when three or four days later my headaches were still there and I needed a damp cloth on my forehead to cool down. That weekend was a blur of headaches and sweating and I was far too unwell to even consider meeting my friends for a drink in our local pub!

When there was still no improvement by Wednesday, the 27th August 2008, I returned to see the GP, my parents accompanying me yet again.

"The headaches are worse now, Doctor. I can't get any relief and to be honest I'm worried. I spent part of a day in A&E last week but I'm still really ill."

"Headaches seem to be going around at the moment," he told me. "One of my earlier patients was suffering so badly I had to give them an injection to ease the pain."

The doctor gave me another prescription – Syndol this time – and explained that I had some sort of bacterial infection that would pass in due course. He also advised painkillers.

Thursday and Friday are a bit of a blur and there was little change. I continued to take the painkillers but got little relief. But Saturday was my sister Kiera's birthday and even though I still felt miserable, I made an effort to celebrate with my sisters and our boyfriends at the Thai Gourmet Restaurant. I looked shocking in the photographs – pale and unwell. I did not drink any alcohol that night at all and I ate very little. My head continued to pound and, though I went on to a bar with the others for a while, I had no relief from the pain and didn't feel able for the disco. This was most unusual for me as I loved dancing.

*

Yesterday, Sunday 31st August 2008, I went to Killaloe for a walk with my boyfriend. We brought Cody with us and I spent a bit of time trying to get him to swim but I didn't have much success. Instead he was more interested in running around and taking off up the hill. I knew he expected me to run after him as I normally would. But I wasn't able. I simply didn't have the energy. We cut the walk short, much to Cody's disappointment.

I stayed in my boyfriend's house but was really ill during the night, vomiting and dizzy and unable to lift my head from the pillow. He was really worried and brought me home very early in the morning.

And now I'm making another visit to the GP's surgery, leaning on my parents and stopping to vomit every few footsteps.

"Let's get her into the car, Pat. I told the doctor's secretary that I'm bringing her to the surgery straight away."

I continue getting sick. It's a relief to arrive outside the surgery. Hopefully they'll give me something to stop the pain and nausea.

"Take a seat in the waiting room."

Mam and Dad are anxious. I feel too ill to be concerned at this stage. I can barely hold my head up.

I'm struggling to stay upright on the chair.

Time ticks on. The waiting continues.

"I need to be sick."

Mam holds me up, carries me really, and gets me to the bathroom just in time. I'm violently ill, hunched on my hands and knees, throwing up into the toilet.

In the waiting room, Dad's patience is running out. "Can't you see her, please? She's vomiting in your surgery bathroom. Her headaches are excruciating."

"Take a seat in the waiting room and Patricia will be seen in due course." The doctor was firm.

Finally, it's my turn but after waiting all this time the GP doesn't even examine me.

"I think your headaches and other symptoms are persisting too long at this stage and you need to go straight to MWRH."

He writes a note for A&E, seals the envelope and hands it to my parents.

"I've mentioned the meds you've been on and how you've been feeling over the last two weeks. I've also asked that they admit you."

Dad doesn't delay and gets me to the hospital as quickly as he can.

I feel worse if anything and barely make conversation. My body is burning up. I need to be sick. We arrive at A&E around 11.00 a.m. and I'm put on a trolley and given yet another bowl so I can vomit. I'm finding it difficult to stay focused. I'm so hot and my head hurts so badly …

The triage nurse examines me shortly after we arrive, recording my temperature at 36.4, my pulse rate at 77 and my respiration at 20. The numbers don't mean anything to me. I'm finding it difficult to concentrate with the heat. My blood pressure and oxygen are also recorded. They ask if I have any allergies.

"None that we know of," Mam replies.

The nurse brings a fan into the cubicle to try and cool me down. It helps a little but I'm still extremely uncomfortable. The vomiting continues. There can't be anything left in my stomach at this stage.

"Here's the doctor to examine you now, Tricia."

He asks me questions and I try my hardest to concentrate and answer him but the pain is so bad. "My head, my head …"

"You'll need a chest X-ray and we'll need to take some bloods." He examines my chest and stomach and instructs the nurses about other tests he wants carried out. "We'll get you on a drip as you seem dehydrated," he adds, checking my neck and asking if it's stiff.

"No," I tell him.

My parents answer his questions about my general health and medical history up to now.

"When she was around two years old, she underwent surgery on her eyes," Dad said. "She had numerous ear infections as a child and eventually, when she was aged five or six, she had grommets put in."

"Anything else?"

"She also underwent some dental surgery and had a bit of trouble with her sinuses when this was going on. But otherwise she was very well and progressed as any other healthy child would. She did very well in primary school."

Dad's pride in my ability is never far from the surface. If I was in the form, I'd definitely tease him at this stage about being his favourite!

"Any other children in the family?"

"Yes, we have two other daughters. Tricia is our youngest."

"Has she ever suffered from migraine?"

"No."

"Anything else worth noting?"

"She was bitten by a rat last year."

"How did that happen?"

"She works in a pet shop. I brought her here for a tetanus injection."

"What type of duties has she in the pet shop?"

"A lot of it is cleaning out fish tanks and cages. They stock a variety of pets and birds. Cleaning the bird cages takes up a lot of her time.

"Do you have animals at home?"

"Yes, a cat and Tricia's dog, Cody."

Dad places a cool damp cloth on my forehead but it's only effective for the shortest time before I burn up again. My sister, Melissa, arrives to see me. She takes over for a while placing the cold cloth on my head. I try to cheer up a little, not wanting to worry my family any more than necessary.

Doctors and nurses come and go, taking the required blood tests and checking my temperature.

"We're still waiting for a urine sample, Tricia," they say, but I shake my head.

Dad continues to reassure me. "You're safe now, Tricia. They'll treat you and you'll feel better soon."

It's difficult to focus on everything. Melissa goes home. Time passes in a blur. A few friends come to see me but I'm not very good company. At around five o'clock that evening, I'm moved out of A&E and transferred to Ward 2D.

There is one other patient in this ward with me and the nurses tell my parents that I'm in the care of the doctor who was on duty when I was admitted this morning.

"Her WCC is elevated to 12.98, with 12.45 a normal reading. Her glucose blood levels are also slightly elevated at 7.2. We're going to rehydrate Patricia and also consider a CT scan, U&E and cervical X-ray."

I've lost count of the number of times I'm given different medicines, dozing in and out of sleep between tests and procedures.

Mam and Dad leave at around 11.00 p.m.

My head still hurts. The comings and goings in the ward make it difficult to sleep and, just as I'm finally asleep, I'm nudged awake again by the doctors. It's after midnight now.

I send Dad a few text messages:

2/9/08 at 00.58 hours – "Stupid doctors woke me up to do a check-up."

2/9/08 at 01.01 hours – "Awake. Was fast asleep. Now crap again."

2/9/08 at 01.04 hours in response to Dad – "No. Glands a bit swollen. I will try to sleep again."

My head feels as though it will burst, the pain is unbearable. The nurses come in and out checking on me throughout the night. I twist and turn but find it impossible to sleep for very long. The pain still kills me even if I move the tiniest bit.

Chapter 2

Patricia Ingle
2nd September 2008
Mid-Western Regional Hospital
Blinding light …

It's September 2nd. I'm glad it's morning. Mam and Dad arrive at around 10 a.m. I'm still being closely monitored and they seem a bit bothered about my GCS (whatever that is). The levels dropped, came back up and now they've dropped again apparently.

I'm definitely worse today. The light hurts. I'm barely able to keep my eyes open and plead with the staff to leave the light off. But even natural daylight is too much for me.

I overhear the medical people talking about me, planning a CT scan.

"Hi, Tricia."

"I must be bad if you're here," I joke, very surprised to see Kiera at my bedside.

Things must be serious! Kiera detests hospitals and always finds an excuse not to visit. She has obviously made an exception for me. I try to show my gratitude by making conversation but the effort is exhausting. I mumble a few words to Kiera, complaining of the heat and grateful when she puts a cold cloth on my forehead.

"It's too bright," I continue to complain, my eyes heavy and difficult to keep open as I struggle to concentrate on the conversation around me.

"The light is already off," Kiera tells me, patting the cold cloth onto my forehead and soothing me as best she can.

Her gentleness and caring nature remind me of how seriously she has always taken her role as my older sister – well, maybe not at the beginning when I entered into the world on 6th September 1988 and stole her place as baby of the family!

*

Born in Limerick Maternity Hospital, I was the third daughter for Patrick and Annette Ingle and little sister to Melissa (6) and Kiera (3). Mam's mother, my grandmother, passed away a few weeks before I was born (coincidentally in the same hospital that I'm in now). It's no surprise there aren't that many photos of me as a baby and sometimes I tease Mam about this, but it's understandable that photos were the furthest thing from her mind after burying her mother.

Mam insists that my sisters were very excited to have a new addition to their family, but right from the first day they couldn't have been more different in the way they welcomed me.

Melissa stepped into typical eldest sister role, treating me as though I were her baby, a real-life doll for her to protect. Kiera, on the other hand, was not a bit impressed that she was losing her place as baby of the family.

Looking back now, I remember a very happy and fun childhood.

We lived at the back of a housing estate in Limerick but, despite it being a built-up area, we felt as though we were cut off from the world. The back garden was a huge oasis. I loved being outdoors with my sisters and friends. We had great fun on the swings and slides and our garden was where we always gathered. We had relatives close by. My grandmother and aunt lived just around the corner and we saw them almost every day.

Birthday parties were tremendous occasions in our house – and still are! Mam and Dad went to great effort every year and threw us huge birthday parties in the back garden. Kiera and I always had a double party as our birthdays are very close, Kiera's on the 30th August and mine seven days later on the 6th September. These were a great excuse for family gatherings and we had loads of cousins and friends to play with. Dad brought the record player out to the garden, ran out of breath blowing up loads of balloons, and then spent his time making sure there were plenty of minerals and sweets to last all day and evening. My aunt, Caroline, acted as DJ and took her role very seriously. She had her own table and chair with a screen around her. It was our very own nightclub! My granny sat in the garden for the entire party, watching the antics going on around her. Sometimes my grandaunt, who lived next door, enjoyed a bird's-eye view from the roof of her kitchen extension, clapping along to the music and taking part in the fun. Kiera and I shared a cake and blew out the candles in turn. The sun seemed to shine every single year and the parties went on for hours.

Mam and Dad always took full advantage of any spells of good summer weather, taking us periwinkle-picking, and on trips to the beach. I was absolutely terrified of seaweed! The day we went to the Cliffs of Moher, Kiera and I were looking over the edge and poor Dad was terrified!

*

I have lovely memories from two family holidays, one in Paris in 2004 and another in Florida in 2005. Disneyland Paris was my first holiday in a warm climate and it was such a novelty to wear shorts and T-shirts without having to worry about the weather. We stayed in Sequoia Lodge on the grounds of Euro Disney. It was only a ten-minute walk to the theme park. Our room had two double beds. I shared with Kiera, and Mam and Dad shared the other bed. Mam's snoring kept us awake at night.

I loved the park but not the roller-coasters or the fast rides. Spinning around on a carousel terrified me when I was just four years old. That frightening experience turned me off for life. It twirled far too fast and though I cried to get off and screamed at the man in charge to slow it down or stop, it kept going around and around. By the time it ended, I was almost hanging off and the terror I felt is as real now as it was then.

But skipping the rides didn't ruin my fun in Disneyland Paris. The castle lit up, it was magical. The car stunt show was another experience I really enjoyed. The Disney parade is a very special memory, in particular when Dad shook hands with Mickey Mouse. Minnie Mouse got in on the act and gave Dad a kiss but she was very flirty so we pulled him away!

Annette's Diner was one of our favourite restaurants in Euro Disney and, Annette being Mam's name, she was all excited and made sure we went there as often as possible. We got her a T-shirt with the diner's logo on it on our last night as a souvenir.

We stayed four nights in total and while we were there we also took a trip to Paris city and climbed the Eiffel Tower. Mam bought us hot dogs to eat while we were walking around. We watched the boats going up and down the Seine. There were lots of birds around and I tossed them bread from my hot dog to encourage them to come closer. But Kiera has a fear of birds and was screaming at me to stop encouraging them. It was her turn to be scared.

It was a terrific holiday and I found the city of Paris to be enchanting rather than romantic. This trip was my first introduction to travelling abroad. I knew I had caught the travel bug. There were so many places I wanted to see but little did I know then how things would change …

*

"Tricia, open your eyes. You have more visitors."

Mam's voice brings me back to the present and reluctantly I let my holiday memories go.

My boyfriend and a few of my close friends are here. I raise my hand and smile. I don't want to be rude but I haven't the energy to appreciate their efforts to cheer me up. Their jokes are wasted on me.

"I'm sorry," I say. "Laughing hurts too much."

My father is becoming increasingly worried.

I'm not eating. I can't face food, not even for Dad's sake.

At around 3.30 p.m. I'm taken for a CT scan. Hopefully this will give the doctors some answers so they can stop this headache. The scan isn't a big ordeal and once it's done I'm wheeled back to Ward 2D once more. Shortly afterwards the scan results are phoned through to the ward and there seems to be a meeting between the doctors and nurses. All I can think of is a miracle to take my headache away.

I slip in and out of sleep, aware that my parents and sister are still here.

More doctors come and see me, a lady doctor among them.

"I think I'm going to be sick again."

The nurse offers me something to help the nausea but I shake my head. Nothing seems to make a difference.

At approximately 7.30 p.m., the doctors decide to do a lumbar puncture.

"I'm going to go home," Kiera says.

I look at my parents.

"We're staying with you, Tricia."

"You don't have to have this test today but it will need to be done so we can get to the bottom of your condition," one of the doctors says.

At this stage, I'm willing to take any advice they give and the sooner they find out what's causing how I'm feeling the better. I just want the pain to stop. I give in to the tears I've been holding back, sobbing as I'm taken for the lumbar puncture.

"We'll be right outside," Mam says.

I'm wheeled into the room.

"You don't need to lie flat," a lady doctor tells me as she commences the lumbar puncture.

Nothing could have prepared me for this. The pressure! It's horrific as they draw fluid from my spine. I've never experienced anything like it.

"Do you want us to stop?" she asks when I scream.

"No, keep going," I respond, determined to get through the test if it's going to help me get ease.

Finally, it's over and again I'm wheeled back to Ward 2D and instructed to lie flat, the doctors promising they will see me tomorrow after they've had a chance to review the results.

"I wanted them to stop, Tricia," Mam leans in close and whispers in my ear, stroking my face. "Hearing you in such pain, I wanted to rush in there and tell them to leave you alone."

Another day passes. I've received various medications, orally and intravenously, and still I feel as though my head is being crushed by a sledgehammer.

I'm spending a second night in hospital with this unbearable headache for company. Throughout the night, I'm examined numerous times. Doctors and nurses talk in loud whispers around my bed. I'm sure I hear the word meningitis being mentioned. Could meningitis take this long to diagnose? I've been sick for weeks now! Could it really take that long to figure out what's causing me to feel so ill if it's something as commonplace as meningitis?

Medication drops into my bloodstream through the IV line, its inability to hit its target (my head!) evident by the incessant throbbing inside my skull. Please make it stop!

To fight against the pain, I grasp at another holiday memory, wishing I had a time machine to return to the magicial world of Disneyland.

*

After the fun we had in Disneyland Paris, Mam and Dad saved up and brought us to visit Walt Disney World Florida in October 2005. I will never forget the burst of heat and humidity that hit us when we came off the plane.

Hiring a car at the airport was a funny memory as Dad had never driven an automatic and, before he dared approach the highway, he drove around and around the airport car park to practise a little before venturing onto the road and following the directions to our villa.

It took us a little while to find where we were staying as the front of the complex was still under construction and we didn't realise our villa was at the back. And, despite Dad's bit of 'driving practice', he managed to back the car into a ditch when he was reversing after we'd taken a wrong turn. It was pitch dark. We got out to push the car back on the road and soon we were on our way again. We had driven past our destination a few times before finally realising that's where we were staying.

The villa itself was amazing. It was a gated community and felt very secure. We swam every morning, Dad heading to the pool before breakfast and Kiera and I taking it at a slower pace and enjoying our swim in a more relaxed way.

We were out every day, seeing as much as we could of Florida while we were there.

We went to dinner shows at nighttime. The Arabian Nights is one that stands out for me, probably because of my love of animals. The horses were amazing.

The Pirate Dinner Adventure Show was another we went to see. Dad got involved in the show and it made our night even more enjoyable and special. He had paid extra money to get us front-row seats. The ship was anchored in an indoor lagoon with amazing lighting that created the illusion of the night sky. There were other ships around it and that's where we sat in the audience.

We had a long table, with our own server. Our drinks were served in goblets. The show was superb. Dad played the part of a pirate. The actors came off the boat and interacted with the audience and everyone got involved in the fun. It's another very special memory.

Shopping played a big part in our trip to Orlando and we visited loads of malls on our way to Disneyland Park. We also called to a number of factory-outlet stores but we found them a bit disappointing and not the value for money we were expecting.

The day we visited Disney Studio, Mam wanted to go to the bathroom as soon as we arrived. Kiera and I pointed out a sign and told her it would lead her there. We were falling around the place laughing as she went down the steps that led nowhere! Mam saw the funny side of us getting her to follow a Disney prop!

We packed so much into our trip. We went to MGM studios and had our photos taken in beautiful cars. Wet and Wild, Busch Gardens and Discovery Cove were fabulous. I swam with dolphins and snorkelled with stingrays and really enjoyed the bird shows. What an amazing experience!

While I still hadn't conquered my fear of roller-coasters and watched with Mam as the others enjoyed loads of rides, I was brave enough to go on Sky Ride.

We were in a jeep travelling through water. For the most part, the jeep was on tracks but not always. My courage was well tested.

Elephants danced along to the music but seeing them chained upset me. My love of animals and concern for them will always outweigh entertainment.

The size of the turtle is another distinct memory. He was over 100 years old and was nothing like the typical turtle we are used to here in Ireland. He looked like a monster by comparison.

We also went to Ripley's Believe It or Not 'Odditorium' which was a museum of all types of oddities from around the world. I can still remember looking through a porthole and seeing my back – strange to say the very least!

In the evenings we went to Downtown Disney and watched the sunset while listening to the music being played on a big screen in the square. The atmosphere was electric.

For the most part, there was no need to worry about warm clothes or jackets because the weather was fabulous. But we did get to experience Hurricane Wilma as well as a tropical storm during our stay. In the villa where we stayed, we were advised to have batteries, flashlights and a supply of water to hand. We were also advised to move all our equipment from the pool area and bring it inside to the garage. The storm kept us busy!

My sister Melissa and her boyfriend at the time (husband now) were also in Florida. They had arrived before us and were staying in St. Petersburg. They had come up to Orlando to spend a day with us and had planned to travel back by bus. The storm affected public transport and Dad said he'd drive them instead when he thought the hurricane was easing. Despite the visibility being terrible and the journey being a bit of a nightmare, we all travelled down to St. Petersburg in our hired car to drop them back, the journey reminding us of some of the scariest rides in the theme parks!

Other fond memories of our holiday are the raccoons I noticed in the area where we were staying. They passed by regularly, messing with the garbage bin outside our front door. I loved watching them and wasn't afraid – at least not from behind the window!

I fell in love with a frog who hung around outside our house. Kiera didn't like him and refused to go in the door if he was there! He seemed attached to the house for some reason and, even though he moved away from the door at times, he always came back.

It was a wonderful two weeks but like all good things came to an end. We left the magnificent villa and returned home.

But, unknown to us, Mam and Dad were already planning a huge surprise for the following year when I was turning 18 and Kiera was turning 21.

I was in fifth year and Kiera was finished school. They presented us with a return trip to Florida as a gift for our special birthdays. Being on holiday on our own was exciting. We flew from Dublin to Philadelphia and were booked on a connecting flight from there to Orlando.

Taking off from Philadelphia, the plane was on the runway building up speed when suddenly everything shut down, including the engines! The plane moved forward again and once more the engines shut down. The captain's voice came over the intercom. "I'm extremely sorry for this unexpected delay. We will shortly be up and running. It appears our cabin crew forgot to close the doors!"

There was a huge cheer from the passengers and the plane soared into the sky. Kiera clutched me as tightly as possible until the seat belt-sign went off and then she started to relax. The rest of our flight was uneventful.

Relieved to touch down in Florida, we got off the plane and made our way through security and into the baggage hall where we were delayed yet again, this time waiting for around 20 minutes for the bags to appear on the carousel. There were all shapes and makes of luggage going around but no trace of ours. We asked in the Information office and were told it was possible our bags would arrive on the next flight.

"Dad has our hotel destination written on the labels," Kiera explained to them. "We may as well go straight to the hotel, rather than waiting around."

"That makes sense. Your bags will be delivered to your hotel once they arrive."

As we came through the Arrivals Hall, a guy was waiting with our name 'Ingle' on a card. Mam had arranged this as part of our itinerary.

We were booked into the Quality Inn Plaza hotel on International Drive. When the driver pulled up outside the hotel, he checked with Reception that our reservations were in order. It was a relief to hear we were in the right place after all the mishaps we'd experienced so far.

"Our bags haven't arrived yet. The airport has promised to send them on whenever they arrive."

"We'll call you once they're delivered."

We went to our room and the phone rang a number of times, both of us expecting each call to be about our luggage. But it was only the travel reps calling with tour details.

The following morning, we met the Rep and received our itinerary.

"Any news on our bags?" Kiera asked, both of us disappointed when there was still nothing.

We had just got back to the room when the phone rang again.

We looked at each other in hope and Kiera answered, delighted to hear that finally it was the call we'd been waiting for and our bags were downstairs.

Back down to Reception once more.

"I can see our bags behind the desk," I told Kiera, pressing the bell for assistance.

This time, returning to our room with our luggage safely in our possession, we felt our holiday was finally getting underway.

Another Florida hurricane, Ernesto, played havoc with our plans, however. We had intended to visit Cape Canaveral, see a rocket launch and take a boat trip through the alligator swamp but were advised against any of these because of the storm. But Florida had plenty of alternatives and we managed to do something even more exciting. There was a helicopter tour area a couple of blocks down from our hotel. We decided to take a helicopter ride. The experience was spectacular, despite Disneyland being off limits for security reasons. We wore headphones and chatted through them. The pilot could hear our conversation. Apparently there had been loads of reports of helicopter crashes around that time but we weren't aware of that back then. Mam only told us about them when we got home! Our parents were panicking a little while we were away, particularly when they heard about the storm.

Once I had turned 18, I called the Glo Ultra Lounge nightclub to check what the age limit was for entry. They told me that girls were allowed in at 18 but weren't allowed drink alcohol. Boys had to be 21! After a great day's adventuring we got dressed up and went clubbing for the first time in Florida.

Kiera was handed a wrist-band as she was over 21. Not being able to have an alcoholic drink didn't bother me as neither of us were big drinkers. It was more about the fun and music than alcohol. Inside the Lounge, everything glowed – just as the club name implied. After our days in the Florida sun, we were almost glowing ourselves with our golden tans!

Kiera and I found a really good seat where we could relax, liking that particular area and thinking nothing of it. After fifteen minutes, other people came in and sat down, glancing suspiciously in our direction and giving us very strange looks. We had a wonderful night there, starting off by playing a few games of pool and enjoying being chatted up by a couple of Americans.

"Your eyes are like the Emerald Isle," one guy told me, ever so sincere.

I had to hold back the laughter, thinking it was hilarious, almost like something you'd see on TV. Then he passed comment on my Nivea Pearl deodorant, saying he loved my perfume.

"It isn't even perfume," I told him, "just scented deodorant."

I appreciated the compliment at the time but now I don't even like that scent.

After a while, one of the bar servers approached us.

"Can I see your VIP invitations?"

Kiera and I looked at each other. VIP invitations? First we knew of it.

It turned out we were sitting in the VIP area. Then it dawned on us that we had stepped over a rope before taking our seats. We probably should have twigged that the area was reserved. Before moving to a different part of the club, we glanced around for 'VIPs' or celebrities but unfortunately didn't recognise anybody famous.

"Take my number," the 'perfume' guy offered, handing me the napkin where he'd written his name.

Mam still likes looking at the photos of us playing pool in the Glo Ultra Lounge with the guys standing behind us looking on admiringly.

We had a wonderful two weeks in Orlando and made sure to fit in a visit to the theme parks we'd missed the previous year. We were out every day doing different things. International Drive was fabulous and we visited as many places as we could but never made it to the Upside-Down House. We put on henna tattoos, giggling as we decided to tell Mam they were real. Kiera got three in total, one on her shoulder, one on her ankle and one on her hand. I was happy with one and chose a tribal script design that went across my lower back. Kiera fell in love with hers and when we came home she had two rosebuds tattooed on her ankle as a memento of the two of us on holiday together.

*

I let go the beautiful memories as my headache worsens. I can't put up with much more.

Chapter 3

Patrick Ingle – Patricia's Dad
3rd September 2008
Mid-Western Regional Hospital
Fighting for life …

A little before 10 a.m. Annette and I arrive at MWRH. Patricia is now in a room outside the nurses' station for observation. This comes as a bit of a shock. Something obviously happened during the night that put her at higher risk. Speaking to Tricia now, her responses are worrying, not only because they're slow but because she isn't making a lot of sense. It's as if she isn't coherent. She certainly isn't herself.

"Tricia's condition seems to have deteriorated," we say to the staff, but receive little in the way of an explanation in response.

Once again we use a damp cloth to try and cool her down, rinsing it over and over to see if it will reduce her temperature. She's burning up. From what we've gathered, she's receiving morphine as a form of pain relief.

"My head hurts," she groans, her eyes mostly closed today.

Watching her suffering is heartbreaking. And frightening.

A specialist lady doctor is introduced.

"I'm a consultant in infectious disease," she tells us.

She proceeds to examine Tricia.

"We'll continue monitoring Patricia every hour," she says when she has finished.

At around 11 a.m. a throat swab is taken, yet another in a long line of tests and still we receive little in the line of new information. Tricia is very drowsy but at least the vomiting has stopped. Her eyes are sluggish. She is slow to react to the light when the doctor examines her. Lymphocytic Meningitis seems to be the diagnosis from what they're saying at the moment.

The word 'meningitis' sends a shiver down my spine. A terrifying illness. A dangerous illness by all accounts. They're still waiting for the results of so many tests.

Melissa arrives around lunchtime, her face dropping when she sees Tricia.

"Why isn't she speaking?" she whispers to us when Tricia barely responds, making indecipherable noises but nothing close to words. She stays a while, holding her sister's hand and soothing her as best she can. Tricia remains oblivious, barely awake and communicating very little.

The afternoon drags on. At around 3.30 p.m. the porter arrives.

"I'll be taking you for an MRI scan as soon as they're ready for you," he tells Tricia.

"The MRI team will let us know when they're ready to do the scan," the nurse elaborates, "but there appears to be a delay."

Annette and I remain at Tricia's side, our concerns increasing as she gets less and less responsive.

Another hour has passed.

"The fan," she asks yet again, her body soaked in perspiration as she continues to burn up. She's extremely confused.

The porter is still hovering – it's 4.45 p.m. at this stage and still no sign of her being brought to have the MRI. More time passes. Tricia isn't speaking by now, merely moving her eyes when anybody speaks to her.

"Stick out your tongue, Patricia," the doctor asks.

She obeys.

"Move your leg."

She also obeys.

Annette steps outside for a break. I'm alone in the room with Tricia, watching her closely. Seeing her like this is terrifying.

"I'm so hot," she mumbles and I watch in horror as her eyes roll in her head.

I jump from the chair and wave my hands in front of her face. She fails to respond. What's happening to her?

"Tricia! Tricia!" I call her.

Still no response. Is she dying in front of me?

"Nurse, please help! There's something really wrong with my daughter."

The nurse rushes in and sees the condition that Tricia is in.

Her two eyes have rolled into the back of her head. I scream her name. I am absolutely petrified. The nurse presses the alarm button. Sirens scream and lights flash over her bed.

"Tricia! Tricia!"

The doctors rush into the room and I'm ordered to wait outside. I'm clammy and dizzy and close to blacking out.

Annette returns. "What is it, Pat?" she asks, knowing by the look of horror on my face that something terrible has happened.

"She's taken a turn – her eyes were rolling in her head," I try and explain as soon as I come around properly, my heart sinking further as the medical team rush out of the room, pushing Tricia's bed past us.

"She needs an emergency MRI," we're told as they hurry along the corridor, holding a bag over her face to assist her breathing.

We follow them, petrified that she has died when they stop running at the entrance to the MRI unit and start working on her, apparently to resuscitate her.

"She's not breathing," I hear one of the team mutter.

A nurse guides us towards a waiting room.

"What is happening to our daughter?"

"Wait here," she advises, proceeding hurriedly to make us tea.

After she has put the tea on the table before us, she leaves the room, saying, "I'll bring you an update as soon as I can."

I pace the room, feeling like a caged animal as we wait for news. I throw my hands in the air in despair, banging my fists against the walls, barely hearing Annette's voice as she pleads with me to calm down. Eventually my fury eases. I collapse into the seat beside my wife.

Annette and I wait for what seems like forever, both lost in separate grief as we pray for Tricia, both unable to believe that she is in a room fighting for her life.

Later, a microbiologist comes to the waiting room to speak to us. She asks us a number of questions about Tricia, her work in Petmania and what animals she has been involved with.

"Has she been in contact with any foreign animals? Or sick animals?"

All we can remember is a story Tricia told us about a sick rat so we explain the little we know and answer as honestly and in as much detail as we're able. She also received a bite from a rat in December 2007 but the hospital would already have that incident on record as I brought her here myself for a tetanus injection when she rang to tell me what happened.

I'm in a blur, a state of shock, finding it impossible to focus on anything. Annette is stronger, holding it together for both of us. We have no idea how our daughter is doing, what's wrong with her or what caused this.

I hold Annette's hand, trying my best to console her but barely able to get the words out, shock really taking hold of me now.

"I'll let the family know," I say, unable to believe that I'm telling our other daughters and our relations that Tricia is critically ill, her chances of survival hanging in the balance. She was absolutely fine a few weeks ago. She is 19 years of age, I keep reminding myself, clinging to the hope that youth and strength will get her through this horrific ordeal.

"There's something seriously wrong with Tricia," I say to my sister, patching the events of the last few days together as I rush to explain over the phone.

Annette calls Melissa and Kiera, her distress evident despite her attempt to remain calm.

"I think you should come to the hospital. Tricia has taken a turn and it's best that we're all here around her."

*

Nurses bring us regular updates, the most terrifying being that Tricia suffered a cardiac arrest while she was being taken for the MRI at 6.00 p.m.

Another lady doctor arrives and asks us to sit down. More bad news.

"We've done a CT brain scan on Patricia and moved her to the Intensive Care Unit. Our diagnosis at the moment is meningoencephalitis. I'm sorry to say the prognosis is grave."

We stare at her dumbfounded and confused.

"She has swelling of the brain," she clarifies, putting it in layman's terms. "Your daughter is critically, critically ill. Her scans are being sent to the Cork University Hospital. Patricia needs to be transferred for specialist treatment."

"Can they do something for her there? Will she survive?"

"It will give her more time but may not save her."

Annette pales. I'm struggling to focus. Things are going from bad to worse. I look at my wife and feel completely helpless.

Shortly before 8 p.m., things escalate further when we're given another update.

"Your daughter is being transferred to the neurosurgical department in Cork University Hospital. If you'd like to see her while we're waiting for the ambulance, you can come with us to Intensive Care."

Kiera and my sister, Deirdre Greensmith, arrive, understandably shocked and distressed when we explain that Tricia's heart had stopped and she'd been resuscitated on more than one occasion.

"I need to see her," Kiera states.

Annette and I look at each other. At this stage, Tricia is hooked up to a ventilator machine and we're concerned for Kiera as she enters ICU, shock registering on her face as she sees her younger sister attached to numerous wires, lying still in her bed, looking nothing like the mischievous girl we all know and love.

"What's wrong with her? Why is this happening?"

I'm not sure if Kiera asks these questions or if I'm asking them aloud. Or are they merely going around inside my head? Either way, we're not getting any explanation from the doctors on what is wrong with Tricia or how she went from being able to walk and hold a perfect conversation to the state she's in now. I cannot take it all in. How can Tricia be lying in the bed, wired up to a ventilator and not responding? How can this have happened?

I can't stand and watch. I rush out and stumble up the corridor, needing air, needing an escape from the nightmare.

"Pat," Deirdre pleads with me, "please calm down. Your family needs you to be strong. Tricia needs you now."

I hear her through the blur in my head, eventually turning and returning to Tricia.

"Will they be able to do something for her in Cork?" I ask again.

"She needs neurological attention," the doctor replies. "CUH have seen her scans. They wouldn't accept Patricia into their care unless they believed there is something they can do to improve her condition or at least give her more time. Her notes and scans will travel with her. There's a letter going with her giving a full record of what's happened up to now."

He talks some more, the medical terms a foreign language to us but obviously painting a very clear picture for the neurological team in Cork. The letter isn't shown to us. It's quite some time before we hear mention of it again but it reads as follows:

Dear Doctor,

Thank you for accepting the above named patient under your care.

Patricia Ingle was admitted under our care on 1/9/8 with a severe fronto-occipital headache x 2/52, + nausea + vomiting.

She had taken migraleve + syndol for 2/52 with no relief. She had attended A+E 2/52 ago + was given antibiotics and discharged home. All of her bloods on admission were unremarkable, except for increased WBC (12.44) ↑

o/e in A+E she had no focal neurological signs + fundoscopy was normal.

She had a CT scan on 2/9/8 – verbal was marginally enlarged ventricles + decision was made that if she was not improving, a lumbar puncture should be performed.

An LP was performed last night. Opening pressure was 26cm H_2O + headache improved following procedure.

CSF showed a lymphocytic picture with increased protein.

CSF has been sent for viral screen + lyme + listeria, HIV I+II has been sent.

Sample sent for herpes PCR + V_2V.

This morning pt was v. drowsy + headache.

Improved.

GCS 15/15

Neuro exam → ° sided divergent squint

↑ reflexes on both lower limbs

An urgent MRI was booked

Pt had been given acyclivor 600mg/tds (started 2/9, amoxicillin 2g IV, ceftriaxone 2g IV, Vancomycin.) Reviewed by infectious dx consultant ++ neuro consultant.

@ 17.00 – clinically status deteriorated – pt developed increasing drowsiness – GCS 13/15 + severe headache.

Neuro exam → ° eye – "down + out"

Up going plantars

No reflexes on both lower limbs

Anaesthetics were made aware of the above pt earlier in the day in case problems should arise. Anaesthetics were called.

GCS 9/15 + pt complaining that she could not swallow

Urgent MRI

– While at MRI pt arrested

– Losec + ° pupil blown

– Intubated + transfer to ICU

<u>*MEDS*</u>
Domperidone 10mg tds
Diclofenac 75mg bd
IV Paracetamol 1g qds IV
Acyclovir 600mg tds IV
Ceftriaxone 2g IV bd
Amoxicillin 2g IV
Vancomycin 1g IV bd

<u>*PMed*</u>
* *Squint repair at 3 yrs*
* *Recurrent ear infections*

Films have been sent to CUH.

Thanking you …

*

We kiss Tricia goodbye. Deirdre hugs us and wishes us the best as we stand at the door and watch our youngest daughter being moved into the ambulance. What is before us? What is before her?

We barely speak, all three of us terrified for Tricia as we drive behind the ambulance. My concentration is wavering. I lose sight of the ambulance. I take a wrong turn. I stop the car, get my bearings, remind myself of my responsibility to get all of us there without incident. I restart the engine and drive steadily towards Cork, hoping Melissa will arrive safely in her car. And despite covering the distance in the shortest time possible, it feels like the longest journey we've ever made.

Chapter 4

Patrick Ingle – Patricia's Dad
4th September 2008
Cork University Hospital – ITU
From minute to minute …

When we arrive at Cork University Hospital, Tricia is already in surgery. She was rushed straight from the ambulance to theatre where the neurosurgeons were ready for her. The Limerick ambulance drivers and helpers are waiting for us. This means so much to us. They had warned us not to hurry on our way down. They introduce us to a nurse and wish us all the best.

"I'm going to bring you to where Tricia is," she says.

Annette, Kiera and I follow the nurse through long corridors, horrified to see porters pushing a trolley with a coffin on it. Eventually we come to a stop and the nurse shows us into a waiting room.

"Take a seat and make yourselves as comfortable as possible."

We wait for what seems like the longest time, our thoughts and prayers with Tricia. Time crawls by, every passing moment increasing our fear. I stare at the walls.

Eventually, the door opens. A neurosurgeon enters the room. It's too much to take in when she explains that they have tunneled an external ventricular drain – or an EVD as it's more commonly known – into Tricia's brain.

"She's in the ITU, the Intensive Trauma Unit. I'm afraid Patricia is still a very sick girl. We can only take it from minute to minute."

"Has she woken up at all?"

"She opened her eyes after the procedure."

We take comfort in that tiny nugget.

"Can we see her?" Annette asks.

"I'll have one of the nurses bring you in shortly."

A male nurse comes out and introduces himself, explaining he will be caring for Tricia tonight. "Don't be frightened by what you see when you enter."

Eventually, we are brought in to see Tricia.

I'm staring at the girl in the bed. She looks nothing like my daughter.

She's unconscious. She's on a ventilator. Her head is shaved and wrapped in bandages. There's an external drain from her brain, liquid dripping into a bag. I can barely see her for wires! They are coming out of her hands, her toes, her face – everywhere it seems.

Kiera's confusion is evident. "Dad, how is this happening to Tricia?"

I don't have any answers.

"She'll go mad when she sees they've shaved her hair," Annette comments, stroking Tricia's face.

The male nurse is kind and considerate and extremely attentive to all of Tricia's needs.

The night crawls by and, despite willing and praying with all of our might, Tricia remains unconscious.

Throughout the night, the doctors come and speak to us, explaining that Tricia's brain is still extremely swollen, particularly on the right side.

"We'll need to perform another operation."

This isn't good news. The thought of Tricia having another brain operation is horrific and incomprehensible. But I sign the consent forms, willing to co-operate in any way.

"This operation," a doctor explains, "will take part of the bone from her skull and relieve more pressure from her brain."

Within half an hour, he returns with different news.

"We've decided against our original plan as we don't believe it would be of any great value. Instead we'll start her on a course of steroids and insert a shunt into her brain to remove the cerebral spinal fluid."

I hear his words but it's as if he is speaking about somebody else, not my youngest daughter. Looking at Annette, I know she is in similar disbelief.

"We would also plan on removing the EVD tomorrow."

We place her in the hands of the experts and hope they make our daughter better.

The shunt is inserted later in the evening.

"All we can do now is hope for the best that she'll make it through the night," we are told.

Little consolation but we cling to it with all our might, relieved when Melissa arrives safely and we sit in silence through the darkest hours.

*

It's Thursday, 4th September 2008, and Tricia has indeed made it through the night. But her condition hasn't altered. She's still unconscious. Her life is still in danger. We maintain a vigil at her bedside, rotating between the four of us and some close family members. We're still in the same clothes we arrived in, barely able to remember whether we've eaten in the past 24 hours.

Various tests are carried out on Tricia throughout the day. We're asked to leave ITU on several occasions while they take X-rays and scans and do numerous tests.

"We need to confirm whether Patricia has blood flow in her brain," they explain.

"What's the biggest concern?"

"There is a possibility that there's no blood going to her brain. If this is the case, we're talking about total brain damage."

I sign yet another consent form to allow further exploratory neurosurgical procedures. But in our hearts we know we're being prepared for the worst possible scenarios – either she dies or she's brain-damaged. Either way, the Tricia we know has a miniscule chance of survival. Together we prepare ourselves but privately neither Annette, Melissa, Kiera or myself have any intention of giving up on our stalwart daughter. We believe Tricia will survive. Her determined personality will hopefully stay with her now when she needs it most of all. We refuse to imagine a life without her.

*

Another night passes with little if any change in Tricia's condition. We persist with our bedside vigil, losing track of time and merely living hour to hour with Tricia.

On the 5th September, the consultant neurosurgeon in charge of her care asks to speak with the family. A shiver runs from my head to my toes and I'm reminded of an episode from Casualty where the family are brought to a small room to be given the worst possible news – that their loved one cannot be saved.

"We have to be prepared," I tell Annette, Melissa and Kiera before the medical team joins us.

We sit and wait.

The consultant neurosurgeon leads the meeting. "We're conducting numerous tests on Patricia as you know and a number have come back negative – salmonella, C-diff amongst them. Her brain is our biggest concern and we're not witnessing any evidence of brain activity."

I'm hearing what he's saying. My heart aches. I hold Annette's hand, squeezing it tightly as he speaks.

"However," he adds, "the latest CT scan is showing some flow through her brain so we cannot be certain that she is brain-dead." The neurosurgeon continues his update, telling us that an infection has caused incredible swelling to her brain and her white blood count is extremely high. He reminds us that she's still in a critical condition and every hour is vital. He crosses his fingers and tells us to hope for the best.

For the first time, I look at my wife and daughters, my distress mirrored in their faces, but there's also a trace of hope in their eyes as they listen closely to the man in charge of our Tricia.

Annette is first to speak. "What happens now?"

"It's a waiting game. We have to wait and see how Tricia recovers. Give her the time she needs."

"And if she does? What can we expect?"

"It's impossible to predict at this stage. She could be in a vegetative state or there's every possibility of deafness, blindness and an inability to communicate indefinitely."

This is frightening, very, very frightening. But we cling to what he said before that Tricia's scan has shown a slight sign of brain activity. We continue hoping and trusting.

"What is the plan, what should we do?"

"We allow Patricia's brain time to heal. For now, it looks like she has locked-in syndrome and could possibly be facing a life where she may not be able to communicate with the outside world."

The doctors leave. We're left in the room to digest what we've been told.

Annette eases her hand from mine, the imprint of my firm grasp and fingernails dug deep in her skin.

I hadn't even been aware of her hand in mine.

She hadn't been aware of her skin being pierced.

We're both numb.

A hospital chaplain quietly enters the ward, blessing all of the patients and approaching Tricia's bedside.

"Why is this happening to my daughter?" I plead with him. "She's only 19. Why doesn't the Lord take me, a middle-aged old git? I would unconditionally trade my life ten times over to give my daughter the chance to live hers."

The chaplain closes his eyes and prays, making the Sign of the Cross over Tricia and nodding at the rest of us.

I watch him leave through tear-filled eyes, his image blurring as he disappears from sight. Even he doesn't have an answer.

We feel lost. And alone. And scared.

Annette refuses to sit still doing nothing and as usual takes a practical approach and starts planning. "It looks like we'll need some supplies," she says, "as there's no telling how long we'll be staying here with Tricia. Time to go to Penneys to get a few changes of clothes."

Annette and the girls go across the road to Wilton Shopping Centre.

I return to sit with my daughter and wait, wondering how they can even consider shopping for clothes when Tricia is lying here motionless. Again, I sink deeper into despair. Even worse is the sense of helplessness that grips me. There is nothing I can do to help my daughter.

*

The night passes. Nothing changes. Another difficult day dawns.

It's the 6th September 2008. It's Tricia's birthday.

"We're taking Tricia for a brain activity test," a nurse explains, instructing the porters to wheel her out of ITU.

I'm filled with fear at the thought of being separated from her, panic impossible to hide at this stage.

"Please bring Tricia back safely to us," I plead. "Today is her 20th birthday. Please don't let anything happen to our daughter!"

Tricia sleeps through my concern.

The nurse stops and turns to look at me, holding my gaze. "Pat," she reassures me, "we will look after her. We'll bring her back to you as soon as the tests have been done."

Chapter 5

Patrick Ingle – Patricia's Dad
September 2008
Cork University Hospital – ITU
The silence is deafening …

Tests, tests and more tests continue to be carried out on Tricia but there's little in the way of any change in her condition. She makes no response. We're oblivious to the time or the day of the week as the activity in the hospital becomes our life. We sleep on chairs, eat when we remember and wash and change in the hospital bathroom.

On Wednesday 17th September, Tricia is fitted with a tracheostomy ventilator to make her more comfortable. The intubation has made her mouth and tongue extremely sore and swollen.

"We made an incision in her windpipe," the doctor explains afterwards, "to fit the tracheostomy tubing."

"Is this more pressure on her?" I ask, hoping it won't add to her suffering.

The doctor shakes his head. "No. It will relieve the obstruction to her breathing and clear the secretions from her lungs."

On the same afternoon a CT brain scan is carried out and the next day we're asked to sign a consent form to allow them insert another shunt.

The hospital staff, though extremely kind and understanding, are getting concerned about the length of time we've spent sleeping in the hospital waiting area. But this room where we eat and sleep has turned into home for us. Returning to Limerick isn't a consideration we're willing to contemplate.

Tricia's boyfriend is heartbroken, making the trip from Limerick to Cork as often as he can. His parents are equally concerned. They've always welcomed Tricia like one of their own.

Family and friends are feeding our cats at home as well as collecting the post and helping us in whatever way they can. We welcome their company when they travel to Cork to see Tricia. The support is helpful, particularly for Kiera and Melissa who miss their friends (and normality) but still refuse to leave their sister.

A social worker brings us restaurant vouchers. She also comes and sits with us – with Annette in particular as I find it difficult to engage. Annette accepts her support and very much appreciates that, while she isn't offering advice as such, she is sensitive and gentle and a very good listener.

"I'm willing to wait until Tricia decides to wake up from her operation," Annette says. "I believe she'll be up out of her bed, walking and laughing as she always was. That's what keeps me going. That's the image I carry in my mind."

The social worker neither agrees or disagrees but sits and listens and offers whatever advice she can under the circumstances.

*

With the help of the ward sister, the same social worker helps arrange a family room in Brú Columbanus, accommodation just across the road that caters for families with critically ill relatives. Near enough to be back in the hospital in a matter of minutes, it's the best solution for us to continue our family vigil at Tricia's bedside.

Brú Columbanus is where we sleep, the waiting room is where we live when we're not in ITU with Tricia. Annette looks after us all as usual, keeping us in food and clean clothes, even going so far as having a constant supply of hot water, tea and coffee in the waiting room, not only for our family but many other families living through similar distress.

She thinks of everything. She's even bought a laundry basket and clothes-airer and has set them up in the bedroom of Brú Columbanus. If only circumstances weren't so serious, we could probably sit back and laugh about this. But considering we arrived in Cork without as much as a clean pair of socks, we now have a collection of clothes from Penneys and are never without a change. It's different to what we've known but it has become our new 'normal'.

We become acquainted with other families in the hospital who are also waiting for news about critically ill family members. We update each other on progress – or lack of it in Tricia's case – and console and support each other as we go through some of the darkest days of our lives. At times we feel more in tune with these new acquaintances than we do with the life we left behind in Limerick.

*

Days turn to weeks and still Tricia lies there sleeping. We are terrified to leave her in case she slips away. We're so grateful to our employers for their understanding and their patience when we can't face returning to work while she remains in a coma. We don't want her to be alone. We don't want her to be afraid if she wakes up. Our family are a terrific support, making the journey from Limerick and other places to support us. Tricia's boyfriend remains a loyal visitor, crying bitter tears with us, their strong friendship making it impossible for him to stay away for more than a day or two.

"We should be on our way to Florida this week," he reminds us one evening. "Tricia was so excited about it. You should have seen the list she'd made. She was non-stop telling me all the places she'd seen before and she was forever on the internet finding new things she wanted to do on this trip. I'm not sure we would have had time to sleep!"

His words set us off again, tears streaming down our cheeks, the sharp reminder of what should have been very difficult to accept. Instead of exploring Florida and living it up like any other twenty-year-old, she's in a coma and on the flat of her back in ITU. Will she ever get to fly again? Will she ever get to travel? Will she live to get the chance?

"There's a letter from the travel-insurance company," Annette comments, flicking through a bundle of post that Kiera had brought from home one afternoon when she'd had to visit the GP to get a medical cert for work. "No refund, despite how seriously ill she is. So unfair." She puts the letter to one side and proceeds through the others, hoping there aren't any more disappointments.

Unfairness is a common theme in relation to Tricia's illness. Nothing is fair. At times it weighs so heavily on me I can't face talking to people. I don't want to be away from Tricia's side but it's agonising watching her in this state.

I'm struggling with my faith.

Annette has renewed hers.

I'm struggling to believe any higher power would leave our young, beautiful, kind Tricia like this.

Annette refuses to give up hoping.

We're coping in whatever way we can, taking strength in different ways and getting through each endless hour. We watch other families in similar distress, the waiting room an environment of shared support.

"Would you like Tricia to receive healing from the Padre Pio glove?" Annette is asked by one of them.

"I'm afraid we're not allowed to go in to her right now," Annette explains. "It's resting time."

"Are you her mother?"

"Yes."

"I can pass healing through you because you gave birth to her. Would you like me to try this?"

Annette nods. "We'll try anything that helps. It certainly can't do any harm. Thank you."

"What part of the body is her injury?"

"Her head," Annette replies.

The man holds the Padre Pio relic over her head and prays silently, the glove never actually touching Annette.

"Thank you," she repeats when he's done.

Melissa, Kiera and I watch wordlessly.

Thirty minutes later, Annette's head is pounding. "Oh my head," she says, bringing her hands to her forehead. "The pain is running from my forehead to the back of my head."

"Will I get you some painkillers, Annette?" I offer.

"No. If this is the Padre Pio glove transferring some of Tricia's pain through me, I'm willing to suffer for her."

I'd like to believe it is. I'd like to believe the Glove is that powerful. I'd happily transfer every bit of her suffering to me. It's so unfair.

"You'd better take charge of the phone calls, Pat," Annette decides. "The phone never stops. It's best if you answer them. You know what I'm like for talking – I'd be on the phone all night."

I'm grateful to my wife. She knows I'm struggling. She knows I'm sinking inside myself. Talking about Tricia to relations and friends drags me out of myself a little. I try and sound strong as I take call after call, even if I feel like I'm dying inside. People are ringing from everywhere, not only here in Ireland. We have family in Southport, Germany and Denmark. Most of my evening is spent outside ITU while Annette, Melissa and Kiera take turns at Tricia's side.

Annette takes a break when her sister, Caroline, or Melissa's partner's mother, Catherine, come to keep her company.

"They're fantastic," Annette remarks every time they've been with us. "It lifts me when they arrive."

"We can't thank them enough for their support, Annette," I agree.

They stay in Brú Columbanus with us at weekends, keep us company, walking through the lonely hospital corridors in the dead of night with

Annette, making it easier to cope in the eerie atmosphere. Their company is a rescue for Annette. It's a rescue for us all.

On Tuesday 30th September, we're asked for our permission to have a biopsy of Tricia's brain be carried out by another consultant neurosurgeon. We're slow to consent at first, unsure if it's fair to put Tricia through this when there's no guarantee that it will benefit her recovery in any way.

"It's to help us investigate why your daughter's condition has deteriorated."

Trusting their explanation, we sign the consent form and allow samples of Tricia's brain tissue to be sent to a laboratory for examination. Though we ask afterwards whether it reveals anything that may help or explain, we're not given any results. The lack of knowledge or explanation is disappointing and frustrating – not that it would change the situation but it might help us understand why Tricia continues to lie there unresponsive.

Continued efforts are made by the doctors to check her responses. Her sedation is reduced and they shine a light in her eyes to see if her pupils react. I watch the doctors and sometimes nurses running a biro along her leg but still she doesn't move. I try this also at times, willing her to respond and disappointed every time when there's nothing. She continues to lie there sleeping, her silence heartbreaking in the midst of the frantic activity of the hospital trauma unit.

Leaving the hospital late at night, sometimes in the early hours, the lights from Cork Airport and planes flying over strike a chord with me. How can they stay up in the sky without ventilation or props while my daughter lies motionless in a hospital bed underneath, a virus taking hold of her body and mind, and nothing it seems can be done for her?

Chapter 6

Kiera Ingle – Patricia's Sister
September 2008
Cork University Hospital – ITU
A light beaming down …

I will never forget the telephone call from Mam on the 3rd September. I was at home. I knew Tricia was in hospital and that she wasn't well but I didn't see any reason for alarm. And then the phone rang and everything changed in that instant.

"I think you should come to the hospital. Tricia has taken a turn and it's best that we're all here around her," Mam explained, the urgency evident despite her attempt to stay calm on the other end of the phone.

I can't remember my response exactly.

She said my aunt had offered to collect me. I couldn't drive there alone. I was still on a learner driver's permit – not that it would have stopped me only for my aunt's offer of a lift. Mam's words repeated in my head as I waited. 'Tricia has taken a turn.' What on earth was going on?

My aunt stayed very calm on our journey to the hospital but obviously saw I was in shock.

"We're going to get you a sandwich and a drink before you go in."

She probably thought I was going to faint. While I ate my sandwich she told me Tricia was in the Intensive Care Unit. She went into a bit more detail but a lot of it went over my head. It was very medical. I was dreading going in to see her. I have a fear of hospitals. Even when my grandparents were dying I refused to stay. But because it was Tricia, I just had to go and see her. I would face my fears and see my sister.

Before entering the ICU in the Mid-Western Regional Hospital, there's an oval-shaped room. I barely remember walking through this area as every footstep took me nearer to my sister. There were a number of beds, each curtained off in isolation. Tricia was in bed number 3. I didn't recognise her. I still shiver at that thought. I can't believe I didn't recognise my own sister!

She had ballooned out, was intensely bloated. She had wires everywhere, a tube out of her mouth, numerous needles, wires coming off her chest, the finger probe measuring her heartrate and lots more monitors I couldn't take in. I know what they are now but was so scared that first visit as I didn't know what was happening. The tubing coming out of her mouth looked horrific. Looking at the monitors and not understanding the numbers or lines on the screen was terrifying. Her eyes were closed. She was in a coma. My baby sister was in a coma.

I caught her hand in mine but it didn't feel like her hand. It was swollen, bloated. There was no response. She was asleep. Her body looked like a shell hiding Tricia away from me. It was so strange.

Everything was why, why, why? I didn't and couldn't understand it. The nurses were busy around me, preparing to transfer her. I was allowed in for only a short space of time. Though I asked, I wasn't told why she was like this, why my sister looked like this person unknown to us. All I was told was that she had taken a turn for the worse. I didn't even know why she was being brought to Cork University Hospital.

What is strange is that my gran had a similar experience before she died but I didn't want to think of that then.

I remember the ambulance man talking to Dad, telling him they would be travelling at speed and advising him not to drive at their pace. Of course Dad didn't really pay much heed as he (and the rest of us) wanted to get to Cork as quickly as Tricia did. We didn't know whether she would survive or not.

I really wanted to take the wheel from Dad and get there faster. Sitting in the back seat, terrified for my sister, I was trying to process everything that was going on as well as trying to remember where the hospital in Cork was, in case Dad got lost.

Arriving in CUH, we went up to the Maternity Hospital waiting room, not knowing where we were. That part of the hospital was new and at the front and we were in such a state we didn't take the time to look around. It was only when we saw a lot of pregnant ladies – and even then it took a few moments to register – that we knew something wasn't right. We were in the wrong part of the hospital. It felt like such a waste of valuable time, crucial moments that might make us too late.

We hurried out of there and eventually found the A&E department.

Once we told the person on the desk why we were there, somebody came to meet us and brought us to ITU. The ambulance people had waited for us to arrive and wished us all the best for Tricia. All they could tell us was that she had survived the journey.

The whole way down the corridor to ITU, we were following the porters. They were pushing a trolley with a coffin on it. It seemed like a terrible omen and made the walk along that corridor even longer if that was possible.

"She's in theatre now," one of the nurses told us.

This was news to me as I hadn't been told she was going for surgery or what type of surgery. Mam and Dad seemed to be equally in the dark.

When the surgeon came to tell us that they had done everything they could and it literally was minute by minute for Tricia, I went into complete shock. I had a lot of questions but couldn't get them out. I was filled with disbelief. I was numb. I was stunned. None of it made any sense. None of it registered. It felt so long from the time I had last seen Tricia in ICU in Limerick until I saw her again. The wait was endless but the medics had their work to do to familiarise themselves with Tricia, stabilise her and make sure she was as comfortable as possible.

Eventually we were allowed in together – Mam, Dad and me. The rules were broken, all three of us allowed in despite the cardinal rule of only two visitors at any one time. This added to our fear.

I remember going in and getting a massive shock. Everything blurred. My only focus was Tricia.

Mam and Dad were the same. There were no tears. We got strength from somewhere. It's difficult to explain.

I can't remember whether I held her hand. But I couldn't stop staring. Because I'd just found out she'd had an operation, I was afraid to touch her and, even though they told us to hold her hand, it didn't feel right to me.

I remember standing next to Mam and hearing her comment on Tricia's head being shaved. The nurses gave us a funny look but I suppose they're used to the way families react in times like this.

Dad was great. He asked multiple questions about every wire and needle attached to Tricia. A lot of it didn't make any sense to me in that moment. I was still coming to terms with what was going on and trying to piece together the bits of information we were receiving.

Tricia was in a coma. She was unresponsive arriving from Limerick. And now she is unconscious.

We were told by the surgeon that Tricia had briefly opened her eyes following the surgery. She did caution that it mightn't mean anything but we chose not to hear that bit. It gave us hope. We grabbed at any nugget at all that was positive to keep us going, to help us fight. Melissa and I were terrified we'd lose our baby sister. Mam and Dad were terrified they'd lose their baby.

*

Over the last few weeks, I have made the corner of the waiting room my personal space, cocooned by myself and slightly apart from my family. One day I don't go in to see Tricia at all. I can't eat. I need some time alone. I cannot accept what is happening in our family. It's impossible to believe that one day my baby sister is living a normal life and a few days' later she is in a coma and on life support.

I need space away from everybody. I curl into a ball, facing the wall. Eventually I sleep.

Darkness is all around me but in the distance a light beams down. There's a swing with Tricia sitting on it, gliding back and forth. I walk towards her. She doesn't say anything, just looks up at me and gives me a big smile.

I wake up. The dream is a vivid image. Whether it's a sign or not, it helps me decide. I'm not going to waste another moment. Every chance I can, I want to be with my sister. I go and sit with her, determined to spend as much time as possible at her side. I have to fight with my sister. I have to fight for my sister. She cannot do it alone.

My aunt is with us today. "Will you come across to Wilton with me, Kiera?" she asks.

I agree and join her, feeling different in myself and aware that I've crossed some invisible line. I am starting to cope. I am starting to deal with this horrific situation my sister is in.

*

Weeks pass. I keep my resolve to fight with and for my sister. I've taken time off work so I can be here in ITU. I work in a factory in Limerick, the same factory that Mam used to work in. I work with circuit boards. My job is to load components onto machines. It's high risk and I know I wouldn't be able to concentrate. Apart from the risk, I just can't leave Tricia until I know she's going to be okay.

My friends are very supportive. They come to see us when they can, mostly at weekends. Seeing them is an escape in a way. They try to encourage me to go back to Limerick but I can't do it. Though I love to see them and know it's helping me cope, my first priority is Tricia. The only time I visit Limerick is to visit my doctor and get my medical cert for work.

My friends understand and accept whatever choices I make. They don't force me to do anything I'm not comfortable with. They're missing Tricia too. She and I shared a lot of friends.

And while they're willing to understand my situation, I also have to understand theirs. I see already that their lives are moving on while time, in a sense, is standing still for us as we congregate around Tricia in the ITU area of CUH.

Tricia and I have always been close and, now she's ill, my older-sister instinct is kicking in and I want to protect her. But how? How can I reach out? How can we connect?

Music is my passion. I enjoy a lot of singer-songwriters and go to a lot of concerts. Listening to music is helping me get through these difficult weeks and I'm sharing that with Tricia in the only way I know how. When it's my turn to sit with her, I put earbuds in her ears, talking to her and telling her about the music filtering through.

As the weeks are going on, we're settling into a routine. Dad is with her in the mornings and then I'm here in the afternoons, with Mam and Melissa also taking their turns during the day, and all of us there in the evenings.

I enjoy having my time alone with Tricia, telling her what I do if I leave the hospital and filling her in on the music I'm listening to on the American radio station I enjoy. I keep her up to date with new songs and artists, sharing them with her through the earbuds and hoping against hope her hearing is intact.

Tricia has a preference for chart music so I keep her up to date with that too even though I'm not a big fan.

Putting the earbuds in her ears one afternoon, I turn on a new chart song.

Tricia's body jerks. I gasp.

The tones are high at the beginning of the track. Her body jerks again.

"Nurse!"

Has the music brought her back? I'm too scared to watch as she's examined.

But the nurse shakes her head. "An involuntary movement, I'm afraid."

I'm gutted, the briefest glimmer of hope disappearing as quickly as it arrived.

*

It's October 2008 and Tricia has been fitted with a PEG feeding-tube. Mam and Dad are weary from signing consent forms at this stage.

The bandage has been removed from around her head. Her hair starts to grow back. It helps seeing her look a little more like herself.

I speak to her as though she is awake and able to answer back. Every day I ask her to move her hand, hoping some day she will surprise me. I look forward to my visits, never dreading spending time with her and gradually getting used to how things are. When I'm not with her, I'm on the Internet looking at new music, reading the newspapers and the Dlisted website to get celebrity gossip. Tricia loved that site so I've started bringing in my laptop and reading her pieces I think she'd like to hear.

The nurses are great to encourage what's good for Tricia, reminding us to continue telling her what date it is and what's headlining in the news. Whether she hears me or not, I know I can't be doing any harm. One doctor reassures me that nurses have convinced him that patients can still hear even while they're in a coma.

I massage her hands in mine. I've started looking into reflexology and pressure points and applying this to Tricia. The physiotherapists visit her every day and she receives some therapy in bed. But my efforts can't do any harm either and I feel close to her as I try out my techniques.

Music has become a constant part of my visit to Tricia. Choosing one of Ashley Simpson's (who is one of Tricia's favourite artists) new songs called 'Out of My Head', a bittersweet title under the circumstances, I place one bud in my ear and one in hers. I wish she could hear me as I tell her this, knowing we'd have a giggle about the craziness of the situation.

I've played so many songs to her over these days and weeks. Miley Cyrus's 'Fly on the Wall', is another title that strikes a chord as I wish I could be a fly on the wall inside Tricia's mind and understand what's going on inside my sister's body. What is preventing her from opening her eyes and communicating with us? Why is she just lying there? Will it ever be any different?

Chapter 7

Patrick Ingle – Patricia's Dad
October 2008
Cork University Hospital – ITU
Eyes open wide …

On a Thursday night, about six weeks after her operation, I'm sitting with Tricia, willing her to wake up. Her eyes give the tiniest flicker of movement. It's the first time there has been anything.

"Nurse! I think she's trying to open her eyes!"

The nurse runs over and shines a light in Tricia's eyes, chatting to her and repeating her name.

"Suctioning might bring her around a little more, particularly if she needs to cough," she says, setting about the procedure.

But unfortunately it doesn't have the desired effect and Tricia falls back into a deep sleep once more.

"But it's progress if she's attempting to open her eyes – she's obviously more alert," the nurse assures us as Tricia's eyes remained firmly closed.

We sit back in our chairs to watch and wait for the next sign of movement. I wonder if it happened at all. I wonder if I imagined it.

Though we do everything in our power to try and entice her to wake up, it's a few weeks more before she opens her eyes again. It's such a turning point for us after weeks of waiting but it's as frightening as it is exciting in reality. Her eyes are open wide. She stares forward, not appearing to focus on anything. After the months we've been sitting with her while she remains in a deep sleep, seeing her with this strange stare in her eyes is distressing for all of us. She doesn't look like our Tricia. She makes no response to our questions. She doesn't look at us. She's like somebody in a deep trance, staring without seeing.

And now we have a new problem. She won't close her eyes. She can't close her eyes. Doctors examine her, noting the absence of tears. They try a number of things to get her eyelids closed. After a time, her eyes begin to swell. The medical team suggests that she gets a number of injections into her eyelids. This is heartbreaking news. She has suffered so much already. We don't want her to be put through any more. Thankfully the idea of injections is deferred and discussions extend to whether or not Tricia's eyelids would in fact require to be stitched to keep them permanently closed as the situation is so severe. Her eyes are any number of colours, changing from green to red, black, yellow and blue.

To try and protect them, the specialist closes her lids and places surgical patches over them hoping this will help. However, they are removed again as it's impossible to see what's happening behind the patches. And her beautiful long dark lashes are also a hindrance in this instance, a beautiful feature that any young woman would want but are now sticking to the surgical patches and adding to her discomfort. How can life be so cruel?

I stand beside my daughter, look into her eyes. "Everything will work out, Tricia. Everything will be fine." My heart is overflowing. Tears spill from my eyes, one falling right into Tricia's eye! I'm devastated, terrified, scared the tear will damage her eye.

I run out of the room. I can't cope. I can't watch this.

My daughter has no tears. She can't close her eyes. I can't stop my tears falling. I can't keep my eyes open.

A specialist comes to treat her with a series of drops, very concerned about blisters that have appeared. He's excellent at his job but it still takes time. We have no option but wait and hope. Eventually, very slowly but very thankfully, her eyes close over a period of five days and the swelling goes down.

It's ironic that after waiting so long to see Tricia open her eyes, pleading with her to come around and let us know she can hear us, we feel such relief when her eyelids eventually close and she goes back to sleep.

Regularly the consultants ask if we think Tricia is aware. Honestly, we don't know but we choose to believe that she is and we continue talking to her and encouraging her in the hopes she will prove us right. Tricia has always been determined in everything she does and, though it's extremely difficult to imagine what it's like being her right now, Annette and I are hoping her determination won't leave her when she is relying on it most and that somehow her inner strength will bring her back to us.

Now that she has managed to at least open her eyes, we're praying she will come around more with time. But the consultants caution us not to be too hopeful in light of the facts facing us. At present she is locked-in and unable to communicate.

Kiera continues playing music in her ears. We hope she's enjoying this but we don't really have any proof. The weeks drag on. We are understandably weary ourselves but in no way will we give up trying to communicate with Tricia.

The consultant neurologists continually monitor her, pleased when occasionally she opens her eyes for a few moments. We're all relieved when she manages to close them too! As part of the examinations, a female consultant takes a biro and moves it up and down and around Tricia's face and eyelids to see if she will follow the pen from side to side with her eyes. Unfortunately, she fails to respond. By now we're watching and learning from the experts and we use our time sitting with Tricia to make similar efforts to reach her, particularly when her eyes are open.

Taking my lead from the consultant, I try the same thing using my glasses. My heart lifts when I see her eyes move, sinking again when she doesn't repeat it a second time. The situation is so difficult to gauge. At times I think I'm imagining her eyes moving and I stop, take a break and then try again. Not knowing what's going on inside her head is heartbreaking. And frightening. We daren't even contemplate how we'll cope if she never comes out of this state.

But we cling to even the slightest response from Tricia and despite it still being very premature, our whole family take great hope that this is just a first step. If anything it makes us fight and work harder to encourage her out of this locked-in state.

Kiera continues using music to connect Tricia with the outside world.

"What song is playing, Kiera?" I ask.

"Demi Lovato's 'La La Land'!"

The choice of song brings a glimmer of a smile to our faces, the song title a parallel to whatever world Tricia must be living in right now. The lyrics, when Kiera shares them, also have a stark resemblance for us as the singer describes a world where everything stays the same and will never change in the La La Land Machine.

"Tricia will be delighted to hear Demi Lovato is in negotiation with Disney at the moment," Kiera tells us, the mention of Disney transporting us back to the fun and laughter we shared in Paris and Orlando. It seems like a lifetime ago now. I would give anything to hear Tricia laugh right now, to hear her voice break through the silence. Even a smile would be wonderful.

Anything would be better than watching her motionless in her bed for weeks on end. Although I must admit I'm not sure what's more frightening and harrowing – watching her sleeping and not knowing if she will ever wake up or seeing her with her eyes open but locked inside of herself and unable to communicate with her family or the outside world.

*

Time and time again, I use my glasses to test her understanding.

"Tricia, see my glasses in my hand," I say, holding them in front of her eyes and slowly beginning to move them. "I'm moving them now. Can you try – even a little?"

Days go by where we try this and very occasionally her eyes do move but afterwards I'm not convinced. What I'm beginning to notice, however, is that she never does it when there's anybody else in the room. She only seems to move her eyes when we are alone. Looking at my youngest daughter, the trickster in the family, I'm wondering if by any stretch of the imagination she could be playing a trick on me, teasing me from whatever bubble she is trapped inside?

Comforted by this thought, I continue this game (as this is what it feels like by now), holding my glasses in front of her face and gently asking her to move her eyes and follow the movement. Though it's excruciatingly slow progress, she is definitely doing it more often when we're alone and eventually, days or maybe even a week after her first attempt, her eyes follow my glasses when there's a doctor present to see the movement.

I let out a long sigh. It's something at least. I finally have a witness. Tricia seems to hear me. She is able to understand what I'm asking. My daughter is still with us. On some level. It's the encouragement we all need to keep going with our efforts to reach her.

More tests follow and more therapists become involved in Tricia's care. The number of scares we get multiply as Tricia takes apnoeic episodes numerous times a day, the alarms beeping loudly to alert the medical staff that her breathing is erratic. We're rushed outside by the medical team, terrified each time will be the last, our hearts in our mouths as we wait to be called back in. We wait while they work on her, fear palpable when the medics come towards us, our own hearts stopping as we wait for them to tell us whether she's pulled through another of these terrifying episodes. But so far she has made it each time. She continues to fight.

A speech and language therapist at CUH becomes a key part in Tricia's care. She pays great attention to her and focuses on ways for Tricia to communicate. In one of her initial examinations, she detects slight but definite evidence of awareness. She works relentlessly with Tricia, repeating instructions over and over, acknowledging each time she opens and closes her eyes, each time she blinks. She works at a slow but regular pace. She visits Tricia (and us) every morning. This continues for weeks.

"Blink once for yes and twice for no," she tells Tricia.

The therapist encourages her to respond to questions. It takes significant time and weeks of perseverance but eventually Tricia starts to blink to the instruction. But even blinking is unreliable for her and it's difficult to watch when it doesn't go according to plan. Tricia struggles at times to maintain control of the movement and blinks maybe three or four times. Everybody, including Tricia we believe, is disappointed each time this happens.

How frustrating and upsetting this is for her, we can only imagine. The therapist repeats the exercise daily, encouraging and helping Tricia to keep trying. Perfecting the number of blinks is hit and miss but it does improve with time and practice and eventually becomes her first escape from the locked-in state she's had to endure.

And then to my horror at first and then delight, Tricia begins to shake her head, shake it and shake it and shake it. That stubborn streak is coming out. She hates when anything gets beyond her.

Once I get over the fright of seeing her so annoyed, I am over the moon. She has moved her head for the very first time since August!

Melissa is beside me.

"I think Tricia's annoyed, Dad," she whispers. "I think my sister is starting to come out of her shell."

"Let's hope."

The speech and language therapist is equally pleased. "You would wait until the weekend to show us you can move your head, Tricia! Lots of exercises ahead to take full advantage. Your family will be busy this weekend!"

I'm happy to work hard this weekend. I'm happy to work hard any time. I'm happy to do anything to help Tricia keep making progress.

Chapter 8

Patricia Ingle
October 2008
Cork University Hospital – ITU
In the blink of an eye …

I have little or no memory of the period between the 3rd September in MWRH and mid to late October in ITU when my eyelids start to flicker open in CUH. This period in itself is a great source of mystery and interest for me. I enjoy listening to my family telling the story. Seeing how recalling it upsets them gives me an insight into how difficult it must have been for them going through every step of my ordeal with me. I have no memory of being resuscitated at all! But I know I have been. It's not like in the movies.

Hearing that I just lay there sleeping for almost two months is upsetting for me too, I suppose … or it would be if I could remember it!

I have visions of me talking to my family while I was lying in the hospital bed in ITU. I can picture us having real conversations but I know this is mere fantasy on my part, images created from the versions of events I've been hearing. I slept for days at a time. This happened a lot. I would wake for a few minutes and sleep for a few days. It was my body's way of healing itself and I needed that time to get better, despite how frustrating it was for others around me.

I'm not sure what happened throughout that time. I had a lot of dreams, dreams where I thought I was doing things that in reality were impossible for me anymore. I dreamt I was jumping from bed to bed, joining in on conversations with my family, watching full-length movies. And these are just the ones I can remember.

It certainly isn't real because I'm no longer able to speak. I'm no longer able to feel or touch. But I am able to think. At least my brain is alert in some ways. I am able to recognise my family and I fully understand that I'm lying in a hospital bed. How or why I'm like this, I have no idea. And so far, nobody has been able to explain. And for obvious reasons I'm unable to ask.

*

My parents and sisters have stayed with me for the entire time I've been in Cork University Hospital. They haven't left me alone at any time. One of them is always at my side. It must be exhausting for Mam, Dad, Melissa and Kiera. And if I could talk, I'd tell them that! My headaches are gone, thanks to the shunt they've inserted in my brain. I don't feel pain. Then again, I don't feel anything!

It's no wonder my family get so excited when my eyelids flicker. That tiny movement gives them hope that I'm going to come out of this comatose state I've been in. But I dash their hopes almost instantly. I'm still not ready to wake up. The effort to fully wake up is too intense. My eyes close again and I fall back asleep as if nothing happened. It seems I'm not waking up today. The attempts being made to encourage me – talking to me, calling my name, holding my hand, squeezing my hand – are relentless but in vain. It requires too much energy that I simply don't have.

Mam is anxious but willing to wait. She tells me so over and over.

"We can see your eyes flickering, Tricia. Open them when you're ready. We're here with you. You have all the time in the world."

Eventually, after weeks, I lift my eyelids a little, managing to get them halfway open.

"Please come quickly!" Dad calls the nurses. It isn't a call for help but a call for a witness to prove he's not imagining this movement after such a cruel wait.

The nurse is excited too and hurries towards me.

But by the time she arrives at my bedside, I've closed my eyes again.

The nurse calls my name, making numerous efforts to entice me out of this locked-in state. She suctions me but still no reaction. I'm dead (not literally I'm glad to say) to the world. The nurse lifts my eyelids but there's nothing.

Another week on, however, I progress a little further in opening my eyes, this time getting them fully open.

I stare straight ahead, focussing on the ceiling. I can't recall this exactly but my family assure me later that it was not a very pretty sight. To their relief I close my eyes again and relapse into yet another marathon sleep. Once again my family are left wondering what's to become of me.

The weeks that follow see tiny windows of hope. I open my eyes for a few minutes every now and again before lapsing back to sleep for days on end. But finally I manage to open my eyes fully. My parents and sisters are thrilled. After weeks of waiting and watching they finally have reason to believe that I'm still in here somewhere.

But I have another problem. Now that I've managed to get my eyes open, I can't close them. I lie in bed, still hooked up to numerous machines, wires sticking out of me, staring at the ceiling, still apparently in a locked-in state, unable to respond to any activity, with eyes that are fixed on one spot. I continue to stare. And stare. This is particularly difficult and concerning for my family, one of the worst experiences they've had to watch me go through. What seemed like progress has quickly diminished and I'm in a worse state than before.

My open eyes become dry and infected. My pupils start to seep downwards. My eyeballs are floppy and oozing out of their sockets. Dad compares them to egg whites expanding when they're cracked into a frying pan. Mam's terrified they won't revert to normal and I'll be left like this. Melissa is consoling Mam and Dad. I can only imagine how disgusting I look. Doctors and nurses are equally concerned and the only possible solution an ophthalmologist can suggest is to tack my eyes shut to protect against further damage and infection. But luck (if you can believe it) is in my favour, and nature steps in just in time. Moments before the procedure is to be carried out, I close my eyes voluntarily. And keep them shut for a very long time after that.

The ophthalmologist becomes a hero in our family's opinion. Dad is so grateful to him for his daily visits. Sometimes he calls really late at night after he finishes a particularly long shift. He examines my eyes and checks on my overall wellbeing, always asking my family if there's anything else he can do to help.

Kindness and support arrives from all corners. I could set the world alight with the number of candles being lit for me. Relics arrive in the post, some from family and friends and more from people who have heard I'm unwell. Word spreads quickly.

Two of the CUH nursing team travel home to India and call to say goodbye before they leave.

"We won't forget you," they promise. "We are going to climb our local mountain when we get home and make a special visit to the church at the top where we will pray for your recovery."

*

My care continues, numerous doctors and specialists taking turns to investigate. Speech and language therapy becomes a constant in my day once I start to open my eyes. One of my most vivid memories is looking into the most beautiful blue eyes of one of my therapists as she spoke directly to me encouraging me to blink!

The importance of being able to blink is significant and I'm being taught (and encouraged strongly) how to use it as a way to communicate. Slowly (and patiently because I keep falling into long sleeps), the therapists, nurses and my family teach me to blink voluntarily.

They ask me to blink any number of times between one and ten and I do the very best I can. This process is repeated over and over when I'm awake for any period of time. It's difficult for me. Concentrating on the count is exhausting. But the exercise helps me gain some control and my responses improve. I begin to blink the number of times instructed, managing to keep count in my head and helped by whoever is with me as they count out loud. Mam, Dad and my sisters are elated. This little bit of progress means the world to them. Controlled blinking marks the start of my recovery. I'm taking charge of one muscle movement and even more importantly I'm giving a response to those around me.

"It's time to try something more than counting," one of the speech and language therapists says.

"What do you have in mind?" My parents are curious.

"Let's see if Tricia can blink as a way of giving yes and no responses. One blink for 'yes' and two blinks for 'no'."

And so begin rounds of questions as Mam, Dad, Kiera and Melissa (and anyone else who happens to visit) take it in turn to ask me to blink to choose different things, like what 'go-go' I want to wear on my head. They hold up different ones and I blink according to my answer. They ask if I want a particular song played and again I blink once for 'yes' or twice for 'no'.

Over the days and weeks that follow we get into the swing of putting my ability to blink to the best use. My family think I'm fantastic at blinking – but of course I am, seeing as I can't do anything else! But I'm bored with the 'yes' or 'no' game after a while. I'm still unable to do anything other than blink. I can't talk so I can't tell anyone what I'm really thinking. All I can do is answer 'yes' or 'no' and this is extremely limiting. And irritating!

The speech and language therapist gives my family pages of facial exercises to do with me, to try to help me make different facial expressions and get my facial muscles moving again. It's something new to pass the time when I'm awake at least.

"Smile, Tricia," Dad says, his face grim as he watches for even the slightest movement.

"Raise your eyebrows," Mam asks and she can't help smiling – along with anyone else who happens to be watching me at the time – when I succeed in raising my eyebrows. It takes a bit of time to lower them again and I'm lying there with that expression, as though I'm extremely surprised, until I manage to drop my eyebrows into their rightful position again.

It's the strangest sensation not having full control over these movements. But my family praise me highly, telling me how well I'm doing – even when I'm not moving my face at all!

Time goes by and the constant therapy begins to make a difference. I respond a little more and now I'm able to move my mouth into a smile. This makes life a little more fun at least, particularly as I watch staff and visitors pass my bed. Any time an interesting-looking character passes by, I look at my family and smirk. One eccentric type of guy is particularly interesting. He passes by my bed regularly as he visits another patient and every time he does I smile. It gets to a point where when Mam or Dad spot him approaching, his purple hair difficult to miss, they make sure to get me to look so I reward them with a smirk as soon as he's in my line of vision. I think my family will always associate my first attempts at smiling with 'the guy with the purple hair'.

I'm able to move my lips now and am managing to mouth words even though I still have no voice. My poor family have had to take a crash course in lip-reading. It's probably as difficult for them to decipher what I'm trying to say as it is for me to move my mouth! Improving slowly but steadily, I regain the strength to nod my head and the therapists seize this as an opportunity to introduce new techniques.

One day in particular is memorable. I wake up to see loads of people around my bed. Mam and Dad are there as always, as are Kiera and Melissa, as well as a number of doctors. The doctors are checking to see if I know family members, testing for brain function no doubt. They ask me to tell them who's with me in the room. I look around and mouth my response.

I look at my sisters, Kiera and Melissa. I look at Dad. I mouth their names. I look at my mother but I don't say anything. I stare blankly. I don't tell them that I know it's Mam. Instead I pretend I don't recognise her. Shock and disappointment registering on her face, my poor mother bursts into tears and runs from the room.

Dad glances at me closely, holding my gaze until my lips shape a smirk. Shaking his head, he runs after Mam but he's smiling too. He knows I'm joking! He's thrilled that I'm still me, the person I always was! I've been so ill, hanging in the fragile balance between life and death, but I've managed to retain my sense of humour. It has survived intact. Being locked-in, my mind a prisoner inside my head and inactive body, has left little room for fun. Tricking my family is the only entertainment I have left! So I cling on tight.

Mam isn't my only victim.

Weeks pass and on occasion I manage to play a few more tricks. Sometimes when a doctor or therapist comes to examine me and test me on various movements and responses, they're surprised I'm unable to respond in ways they expected or hoped, considering the amount of time elapsing. But my family starts to recognise differences in my responses. They're reading my expressions, watching me closely during these examination sessions and seeing a lot more in my eyes than the unsuspecting professionals.

Colours and alphabet letters are next on my agenda. Honestly, it's like being back in school! Although I can honestly say that learning the alphabet and using colour charts is far more enjoyable and less frustrating as a small eager child than it is as an adult locked inside her own body.

*

Starting primary school wasn't very strange for me as I had been there with Mam when we collected Kiera and Melissa. I was thrilled when my turn finally came to be part of the school scene with my sisters rather than waiting outside the gate.

Dad took me to school on my very first day and Mam collected me. The classroom was set up so that we all sat alone at single desks. Patrick was my best friend in Junior Infants. Mostly I played with Kiera at lunchtime but Patrick also joined in. We were best friends right up to second class when we got our Holy Communion. There's a photo of us together outside the church that morning. Unfortunately, after Holy Communion class, boys and girls were moved on to separate schools and we were split up.

But that wasn't the end of our friendship as he lived close by. For some reason I remember the times he was grounded best. I used to sneak around the back and we'd meet at the wire fence separating our gardens, chatting for ages through the mesh.

My family were used to seeing us together.

"Where's Patrick today?" Nana would ask when he wasn't by my side.

"I think Tricia has a little boyfriend," my aunt teased on her visits from Southport. She slept in the back bedroom when she visited and often heard us through the window. "I heard ye chatting in the garden – ye sound like a right pair of lovebirds!"

At the time I didn't get the joke – but my family were highly amused!

My teachers said I was quiet, one of the good girls in our class – at least that's Mam's version. She also says I liked school!

Primary school brings back other memories too, in particular the pets we had at home. Cats and dogs were a permanent fixture in our back garden. It was great fun playing with them. I can't remember a time when I haven't had an obsession with animals – mind you, at the moment, there's so much I can't remember that this statement is slightly exaggerated.

One afternoon Kiera and I were playing in the garden when we heard animal cries. Both of us ran to the boundary fence and realised the cries were coming from next door. We pushed our way through the fence and, following the crying sound, we found four tiny kittens in a hedge and rushed home for help.

"Mam, Dad, there are four little kittens in trouble."

Dad came with us to take a look. He didn't really have a choice. We wouldn't let him have any peace until he agreed.

"I think their mother is dead, so the poor little things are on their own," Dad told us.

"We have to give them something to eat, Dad," Kiera and I insisted.

We started to feed them and little by little they got stronger. After a while they followed us home. We weren't allowed bring them into the house. Mam didn't allow cats inside. But she didn't mind us keeping them in the garden and she helped us make a home for them in the shed. We named them and wrote their names on the shed wall. Unfortunately, three of the little kittens died from cat flu but the fourth one, Rachel, survived. She was named after Rachel in Friends. She settled into life in our garden and only four months after we found her she became a mother herself and had a litter of kittens.

"You can only keep one," Dad cautioned, watching us fall in love with the little furry creatures.

We found homes for the others and kept 'Ross', sticking with the Friends theme for a name. The fact the kitten was a girl didn't matter to us. We wanted to use the name, Ross, regardless!

But then the breeding continued and Ross started having kittens at the same time as Rachel! We had up to 12 cats at any one time. Kittens went from one mother to another to feed and, as soon as they were old enough, we were always careful to find lovely homes and lovely people for our kittens.

We built up a relationship with Animal Welfare in Limerick. They often approached us to keep additional cats. When we could, we helped out.

Many of them were very skinny when they arrived but, in a short space of time, with proper feeding and nourishment, they filled out and grew. Male cats regularly disappeared for a day or more and then returned starving. No doubt they had left their mark on another family with a new breed of kittens on the way!

I enjoyed naming the cats. I called one little guy Mask because of the patch on his face. We had one called Felix, and another called Terry, after Terry's Chocolate Orange, a nervous cat called Shivers because he was forever shivering, and one called Nikki just because I liked the name! Midget was one of the cats we took in. We found him between fences. Though it might seem an unusual name for a kitten, I heard the vet calling him a tiny little midget when we took him to be checked out. The name stuck.

Cats came and went but in the last few years the number of cats living in our garden has whittled down to four. Three stay with us all of the time but the fourth is a bit of a rambler and definitely visits more than just our house!

Though I wouldn't consider myself a tomboy, I have to admit that playing with cats was far more enjoyable than playing with dolls. I feel comfortable with animals. Maybe it stems from being shy as a child. If I was asked to say something very simple to somebody I didn't know, I found it impossible and clammed up. Even at home, around people we knew, I hated the spotlight and found attention uncomfortable.

I couldn't get the words out to answer a question. It's so ironic, considering my inability to speak now when I'd give anything to open my mouth and use my voice.

Shyness held me back a little when I was younger. I had a small circle of close friends and that was more than enough entertainment for me. One of my friends lived on a farm, something very different for a city girl like me! Playing on the farm was a novelty at first but the agricultural aromas were too overpowering for me! I did acquire a taste for warm unpasteurised milk though!

With my two sisters and lots of cousins living nearby – not to mention our pets – I was never short of company. And eventually I got over my shyness, thanks in part to being the youngest of three sisters and needing to be able to speak up and fight my corner at times!

In sixth class, I opted to attend French classes after school. Learning a new language came easy to me and taking the class gave me a headstart when I went to Secondary School as I already knew some French words and phrases. A few new boys joined the boys' school when I was in sixth class. Little did I know when one of them smiled at me that I would bump into him again when I was 17 and he'd become my first boyfriend! I don't think I had a crush on him when I was 12 – well, maybe a little!

Secondary School was an all-girls school. Languages remained top of my list with Geography and Art next in my order of favourites. I studied Art from first year through to fifth year. Mam still has lots of pieces I made on show around the house but some of my best pieces are in the school display cabinet as they were considered high calibre!

Computer class was also a lot of fun. Because I enjoyed the subject, I often found myself helping some of the others in the class with their homework. I showed them what they needed to do and they called on me if they needed help. There was a benefit for me too as some of the people I was helping were considered bullies in the schoolyard. Helping them with computer work kept them off my back! The Spanish teacher also relied on me for help in class. And on a few occasions, I was actually left in charge when she had to leave the room!

Maths was a different experience, however. The tables (pardon the pun) were turned and I was the one needing help. Dad came to my rescue and after a hard day at work he never complained when he had to sit and explain the rules and method of trigonometry or theorems! Luckily he'd been doing a course himself to help him get promoted at work. Maths were fresh in his mind. Maybe he missed his calling as a teacher. With his help I passed my exams and went on to win a Leaving Cert Overall Award as well as Best Student Award in my final year. Kiera was also an award-winner in school. And Melissa was a top student too, and a great example to her younger sisters!

Pat and Annette Ingle were very proud of their girls.

*

I look at my parents now. They're busy arranging letters on a spell board, there to help in whatever way they can as has always been the case. I focus on what I need to spell, the grins on their faces worth the effort of concentration when I register their surprise at the first word I succeed in spelling: 'Cody'.

All the hours Mam, Dad, Kiera and Melissa have spent with me and I don't choose one of their names! Even my boyfriend is a little put out! However, spelling that one four-letter word takes it out of me. I lapse back into a long sleep once more, too exhausted to keep up the good work until I've regained some energy. It'll be a while before I'm getting any 'best student' awards if I keep this pace up!

But Mam, Dad and the girls are kind and patient teachers. They continue working with me, coaxing me to choose the letters by nodding and blinking. They encourage me to try new movements and responses, grateful for something as small as a smile, exhilarated when I succeed in doing something better than my previous attempt.

Being here for me is so difficult for them. The number of times in a day they are hurried from ITU when I take apnoeic episodes and my breathing fails, how scared they are while waiting outside to be called back in. Will I still be alive? Will this be the last time they see me? It's cruel they have to go through this. It's upsetting. It's heartbreaking. It's terrifying.

I see the relief on their faces when they're brought back in. I see it in Dad's expression, the look of terror remaining in his eyes. It doesn't matter how many times a day this occurs. Each is as terrifying as the one before. Each time they're scared I won't come round.

But I'm still here. I'm stubborn. I'm not going anywhere. I wish they'd believe this.

I know they're happy that their Tricia is still here with them. I'm not just a shell lying in a bed, strapped to machines. I am somebody.

Chapter 9

Patricia Ingle
Christmas 2008
Cork University Hospital – ITU
Season's greetings …

In December 2008, there are mumblings about transferring me back to ICU in MWRH in Limerick. This is worrying. My family panic and object strongly. They're scared my therapy will be reduced (or non-existent) if I'm moved from ITU. At least here in the CUH, rehabilitation is constant. Physiotherapy, occupational therapy and speech & language therapy have replaced breakfast, dinner and tea! The therapists arrive to me as regular as meals to most of the other patients. I can move my eyes and I have a tiny flicker of movement in my right hand. I'm also able to shrug my left shoulder! I'm able to sit in a special chair for a short amount of time if I'm strapped in.

Sitting out in a chair is a big ordeal. Getting there is an even bigger one as they use a hoist to take me out of bed and onto the chair! When nurses are moving me from bed to chair, I'm completely helpless. Being powerless is frightening. Being fully reliant on others is equally concerning. Will I ever be able to get myself out of bed again? I'm strapped to the chair. I must look fabulous sitting there, a series of buckles and straps holding me together, the collar around my neck still needed to hold my head up! Thank God there are no mirrors anywhere. At least I'm saved the upset of having to look at myself.

The dizziness continues. Will it ever stop? Sometimes I only last in the chair a few minutes before I'm put back into bed again. It seems a bit of a waste. There's such effort required to move me from the bed to the chair. The nurses have to make sure my vent and other tubes and wires remain attached. They have to make sure I don't pass out during the transfer!

"It will all be worth it," the nurses reassure me.

I'm not exactly in a strong position to object loudly. Mouthing isn't very effective when there isn't anybody looking at my face! But one day I manage to sit out for a little longer than normal and I begin to believe the nurses. Maybe in time it will all be worth it.

Each of the staff encourage me, all of them working together to ensure I'm getting the best support possible.

My dreams are particularly vivid, probably because there's so much going on or maybe because there are so many thoughts stuck inside my head and it's too difficult to get them out.

On December 3rd I wake suddenly, feeling very confused. Why hasn't Grandad come to visit me? I've been asking Mam why. My memory is fuzzy this morning. But I remember my dream perfectly. Grandad was standing in front of me, the air around us hazy.

"Tell your mother and aunt I'm doing well," he tells me. "I'll be fine. They're not to worry."

Mam is beside me now. I describe my dream.

"Grandad's gone, pet. Remember?" This isn't the first time she has had to remind me of this. "But today is a special day to remember him. It's his first anniversary."

The memory comes back to me. Again. Between them my parents have been patient and kind when explaining that Grandad died last year. They described the funeral and mostly it jogs my memory.

My face crumbles. Seeing him standing there was such a relief. In those moments when I woke first I was convinced he was still with us. Now I have to miss him all over again. Whether he was really visiting me and sending a message to Mam through me, we'll never know. But despite feeling a little sad, his face is clearly ingrained in my mind. I hold onto it as long as I can. It's good to feel support from a higher level.

The doctors continue their pleas to get us to agree to a move back to Limerick.

"The level of care you get here will continue when you transfer to MWRH," we're told by a number of experts.

But Dad fights to keep me here, digging his heels in and pleading for more time. He has no confidence in the Limerick hospital. And he's not alone. Mam feels the same. They're still haunted by the experience we had when I first became ill – nurses and doctors ignoring my parents' concerns when I was sluggish and unresponsive. There was no sense of urgency, despite their pleadings.

The move to Limerick is delayed – for now at least – but there's a transfer to a different hospital being negotiated. Mam and Dad are pleased with this second option. It's the National Rehabilitation Centre in Dún Laoghaire, Dublin.

"It provides specialist rehabilitation services," Mam explains. "It's exactly what you need to speed up the progress you're making."

"I'll send them a letter requesting an in-stay for you, Tricia," a consultant offers.

"Thank you," I mouth.

*

Dear Doctor,

I would be grateful if you would consider this young girl for rehabilitation in your Centre. She became unwell in September of this year. She was previously well with a background history merely of recurrent sore throat, surgery in childhood for divergent strabismus and grommets bilaterally in childhood.

In August of this year she began to complain of headaches associated with nausea and vomiting. She attended A&E in another hospital a number of times and was admitted when the headaches increased in severity. She was mildly photophobic at the time and a CT brain scan showed mildly enlarged ventricles. A lumbar puncture was performed to assess for meningitis. This showed a markedly elevated white cell count of 335 with 100% lymphocytes. The day after the lumbar puncture she became drowsy and deteriorated throughout the day. Her pupils became unreactive and her speech began to become impaired. She had a respiratory arrest that lasted 10 seconds after which she was intubated immediately. A CT brain scan was performed which showed increasing size of the lateral and third ventricles and she was transferred down to CUH for insertion of a VP shunt. She has remained in ICU ever since.

The working diagnosis is of lymphocytic meningitis (cause unclear) whith evidence of severe brain stem dysfunction. An MRI brain scan which has been repeated twice shows diffused swelling and increased signalling throughout the cerebellum with distortion of the brain stem. Her CSF has a lymphocytic picture with decreased glucose. TB culture to date has been negative, as has India ink stain, Cryptococcus antigen, lyme and listeria. A meningeal biopsy has been performed also which showed non-specific inflammation. Patricia Ingle is

*on treatment for TB meningitis and has also been treated for
listeria and for bacterial meningitis.*

*Since her initial transfer to CUH when her pupils were
fixed and dilated, she had a GCS of 3/15. Patricia Ingle has
shown significant neurological improvement. Currently she
still has a tracheostomy in and is requiring full ventilation.
However, she is alert, moves her eyes and has good facial
expressions, she communicates with mouthing words and
with spelling words out on a spell board. She has a slight
flicker of movement in her right and can shrug her left
shoulder. The exact cause of her lymphocytic meningitis
and cerebellitis remains unclear but peripheral bloods are
normal and she is improving neurologically. She remains on
anti-tuberculosis chemotherapy. She has undergone extensive
rehabilitation with our speech and language therapists and
has achieved a good level of communication. She was also
seen by our physiotherapist and occupational therapist. She
has her own chair and recently has managed to sit out for a
few hours each day.*

*Clearly Patricia Ingle is a very difficult case. Initially
we felt that her prognosis was extremely grave and that she
was in fact locked-in. However, this is now clearly not the
case. She has had nerve conduction studies which do show
evidence of a critical care neuropathy but we feel most of
her neurological deficit is from her central pathology. As she
has made such improvements in the last number of weeks
we do feel that she should be assessed for rehabilitation in
a specialist Centre such as your own. I have arranged for
physiotherapy, speech and language therapy and occupational
therapy to send reports on to you regarding Patricia Ingle.
I understand that it is a difficult case given the fact that she
has a tracheostomy in situ and still requires ventilation but I
really would appreciate your opinion with regard to arranging
ongoing rehabilitation for Patricia Ingle. At the moment
she remains in our Intensive Care Unit and is gradually
improving.*

*

I wait for news. I hope they can take me. With more therapy, they might
make my hands and legs work. Or at least move a bit. And my balance – I

can't even hold my head on my shoulders! I'm only 20 years old – how can my body be giving up like this?

"I'm sorry, Tricia," the doctor tells me when he hears back from them. "I received a response from the NRC. But it's not what we were hoping for. It's more complicated than we realised because of the ventilator."

> *Dear Doctor,*
>
> *Thank you for your telephone call and for your Registrar's on the above named lady.*
>
> *She is currently in a very high dependent state although it is clear that she is making slow improvements.*
>
> *Normally I would arrange for our brain injury liaison nurse to review this lady but unfortunately we do not have anyone in position at the moment. However, either myself or one of my colleagues may be in a position to review Ms. Ingle sometime in the New Year.*
>
> *We currently only have three beds dedicated to the high dependency service and because of this, we have a very protracted waiting list. However, I will list Ms. Ingle for admission under this service and hopefully by the time we have a bed available for her, she may be weaned off her ventilation. She would require to be non-ventilator dependent prior to admission to the National Rehabilitation Hospital.*

*

"Surely there's something that can be done?" My parents are as persistent as ever but the response is still the same.

"Tricia needs a special bed as well as dedicated nurses to make sure her ventilator tube stays connected when she's being moved. Unfortunately, the NRC have only three high-dependency beds and a very long waiting list to get into them."

"Will she ever be called?"

"I've asked them to include Tricia on the waiting list but they've indicated that she will need to be non-ventilator dependent prior to admission. I'm sorry the news is disappointing."

The air is tinged with despondency. The hum of my ventilator fills the silence. Intensive rehab slips from my non-existent grasp.

*

Christmas 2008 comes and goes.

We have our first family outing from ITU. I'm wheeled with my entourage – three members of staff, my parents and sisters – to the hospital's first floor to see the Christmas tree. From my restricted vantage point, it's difficult to see the twinkling lights and glistening decorations. I can't move any part of my body. I have a conglomoration of medical equipment and apparatus attached to me. And there's no escaping the ventilator!

To keep my head from flopping forward, Mam and Dad take turns in supporting me while the girls take some photographs and I do my best to smile on demand. I won't be in any rush asking to see those photos!

This time last year, Christmas 2007, we shared a quiet Christmas at home. Granddad had died on 1st December and understandably Mam was finding it difficult to get into the festive mood. But as always she kept her spirits up as best she could and created a Christmas atmosphere nonetheless. Thinking back on visiting Grandad in ICU, the experience of walking in and sitting with him was very much like looking in. But being a patient is a completely different situation. I feel I'm looking out as I watch my family come and go and able to leave when they want while I have no choice but stay.

Instead of having a real tree, Mam and Dad bought an artificial tree in the last days before Christmas.

"Oh, it's a black tree!" Mam said, pulling it from the box. She hadn't paid any attention in the shop. "And it has red berry lights."

Though it was a surprise to all of us – even Mam – it was as if a black tree was what was meant to be on our first Christmas without Grandad.

This year stuck in ITU feels as though it's another occasion for a black Christmas tree! But our relations have other ideas and shower us with gifts on Christmas Day. They arrive at the hospital and do their best to help create a sense of festivity for our family. But Dad's worried we'll break hospital rules. I'm only allowed three visitors at any one time and he has a hard job organising a rota when they arrive laden with presents.

My aunt, Deirdre Greensmith, and her husband, Joe, arrive. Dad is thrilled to see his sister and brother-in-law. What a great surprise.

"I've brought you a present, big brother," she says, handing him a gift.

"You're so good to have taken time away from your own family day." Having her and Joe here means a lot to him and he really appreciates the effort they've made.

Deirdre has three children of her own that she has left behind to come and visit us and cheer us up this difficult Christmas.

Seeing the bundles of pajamas, slippers, dressing gowns and teddies on the bed, she smirks as she takes her turn to sit with me. "I guessed you'd be overloaded on nightwear and cuddly toys so I thought I'd get you a little collector's item instead."

I'm thrilled when she unwraps the gift for me and takes out a Newbridge Silver Christmas-tree decoration. I smile and mouth "Thank you".

She stays a while and then says her goodbyes as she leaves to let others in.

Though it's a very tiring day, I'm pleased Mam and Dad get to see close family on Christmas Day.

*

Melissa has kept the Christmas atmosphere alive all day. She must be as exhausted as me tonight.

"I brought you some new music, Tricia." Kiera plays a music video on her laptop that evening when it's just us again.

Melissa massages hand cream on to the palms of my hands.

But the effort to stay awake is too much. I slip into a dreamless sleep. The music is wasted on me but the massage at least is good for my skin.

*

In the days following Christmas, I sleep a lot, sometimes for a few days at a time. It's peaceful for me but hard on those sitting around watching my every movement.

"Rest is a large part of Tricia's healing," the neurologist assures my concerned family. "It's all going to take time. Keep working with her at a slow pace. Her brain is healing so it's one question at a time. Give her time to grasp the message. Otherwise it'll be too confusing and while you're asking a second question, she may already have forgotten the first!"

And that describes my memory in a nutshell. I can hold one piece of information but if I let it go there's no guarantee I'll be able to catch it again. It floats in a bubble but once it floats away it's next to impossible to get it back.

The chaplain visits regularly, chatting to me and my family, his gentle tone soothing in the midst of the busy ITU. Though I'm not overly religious, I enjoy his visits. Sometimes a lady chaplain does her rounds, her words of assurance equally welcoming. We soon become familiar with both visitors, sharing our news with them and listening to any advice they have to offer. Their belief instils hope. Their understanding offers a neutral opinion. And their faith is encouraging as they accept rather than question what life throws at us.

Kiera is adamant I will recover in my own time. She is willing to wait it out, talking gently to me and encouraging me to squeeze her hand. The Ralph Waldo Emerson slogan, 'Adopt the pace of nature, her secret is patience', is tattooed over the rosebud symbol on her ankle. It's the motto she applies to my recovery, strengthening her belief that I'll learn how to speak and move in my own time.

I hear her asking me to grasp her fingers. Her patience is endless. She remains at my side, creating an invisible path of communication between us. I know she's there. I hear her voice. I try. I try. I try.

"That's it, Tricia. Squeeze my hand, just a little more. You're really doing it – I know you are."

Kiera calls the nurse. "I felt her fingers squeeze mine. Isn't it great?"

"I know you believe you felt something. We have to be sure it's not an involuntary movement."

My sister's excitement is crushed.

*

My stay in ITU continues. More intensive physiotherapy sessions start. Mam and Dad chat to the other families and parents of patients and compare notes about our care and recovery.

"How long is Tricia in ITU?" one lady asks Mam.

"Four months now."

"You should ask the doctors why she doesn't have boots for her feet."

"They haven't been mentioned. I suppose because she's not mobile?"

"Her feet will drop if they don't put boots on them. If that happens she might never walk again."

As usual, Mam is quick to act. She makes enquiries and finds out that foot drop results from weaknes or paralysis of the muscles used to lift the front part of the foot. She isn't going to let this be ignored. Or get any worse if it has already started to happen.

She asks the nurses about it. "Can Tricia be tried with boots? We're worried that her feet will drop."

The nurses nod and promise to look into it.

The boots are made to measure using heated plastic moulds – rather strange but apparently effective. "You'd think somebody would have suggested this for Tricia, instead of us having to ask," Mam comments to Melissa.

"At least we found out," Melissa says. "Hopefully in time to make a difference."

But where's the point in complaining? As soon as they're available they put them on my feet. Unfortunately, they're not the most comfortable. My feet have already dropped a little it seems, so they're strapped to my legs to keep them on. They're a million miles from the knee-highs my friends are wearing this season but, if they protect my feet, I'll put up with the discomfort and the fashion disaster!

Sometimes my arm twitches. Dad notices even though I'm oblivious. He runs to tell the doctors but their response is less enthusiastic than we expect.

"I don't want to disappoint you but it's likely they're just involuntary movements. This would explain the twitches."

I smirk when Mam and Dad share a look that says something entirely different. I can't be sure of course but I really do think I feel a tiny tingle of movement every now and then. Or am I imagining it?

Dad isn't put off by what the doctor says. He decides to play a new game with me to prove otherwise.

Taking one of my many teddies (my collection is rapidly increasing), Dad sits it on my leg (and sometimes on my arm) and tells me to knock it over. This is very funny at my age so I try really hard to move my leg or arm and give the teddy a bit of a jolt.

I know what Dad wants me to do. I want to do what he's waiting for. But the message gets lost between my brain and my leg. It often takes several attempts but eventually I get either my leg or arm to twitch and to our great delight the teddy falls. It sounds silly but this tiny movement creates a bit of light relief all round. It's so good to see my family laughing. I manage a quirky smile too.

Dad is so pleased he calls a doctor to show him my new trick.

The medical team come in.

"She's able to move a bit," Dad insists. "Watch her knock the teddy off."

But, much to his frustration, I don't do my latest trick in front of the staff.

Mam knows I'm teasing, just as I always did.

Melissa and Kiera are also suspicious. They know my humour better than Mam and Dad at times.

I hold out a while and then feel sorry for Dad and give in. The medical team note my latest bit of progress, smiling as they write up the details on my lengthy chart. If I could laugh, I would!

The nurses and doctors talk to Mam and Dad a lot about me. Mostly I tune out and let them at it. Hearing discussions on every aspect of my care isn't very interesting. And so much of it is very embarrassing at my age. Having your parents washing and cleaning every bit of you at 20 years of age isn't something I want to hear too much about.

"Your medication is being reduced, Tricia," Dad shares with me. "The doctors don't think you need to be on the drug for fits and seizures anymore. And you've stopped slipping into those long trances too. So they're going to try you without the meds."

If I could shrug my shoulders, that probably would be my response. Though it should be good news to hear my medication is being reduced, it's still not the news I really want to hear – that I can get out of bed and jump around and be normal!

Melissa reads fashion snippets from the magazine she's reading.

Kiera gives me one of her regular music-news updates. "There's a new artist out in America called Lady Gaga," she says, as she places the earbuds in my ears and presses the play button on the iPod.

'Just Dance' plays, the opening lyrics describing the fog inside my head.

I'm not sure if I'll be a fan of Lady Gaga's music but I hope, hope, hope her lyrics have a message for me and it will be okay for me and that I will remember and dance.

Back to reality, however, and I have as much chance of dancing as I have of visiting the moon right now.

"The doctor has advised we get you a TV," Mam tells me. "He thinks it will be good distraction."

This had already been suggested but the television hadn't materialised.

I mouth "okay" and Mam and Dad go to Argos and buy one, installing it in the room. It's difficult to position it so I can see it perfectly but he does his best. The doctor encourages Mam to leave it switched on.

"We believe it's good for stimulation," he explains.

It'll be better than staring at the wall or the ceiling, I suppose, particularly since Dad started pointing out black marks on the ceiling and letting on they are racing spiders! He's trying his best to amuse me, trying anything to get a reaction. And there are times when I'm staring upwards for hours on end that I begin to imagine the 'spiders' are moving!

*

It's a few days into January 2009. I'm lying in bed. It's one of the rare occasions I'm alone. The ward sister leads the medical team to my bedside.

"We think it's time you're transferred back to Limerick, Tricia. You'll be near your friends and extended family. More people will be able to visit. It will be convenient. What do you think?"

I'm too weak to fight against it. They've caught me at a particularly vulnerable moment. I think I'd nod my head and mouth 'yes' to any request!

And so I mouth my answer: "Yes, I will go back to Limerick." Maybe it is time to give in. It would be nice to get nearer home. It would be even nicer to get home.

As soon as I've given my agreement, the ward sister and team move away, only to return a few minutes later with four chairs. Placing them around my bed, the ward sister steps outside and asks Mam, Dad and the girls to come in.

I look around. The scene is set. They want me to repeat my answer. They want me to agree to being moved to MWRH in front of my family. Is it the right thing for me? Is it the right time?

I've been in the trauma unit in CUH for four months, much of it lost on me. My parents have stayed the entire time, Melissa and Kiera also apart from a few occasions when they needed to return home to let their employers know what was happening. Luckily, their managers are sympathetic under the circumstances. My boyfriend is another regular, taking his turn to sit with me and reminding me of the hours of fun we had snorkelling in Ballyvaughan, not to mention our afternoons and evenings in his father's garage tinkering with cars, trying our hand at panel-beating and respraying bonnets and boots. His family are great, always so warm and welcoming when I'm in their house. He's so much more than a boyfriend. We've been together four years. He's my closest friend after family. I can't imagine how hard this is for him, spending endless hours in a hospital. If the situation were reversed, it would break my heart to watch him unable to move, unable to speak, unable to breathe without a machine. I hope he knows I appreciate what he's doing for me. I hope everyone who makes time for me knows they're helping carry me and the rest of my family through this nightmare. I've had visits from aunts, uncles, cousins and friends. I've received hundreds of cards wishing me well – and even some praying for my survival.

I was expected to die. I'm very grateful to everyone who took the time to think or pray for me. I'm very grateful to be alive. I'm very grateful for the kindness and care I received in the CUH. I will always appreciate everything the nurses, doctors, consultants and surgeons did to release me from a locked-in state back into the real world.

They didn't rush me. They waited for nature to take its course. They waited for me to be ready.

And now they're waiting for me to vacate the bed so they can offer somebody else a similar chance.

Chapter 10

Patricia Ingle
January 2009
CUH to MWRH
Time for a move … Bed Number 6

On the 6th January 2009 my dad's efforts to extend my stay in Cork University Hospital are brought to an abrupt end. I'm transferred back to ICU in MWRH Limerick, still with a tracheostomy and completely dependent on a ventilator to help me breathe, still unable to speak or move, still unable to eat or drink by mouth, fully reliant on PEG feeding for nourishment. My balance has gone. Without a neck brace, my head flops.

But I try not to dwell on the upsetting parts. I try to focus and do what I'm asked by the therapists. I am determined to keep improving.

*

Transferring me from bed to chair is a series of tried and tested escapades. Tom, one of the physio team, gets me working with a tilt table. I've nicknamed him Tilting Tom. He laughs when I mouth this to him. He's amused but not deterred.

"I hope you're well rested, Tricia. I'll be spinning you shortly!"

The tilt table is the first step (pardon the ironic pun) in my very long journey of getting into an upright position.

The physiotherapists put me lying on the flat of my back.

"We're going to strap you to a table."

I don't move. I can't move.

Once I'm secure, Tom tilts the table ever so slightly – just a couple of degrees. My head starts to cloud, the pressure of the movement building inside my skull. I want to grab the table. But my hands won't move. I know I'm strapped in but it's scary – one hundred times scarier than the carousel that turned me off roller-coasters for life.

'Tilting Tom' gradually moves me into an upright position, a little bit at a time until I can cope with the pressure inside my head. But the tiniest movement is terrifying. I feel as though I'm spun 360 degrees at top speed. My head is cloudy and muffled. I can only manage a few seconds. I faint. It's exhausting and terrifying.

I open my eyes. I'm back in bed, no longer strapped to the tilt table. I sleep for hours after my tilting adventures.

The therapy continues. Every improvement is noted on a chart.

"How many degrees today, Tricia?" Dad takes special interest in my progress and looks at my chart to see what's recorded, often looking at the chart before even saying hello to me!

I'm literally working my hardest, doing my best so that someday soon I will achieve the full 90 degrees, a fully upright position!

My physiotherapists, like my family, are relentless. They persist with the tilting-table exercise, motivating me as best they can and measuring the extra movements I manage. My progress is slow but the look of delight on Dad's face when the physio announces I've moved a few extra degrees encourages me to keep trying. And finally I reach a point where, strapped to my old friend the tilt table, I'm tilted fully upright and I'm able to look people in the eye instead of staring at the ceiling.

"Now you're ready to sit out in a chair for longer periods," Tom tells me.

Sitting out for longer periods of the day is like climbing another mountain. It's tiring. I can't control any movement of my limbs. Everything is such an effort.

*

I'm not long back in Limerick when it's obvious that, despite the promises and assurances made in Cork, the MWRH have no plans in place to continue providing me with an occupational therapist or speech and language therapist.

This is devastating. It is so disappointing for all of us. We feel cheated. We feel tricked. We feel we have taken several steps backwards. We finally agreed to come back to Limerick with the expectation that, at the very least, I would be getting the same therapy as I had been receiving. But now I've arrived, there are no services in place for me.

What's going to become of me? Is this it for me? Am I to spend the rest of my life mouthing a few words and unable to do anything for myself? It's frustrating. And I can't show my frustration! I can't scream. I can't shout. I can't even clench my fists. I can only lie here in a hospital bed strapped up to machines, letting a machine breathe for me, letting tubes feed me, waiting for others to make decisions about me and, worst of all, I have no control over anything that happens to me.

Fr. Coffey and Rose, the hospital chaplains, pay regular visits, listening to our woes and mostly finding a way to make us smile. I look forward to seeing them, each of them calling in their turn when they are on duty. As the weeks pass, we become very familiar and they're happy to be a sounding board for the latest happenings.

"You won't believe what's happened now," is a frequent opener to our conversations.

Fr. Coffey and Rose are two of the most patient people I've ever met. And in their own gentle way, they allow us offload some of our anger and frustrations.

My parents take on the therapy fight for me. Thankfully their pleas are heard, but we're told we have to wait. And while we wait, my family settle into a new routine, arriving in ICU as early as 8.30 a.m. every morning and staying until almost midnight.

And they're not going to sit around doing nothing. Waiting for therapists is no excuse for me to be lazy. They're hard at work repeating the various routines they'd watched my therapists carrying out in Cork. Alphabet letters, spelling words, attempts to get me moving my limbs are part of every hour of every day now – at least every hour I'm awake.

I sleep a lot, the effort of concentration and trying to get my body to respond exhausting. But I have a very resilient group of people around my bed. Even the tiniest effort I make has them applauding my success. I try to nod my head as a thank-you. And even that sometimes is virtually impossible, the simple gesture beyond my capability.

Dad taps his fingers on the table and places a clipboard under my hand.

"Come on, Tricia, see if you can tap the board with your fingers."

Mam, Dad and the girls practise their lip-reading. They encourage me to mouth out words, determined to communicate, equally determined to prevent me from retreating back inside. They use the alphabet letters to spell out what I'm saying.

"Is it an A? Is it a B?" The routine is a bit like cheerleading as we create words together on the spell board.

"Can you mouth this word?" Melissa asks, showing me the board.

It's an easy one. I know this. It's 'dog', my favourite animal. It reminds me of Cody. My boyfriend has him at his house. I hope Cody's happy. I miss him so much.

Between them, they create lists of words.

"I'll spell it on the board, Tricia?" Mam says, using the alphabet letters to spell out a word so she knows what I'm trying to say instead of guesswork. "Nod if it's the right letter."

I get bored after a while. I close my eyes. I tune out.

Mam is keeping a diary. Everything is recorded. My visitors are asked to write down anything I do while they're with me. If I watch television or move my legs, it's noted in the diary. Though little things might not sound very important, seeing it all come together shows the distance I have travelled and the hurdles I am overcoming.

Improvements are barely visible. It's very hard work. My chart and Mam's diary list a shrug of my left shoulder, a slight movement in my right hand, facial expressions, sleep patterns, everything single thing.

*

Moving me out of ICU is mentioned to Mam and Dad.

They're devastated. And worried.

"We need the bed for another patient who is critically ill," they're told when they object.

Dad hits the roof. "Tricia is on a life-support machine! She needs a nurse with her at all times in case the tracheostomy tube falls out. She can't talk, she can't shout for help!"

I see the look passing between my parents, their fear that I won't get the attention I need if I'm moved out of ICU. I hate seeing them upset.

"What if the ventilator doesn't work? Or if she requires suctioning?" Dad points out.

His pleas and concerns gain me a little more time in ICU. I'm relieved too. As much as I hate being in hospital, at least I feel safe here with the ICU nurses. They're never further than the end of the bed. No matter what happens, they notice. I can't imagine being alone.

*

Life in ICU continues. The doctors run tests, take blood and serum samples, analyse any progress and change in my condition and provide us with updates on some of the findings. My dependency on the ventilator is raised for discussion on a regular basis, with a few attempts to wean me off ending in disaster. The doctors and nurses have explained the reason behind my inability to breathe as best they can. I've had to hear it a number of times and sometimes I remember but other times I forget. Maybe that's a good thing. It stops me from being angry.

I understand that damage to my brainstem is preventing my brain sending the correct messages to my body. Obviously the 'breathe now' message from my brain to my lungs and airways is getting lost along the way and as a result I'm reliant on the ventilator to do the work for me. But it doesn't stop the doctors trying or testing for improvements.

Mam and Dad get a brainwave. They make a sign and paste it across the television screen, reading: 'Don't forget to breathe.' At least the television is used for something. I can't see it very well because of the angle it's at, so we don't bother with it. But even the sign isn't enough to remind me to perform the task most humans take for granted: breathing. The miracle I need to breathe by myself doesn't seem to exist. The possibility of weaning me off the ventilator is kept alive and tried repeatedly. But my body just isn't up to it. If only the 'breathe now' message could be transmitted as simply as sending a text or Facebook message. If only I could breathe independently. If only …

*

In the third week of February 2009, the doctors call my family to another meeting. They have an exciting announcement. I'm being transferred to St. Thomas' Hospital in London for assessment. Their Lane Fox Unit specialises in acquired brain injuries.

"This will give you a chance to make better progress," one of the doctors tells me.

This is very exciting news. My progress has slowed down and I'm eager to get going and try something new. Travel arrangements are in place and we are all packed and ready to go. But there's a cruel twist of fate again at the very last minute. The plan is abandoned.

"But why? Can't you see she really needs every bit of help available?" Dad is devastated.

"Funding issues unfortunately," is the only explanation provided, a very lame excuse in our opinion.

And that's it, our hopes dashed yet again, and all I can do is make the best of the therapy I'm getting in ICU, along with the continued efforts from Mam, Dad, Melissa and Kiera. They've become expert learners. They watch everything being done for me by the professionals so they can keep it going throughout the day and night in the hope that it will bring me on faster.

It's so frustrating that so many obstacles are put in my way. Nobody takes the time to explain why. And without a voice of my own, I'm completely reliant on others to speak on my behalf.

Another month passes with nothing much changing for me and now we're into March 2009 and for the very first time the magical word 'discharge' is mentioned.

"While Patricia is fit for discharge home, it's going to be a very complex process," the professor explains. He's the consultant physician in charge of my care.

This prompts serious consideration about the unsuitability of our home in Ballinacurra, Weston.

"We'll have to move house then," Mam and Dad decide, making an appointment with their bank manager to apply for a mortgage.

Dad gives the bank details of their earnings, then waits with Mam while the bank assesses their application. They are devastated when the bank declines the request for a mortgage. Dad takes the refusal documentation with him, wanting it as evidence that he has made every effort to secure housing independently.

Even the bank collapse and the current state of Ireland's economy is working against us.

The professor's team send a letter to the housing unit to support our need for alternate accommodation.

Intensive Care Unit
Mid-Western Regional Hospital
Dooradoyle
Limerick

To Whom It May Concern
Re: Patricia Ingle, Ballinacurra, Weston, Co Limerick
Ms. Ingle is currently an inpatient in the Intensive Care Unit of the Mid-Western Regional Hospital, Limerick. She was admitted following an episode of meningo-encephalitis that has rendered her quadriplegic and ventilator dependent.

Her family are currently trying to make arrangements for her future discharge home. Unfortunately, their present accommodation is unsuitable for Patricia's care needs. Most notably, their front door is unable to accommodate the passage of a wheelchair.

Furthermore, the house is unable to hold a hospital bed or the necessary ventilator equipment together with the nursing team that will be needed to provide twenty-four-hour care. The bathroom is also unable to accommodate the necessary equipment for Patricia as she will need a hoist transfer for basic tasks such as bathing.

We would appreciate any assistance that you could provide for both Patricia and her family in relation to this critical matter. If you have any further queries, please feel free to contact a member of our team.

Yours sincerely,

Medical Senior House Officer, MWRH, Limerick

*

It's hopeful that real efforts seem to be in place to progress plans for my discharge. Equipment is high on the agenda of requirements and on May 19th one of the professor's team sends a letter to detail these and put a request in motion.

To Whom It May Concern
Re: Patricia Ingle, Ballinacurra Weston, Limerick

The above named young lady has suffered from a lymphocytic meningo-encephalitis complicated by obstructive hydrocephalus, necessitation VP shunt insertion. She is currently ventilator dependent due to her central apnoea and is tetraplegic.

She was originally admitted under our care on the 2nd September 2008, travelled to Cork University Hospital the following day and was readmitted to Mid-Western Regional Hospital Limerick on 6th January 2009. She has been under the care of a multi-disciplinary team throughout her stay in MWRH, and we continue to see small improvements in her abilities.

*We are now at a stage where we are planning her
complex discharge. To facilitate this, Patricia will require a
wheelchair and ventilator support. We have already organised
an assessment of Patricia for her wheelchair through the
multidisciplinary team and have received a quotation from
O'Neill Healthcare Ltd. The team are satisfied that this is a
suitable wheelchair for Patricia and her needs at present.
We will be organising a motorised wheelchair for Patricia
in the near future to allow her independence but this is not
a suitable wheelchair for Patricia to start with for safety
reasons.*

*Patricia will require two ventilators prior to her discharge.
We have been in close discussion with consultant ICU
physicians about the most suitable ventilator for Patricia and
prescribed her a NIPPY 3 from RespiCare Ltd.*

*We are in full support for any help that she is entitled to.
Please don't hesitate to contact me should you require further
information.*

Yours sincerely,

Medical Senior House Officer, MWRH, Limerick

*

My parents' responsibilities increase. As well as taking care of me, they set about the difficult business of selling our home and finding alternate accommodation. This must be so hard for them. They own our home at the moment and are enjoying the financial freedom it gives. But now they may be facing a financial step backwards and either need a loan or a rental agreement to get somewhere suitable for my needs.

Following the loan refusal from the bank, Limerick City Council and the Regeneration Agency are their first points of contact. Our house is in the Regeneration zone and subject to the Regeneration Programme currently being planned across Limerick City.

"We'll ask if they'll buy our house in exchange for one that's wheelchair accessible," Dad decides, putting his request in writing and sending it off. He also asks the professor to contact the Regeneration Agency Offices on our behalf. On 27th May, the professor sends a letter to this effect.

Dear Sir or Madam,

I am writing to you at the request of Mr. Patrick Ingle whose daughter, Patricia, is a patient of ours at the Regional Hospital. Patricia is a 20-year-old lady that presented to the Regional in early September 2008 with a headache that subsequently transpired to be a lymphocytic meningo-encephalitis. This is a form of meningitis that was confined largely to the cerebellum. This resulted subsequently in an obstructive hydrocephalus, which meant that Patricia needed emergency transfer to the Neuro-surgical Unit in Cork to have a shunt put into her brain. All of this has left her very highly dependent and she is now at the Regional in our Intensive Care Unit. She will need ongoing ventilator support for the rest of her life. She has a tracheostomy in position and specialized wheelchairs. She has the input of a very large multi-disciplinary team and she continues to make steady progress but I think she will need very significant and ongoing support if she is to return home.

We have come to know Patricia and her family very well over that time period and as you can well imagine it has been an extremely traumatic period for the whole family. They have been excellent in their support of Patricia and are extremely willing to do everything that they can to make her life as normal as it can possibly be.

We have recently had a full multi-disciplinary meeting and it is clear that Patricia and her family are going to need new accommodation. They are currently living in Ballinacurra Weston and it would not be appropriate for her to return there. She will need level access housing so that she can move her wheelchair and ventilators in and out with ease and which would be able to accommodate the care that would be necessary in the long term. We would be very grateful for anything that you could do to help in relation to the accommodation issues and would happily keep you updated on her progress if you feel it helpful.

Yours sincerely

Professor of Medical Science and Consultant Physician
cc. Limerick Enterprise Development Partnership
cc. Mr. Patrick Ingle

The Regeneration Programme response arrives, the reply very disappointing.

"Funding issues," Mam tells us. "They've said they can't trade ours against another."

"What will we do now?" I mouth.

"They'll try and work with the City Council to see if there are other options."

"I'm not giving up, Tricia," Dad insists. "I'll try everything I can think of to get us a suitable house. We'll get you back home. We will get you out of hospital no matter what it takes."

I hope he's right. Being incapacitated is getting more and more difficult to cope with and the only thing that helps me stay positive is the hope that I will get out of hospital and home to my family. I'm not thinking beyond that, not worrying about the harsh realities of coping without the hospital staff. I'm not thinking about the amount of equipment I need to stay alive.

Instead I'm thinking of a real life in the outside world, not the life I am living now as a patient in hospital.

Chapter 11

Patricia Ingle
May 2009
Bed 6 ICU – MWRH
Dear Sir or Madam …

Dad has been researching support services. He emails the West Limerick Independent Living Division of the National Advocacy Service. Thanks to his efforts, Grace Moore is nominated as my personal advocate. Grace is kind and patient. She makes such a difference. Until I met Grace I had never heard of the Advocacy Service.

Grace explains her role. "Technically a patient advocate is a case worker who acts on the patient's and sometimes their family's behalf when dealing with the hospital or healthcare service."

It's such a relief to have somebody working with us who understands the health system. My family is just a normal family. Dealing with all the hospital teams is complex and confusing. There are times we feel like the doctors and specialists are speaking a different language. And I know this isn't just an issue for my family. At least now if we are looking for information or if we have a complaint or concern, Grace will speak up on my behalf.

Within the shortest time, Grace becomes the voice I've lost since this horrific illness robbed me of my independence. She quickly learns how to communicate with me as I mouth the words I would like to be able to say out loud.

"Can you help me get out of hospital and be allowed home to my family?" is my first question and request for Grace. Not an easy one to resolve, I'm sure.

"I can certainly try, Tricia. The first thing we need to do is make an application for Personal Assistant services," Grace says.

As with all official processes, there are numerous forms to be filled but thankfully Grace is an expert and more than willing to help out. Together we complete the application. She also helps me write a letter to the HSE Disability Services Manager and both are submitted in June 2009.

"The letter will support the application for PA services," she explains. Together we get to work.

I.C.U.
Mid-West Regional Hospital
Dooradoyle
Limerick.
18th June 2009

Dear Sir or Madam,

I am in hospital nine and a half months and I want to go home. Everyone comes in to see me. My family practically live in ICU with me. I will need a lot of help and support when I go home.

My family have been in touch with Limerick City Council and lots of people to help organise a new family home that will suit my needs and equipment. When this new home is ready I will need you to provide me with a care package so that I can go and live at home with my family and hopefully two St. Bernards.

My professor said that when I am discharged it will be a complex procedure and that my case is very unique. I use a ventilator to breathe for me all the time. If you want to give the professor a call to discuss my situation that's okay with me.

You are more than welcome to visit me wherever I am.

Yours sincerely,

Patricia Ingle

*

The staff in ICU mention transferring me – but not home – no such luck! Instead they're considering moving me to a room in the High Dependency Unit.

Yet again, the air is charged with apprehension. Any mention of change is frightening, not only for me but also for Mam, Dad and the girls. A reduction in the level of care I receive from the hospital is a direct increase in the level of responsibility of my family. And the biggest worry of all is that any kind of transfer will jeopardise the services I'm receiving and the progress – albeit painfully slow – I'm making.

"It's still too soon," Mam and Dad object loudly. "She's in no fit state to be moved. We have fought so hard and waited so long to get the level of therapy she is receiving now. We are not about to put that at risk."

Discussions continue and for now at least I stay in ICU.

"We need the hospital and Community Care working together," Dad insists. "Otherwise this will go on indefinitely."

They're worried about the lack of communication. Even the slightest bit of communication between the hospital and Community Care would show us that something's being done about getting me home.

True to his word, Dad is relentless with his personal campaign to resolve our housing need, canvassing on my behalf to try and get the authorities to address the issue as a matter of urgency.

He spends ages wording emails, reaching out for support from local and national organisations to get them to acknowledge our genuine need and put the services in place so I can go home.

"Are you happy with this, Tricia? Annette?" Dad reads the email aloud before sending it, looking from one of us to the other to seek our approval.

June 25th 2009
To the Minister for Environment

Dear Minister,

My daughter Patricia (19) stopped breathing on Wednesday 3rd September 2008 and has not taken an unassisted breath since then. Two weeks prior Tricia had started to complain about headaches and nausea and dizziness. This ended with her brain swelling and damaging her brain stem, which has now left her on a ventilator (breathing machine). As well as not being able to breathe, Tricia is unable to speak or swallow and has restricted use of her limbs.

As I try to focus on Dad's email, I'm sort of horrified that he is describing me. It also makes me realise how much of this I have forgotten. Concentration is still difficult for me and my memory isn't very reliable. Hearing Dad reading aloud is like being told a story, except unfortunately I am playing the leading role. I tune back in to his email, almost afraid to find out what happens next!

Tricia is now almost ten months in intensive care, three days initially in MWRH, four months in ITU in Cork University Hospital, and has been here in Limerick Mid-Western Regional Hospital for five and a half months. Despite all of this, Tricia is fully aware and alert and can somehow communicate by mouthing words (no sound) and we the family now communicate with Tricia through lip-reading but we find it difficult at times. Tricia is well taken care of by the nurses and staff of the ICU.

The reason I am emailing is that in March of this year, the professor in charge of her care, the multidisciplinary team (anaesithists, dieticians, physiotherapists, speech therapists, occupational therapists, respiratory experts and social workers) and all involved in Tricia's care held a meeting which Annette and I (her parents) later joined. It was decided that Tricia is long enough in hospital and at this stage would benefit better by returning to her family and we are grateful for this after ten months. Tricia will be left home under a complex discharge plan.

Our problem is our present home is unsuitable even with extensions to accommodate Tricia's needs. We will require a bungalow that will be suitable for Tricia's special needs as documented by her occupational therapist and medical consultants.

For this we have had some meetings with Limerick City Council and the Housing Department. Our present home is in the Limerick Regeneration Area so we contacted the Director of Regeneration. These people, although sympathetic, are limited in the help they can give us.

I am asking you as Minister for Environment and Local Government, that you and your department will help us and treat Tricia as a unique and special case in funding for accommodation suitable for her needs. I am asking that you personally will take this case in hand and talk to Limerick

City and County Councils, the Limerick Regeneration Board
and HSE Limerick.

As I have earlier written, Tricia is still in ICU in Limerick
Regional Hospital and she would dearly love to return to
her family. The ICU is occupied mostly by elderly patients
and Tricia has turned 20 and is witnessing at least three
deaths per week. Minister, I am sending attachments of
documentation of her case and you have my full permission to
enquire about Tricia.

I have also contacted our local TDs who have been great
help and seem to take a special interest in Tricia's case. These
people would have more details on our daughter.

As you can tell, we are in need of help but we want our
Tricia back to us. I pray that you can help us.

Mam doesn't say anything but looks to me for my reaction.

I mouth my questions to Dad. "Is the Minister the only person you're contacting?"

"He's one of many, Tricia. I'm emailing Councillors, TDs, other Ministers and anyone that has a bit of influence to get us a wheelchair-accessible house. There's a lady in Limerick City Council who might be able to fight our corner. I'll try her too."

He rewords his request and sends a version of the email to numerous influential people between June and July 2009. But, despite Dad's persistence, his requests are met with one silence after another. The responses from those that bother are sympathetic, but in reality offer nothing real to help us.

It's so disheartening. I'm scared I'll be left here for the rest of my life. I'm miserable a lot now, particularly at nighttime, scared things will get worse if that's possible. What if we can't get a new house? What will my options be?

The situation causes us all quite some grief, the mood around my ICU hospital bed subdued as we look at each other and wonder if I will ever get out of this hospital. And if I don't get out, neither do my family. They will be imprisoned as much as me.

*

Dad rejects the silence and lack of response, leaving no stone unturned until finally our luck changes. Following a succession of meetings between various parties, Limerick County Council eventually agree to come on board. A number of houses are suggested for consideration. But it's more pressure (and frustration) for my parents as they're expected to go through lists of almost every property in the City and County districts to confirm whether each property has already been considered and, if so, whether it is suitable or not.

Time passes. Every step seems to take so long and still I remain in hospital.

In the outside world, the economic crisis worsens. Funding is exceptionally scarce. So many barriers, so much uncertainty, so many hurdles blocking our path.

*

Dad's life has become one series of requests after another on my behalf. As well as pleading with the Council to get adequate housing, he continues his pleas with the hospital to put more dedicated rehabilitation in place for me.

"We know that MWRH is a general hospital and not a neuro-rehabilitative hospital," he says to the professor when this is used as an explanation regarding the lack of appropriate therapy.

He tries to stay patient when the doctors explain the difficulties. But in no way is he going to give up asking or pointing out the facts any chance he gets when speaking to my care team.

"The therapists here are very attentive but might not have the necessary training to deal with someone like Tricia. We're worried she is losing out. What about trying the National Rehabilitation Hospital again? Have you told them the progress she's making? Would they reconsider?"

Dad takes a picture of me using one of the physiotherapy bikes (I'm really moving on from the tilt table at this stage!).

He shows me the caption he adds to the photo, appealing to politicians for help and using the photo as proof that I am getting better.

'Look at her now – she may be on a ventilator but she is on a bicycle!'

I nod my head. He's trying everything. I can't ask for more. But unfortunately it doesn't appear to be making a difference, at least not that we can see.

*

Facing the reality of my situation and indeed my future, Dad is considering his ability to continue in employment and care for me as well. The ESB have been wonderful to him, allowing him flexibility to be at the hospital as much as possible. But he isn't a person who takes advantage. He needs to make a choice. He makes enquiries into taking early retirement. He also books an appointment with a solicitor to discuss making a will.

In the course of conversation, Dad tells the solicitor about my illness and his reasons behind his decision to apply for early retirement.

Mam is at the meeting too and, between her and Dad, they outline the length of time I have been in hospital and the difficulties we are having in relation to my discharge.

The solicitor listens very attentively, his curiosity piqued.

"But how did your daughter's condition go from severe headaches to life support in such a short space of time?"

My parents are unable to answer why my condition deteriorated so severely.

"But surely this has been explained to your daughter? Or indeed yourselves?"

They turn to look at each other. His questions awaken something in both of them. With the seriousness of everything going on, they've accepted what they've been told.

"How much has been explained to you?" he prompts them. "How is Patricia's illness being described? Is it a virus? A result of complications?"

They don't have any answers. What they do have all of a sudden are lots of questions themselves. They are suddenly very aware that the cause of my illness and subsequent disability has never been disclosed.

They recap on the events of my visits to the GP and admissions to both Limerick and Cork hospitals, sharing the telling of the story between them.

The solicitor listens attentively and, when he is brought right up to date, he strongly suggests they consider legal representation.

"These types of cases aren't really my area," he admits, "but I can recommend Cantillons Solicitors. They're experts in medical cases like your daughter's. Their offices are on the South Mall in Cork City."

Mam and Dad nod in unison. It seems so obvious now he has pointed it out to them. Of course they deserve answers. We all do.

"Hopefully, in time, this will give your daughter a better chance at gaining access to the relevant supports she will need to live outside of the confines of hospital."

Mam and Dad don't need to hear anymore. They take the contact details he offers, along with the tiny glimmer of brightness and hope that comes with it. They waste no time in contacting Cantillons Solicitors and attend a preliminary meeting with the solicitors at the end of June 2009.

Ernest Cantillon and his colleague, Susie Elliott, listen to my parents' account of every stage of my illness. Mam and Dad recount as many details as possible from the onset of headaches in August 2008 to the present day. The telling of the story makes my discharge sound like a game of volleyball, constantly being punched out of reach by the various players on either side.

"We just feel something's wrong," they say, putting their innermost fears and thoughts to the legal team, hoping they will agree I have a case. More importantly, they hope that this expert firm will offer representation and help get me the services and supports my family need if I'm ever to leave the hospital.

"Could it be that one of the doctors didn't pick up on something? Maybe she should have been on a course of antibiotics earlier than she was? It doesn't make sense that she has become so critically ill, despite the number of times she went to the doctor and hospital."

The solicitors probe further, their questions seeming cold and clinical and a bit daunting for Mam and Dad. But the more information they share, the more natural the conversation becomes and soon Mam is interrupting Dad at her usual pace!

"What information were you given at these GP visits?"

"He diagnosed her with flu or a viral infection. And when he did refer her to hospital, she was sent home again. Something must have been missed."

The first meeting ends with some questions about the working conditions at Petmania. Mam and Dad tell Susie and Ernest what they know about my employers' premises, which in reality was far from perfect and left a lot to be desired.

"Tricia is a real animal-lover and sometimes the conditions for animals in the pet store annoyed her."

"Anything of major significance you can recall?"

Again they share the snippets I had told them, in particular an incident where I was bitten.

"She was bitten by a rat in December 2007. It broke right through her skin. She phoned me and I left work to take her to the hospital."

"Did anybody from the store offer to take her?"

"No. I was furious about that," Dad states.

No matter how unreliable my memory might be at times, I don't think I'll ever forget that particular experience! There were two rats sharing a cage, one sick and another healthy. I was trying to separate them and put them in individual cages. But as I went to lift the sick rat, he bit my hand and broke my skin.

I contacted my parents to see what I should do. Dad was appalled. Working with the ESB, he was very aware of the dangers associated with rats. The ESB insisted their employees wore gloves at all times. But this wasn't the case in Petmania.

"You'll have to go straight to the hospital and have a tetanus injection, Tricia," he told me on the phone.

I explained this to management but there were difficulties.

I call Dad again. "I can't get away from work to go to the hospital."

He came to collect me straight away and insisted that I go to the A&E Department of the MWRH for the correct treatment after the bite.

Following this incident, Dad asked me numerous questions in relation to personal protective equipment. "So you don't wear gloves?"

I shook my head. "We don't have any. They're not provided."

After the rat incident Dad brought home some disposable gloves like the ones he used himself at work and issued me with strict instructions. "Make sure you wear these, particulary when you're cleaning out the cages." He handed me several pairs. "And give some to the other workers too."

I did what he asked and when his supply of gloves ran out, I went to Dunnes Stores or the hardware store and bought more. And though I always tried to have a supply there were still occasions when I had to clean the cages with my bare hands.

Dad couldn't understand why it wasn't compulsory.

"The only thing they insist on is that we wash our hands before working with fish if we have been handling other animals. But this precaution is more about the protection of the fish than ourselves!"

"What about antibacterial hand gels and disinfectants?"

Again I shook my head. "Nothing."

"When you're cleaning out the cages and floors, do you wear masks?"

"There aren't any provided. No masks, no gloves. We don't even have aprons to protect our clothes from the dust and dirt."

Mam and Dad give Susie as much background information as they have.

And there were other things they didn't know about, the most important to me being the care and condition of the pets.

Animals have no voice.

While I worked in Petmania, I tried to be a voice for them.

And, ironically, since my illness, I have lost my voice and am now in the same place as the animals. I'm dependent on others to be a voice for me.

*

My parents continue to answer Susie and Ernest as best they can at that first meeting.

Susie is understanding and supportive and takes plenty of time to explain the avenues they are considering. "We will look into the possibility of a zoonotic cause," she explains. "We will have to investigate the possibility that Patricia contacted an infection or virus from infected animals. From what you've described, there is possibly a potential Employer's Liability aspect to this case."

Mam and Dad listen attentively. "How do you go about that?"

"We'll start by requesting Patricia's medical records."

"From the hospital?"

Susie nods. "Both hospitals – the CUH and MWRH – as well as the GP and any others that are directly involved."

My parents sit back in their chairs. Letting the legal experts take control is a huge source of relief – and concern – for them. The stark facts already outlined by Susie and Ernest are grim. And that's only for starters.

"The clinical files from the rat-bite incident might give us some relevant background to the case," Susie adds. "And we'll need to carry out a thorough investigation on Petmania's health and safety standards as well as the conditions Patricia was working in."

"You really think it might have something do with her job?"

Susie nods. "Possibly. Combined with the question mark over Medical Negligence if your daughter's illness was mismanaged at any stage. There were a lot of admissions and discharges during the time Patricia's condition deteriorated. Until I read all the notes and reports, I can't put it further than that."

Mam and Dad are overwhelmed. It's a lot to take in.

Susie's confidence provides reassurance, however. "It's a blank canvas until we start intensive detective work. But that's for us to worry about."

"Thank you."

My parents' gratitude is heartfelt.

"Susie will lead Patricia's case," Ernest states at the end of the meeting.

From that moment on, Susie becomes a tremendous support and, along with the help we are receiving from Grace, some of the distress and confusion is lifted from our shoulders.

*

Susie prioritises my case. By now, Susie and I have been introduced and she's already calling me 'Tricia'.

The first letter she sends on our behalf is to MWRH.

"I've asked them to furnish every document and piece of information of any nature and description in relation to Tricia," she tells Mam and Dad. "As well as MWRH and CUH, I've contacted the HSE headquarters for every record and a list of doctors, hospitals and organisations you've been in contact with."

"Will they send them on?" I mouth.

"They've all promised to send them as soon as they have them to hand. They'll drip-feed them to us in other words. But I've agreed to receiving them like this."

"Did any of them object?"

Susie shakes her head. "Not exactly, but MWRH did try to exclude some records because you're still an inpatient, saying it would be risky to remove them for photocopying."

"Oh. What did you say?"

"I've insisted I need everything."

Susie's extremely busy gathering information but nothing changes immediately. Our lives continue within the confines and restrictions of hospital.

*

Multidisciplinary meetings continue between my doctors, speech & language therapists and occupational therapists to discuss the complexities of my discharge. My parents are invited along on occasion. But the metaphorical volleyball game remains in play. There's no plan in place and we're merely passing the ball back and forward over the net.

I'm still stuck in hospital.

On 22nd July 2009 I receive a disappointing response from the Disability Services Officer. She explains that the Independent Living Division cannot get involved in, or comment on, a discharge plan for me until direct contact is received from the hospital.

More correspondence follows with Grace's help but unfortunately the next letter also contains bad news.

> *In the absence of clarity on where you will be living and a time frame for your discharge, it is not possible for us to plan appropriate supports for you. Service will be planned and delivered based on your home address and functional abilities at discharge.*

I'm gutted.

Mam, Dad and the girls are furious.

*

By now my family rotate the time they spend with me, and one evening Mam decides to make a nice meal for Dad at home. This is the first time she has cooked for him since I've become ill, the first time in almost a year. It's probably the only time they have had a break from the hospital together.

Kiera and Melissa are by my bedside for the evening instead and we're all surprised when a doctor pops her head around the curtain and asks if she can have a word.

"Patricia, we've decided to move you up to the High Dependency Unit."

The suddenness of both her visit and suggestion startles us.

My heartbeat quickens. I look at my sisters for help.

They see the fear on my face.

I see the fury on theirs.

I have no control, no say over what happens to me. What if my tubes fall out? What if the nurse doesn't get to me quickly enough in the HDU? I could die without them noticing.

I can't move. I can't call out. I have no sense of touch. I can't ring a bell. How can I alert somebody if I'm left alone? Thoughts whir at top speed, none of which leave my mind. They're trapped inside my head. Just like me. I'm trapped inside myself.

But Melissa's voice interrupts my panic.

"I'm sorry but you can't move my sister until my parents are told what's going on. Mam and Dad have to be here," she insists, already dialling Dad's mobile number.

Poor Dad, he doesn't even get to enjoy one home-cooked meal without having to rush back to help me and bear the burden of responsibility once again. It's very difficult for my parents. And it's becoming equally difficult for Melissa and Kiera. Their lives are completely disrupted. They barely get to meet their friends, choosing instead to spend as much time as possible with me.

As for me? How has this impacted me? There are no words. And even if there were, I cannot say or shout them aloud! I cannot even scream to relieve my frustration. It's impossible and unbelievable. It's cruel. We are just a normal family. Why has this happened to us?

Tension builds around my bed. Dad phones. He's on the way back with Mam.

He asks Melissa to put the doctor on the phone, arguing that our family should have been consulted. "You can't move her without her professor's permission. He needs to be here."

The doctor instructing the move is equally annoyed. "I'm sorry but it isn't your place to dictate the ICU bed allocation."

When my parents arrive, Dad's invited into an office to discuss the issue. He's kept out of earshot of other patients and families.

His face is like thunder when he rejoins Mam and the girls at my bed. "I've just been told that Tricia is now well enough to go to the High Dependency Unit. Just like that!"

Mam looks on while Dad continues, his gaze fixed on me, the pain he's suffering etched in the worry lines on his forehead.

"I reminded the doctors that you're still on a ventilator, a life-support machine, and need a nurse with you 24-7."

"And what did they say to that?" Mam asks.

"They went off to discuss it. After a while one of the professor's team came to get me and brought me to them. It appears that the team is united in their decision to move you to HDU. They seem to think that you're well enough and the space in ICU is needed for somebody else."

Dad's upset is obvious. But his anger is still bubbling under the surface as he continues. "I told them I will not stand back and let anything else happen to you, Tricia. I'll do whatever it takes to get you the best treatment and care available."

"Calm down, Pat," Mam says but she is upset too.

"She deserves the best treatment, Annette. She hasn't been looked after properly in the past and this is probably what led to the condition she's in now."

"What have the doctors suggested?" Mam asks.

My sisters don't interrupt.

"They suggested St. John's Hospital as an option. I'm not having it! It's out of the question."

I can see how shaken Dad is. I'm scared and finding it hard to take it all in. There's so much going on. And no certainty about what's going to happen to me. St John's is a General Public Voluntary Hospital in Limerick. What on earth can they do for me in St John's?

"I gave them two options – either move her home with ICU nurses, or transfer her to the National Rehabilitation Hospital in Dún Laoghaire. I told them not to move her to the HDU and certainly not to a normal ward. As for St John's …"

He leaves the statement hang. The air is charged with a mixture of anger and fear, our trust in the hospital disappearing after the underhanded way they attempted to move me to HDU this evening. If we can't trust the professionals in charge of my recovery, how can I get better? Am I safe here anymore?

Dad senses my fear and takes my hand in his. "If I have to sit with you 24 hours a day, Tricia, to make sure you're not moved out of ICU, I'm prepared to do that."

The evening is ruined for Mam and Dad. I feel guilty about this. They shouldn't have to mind me like I'm a toddler. But unfortunately that's how it seems to be.

The doctors don't visit anymore this evening.

I spend another night in ICU with my parents either side of my bed, weary with exhaustion I'm sure, but too afraid to leave in case another attempt to transfer me occurs during the night.

When the professor leading the team is back on duty, Dad explains what happened. And though it is much easier for Dad to discuss things with him as we've become familiar with him during my stay here, he doesn't respond as Dad expects.

"I know it is difficult right now but you have to understand that the anaesthetists have full control over the ICU. Neither I nor any other doctor has any say in it."

"But that night they mentioned sending Tricia to St. John's Hospital."

The professor shakes his head. "There is no question of Tricia being moved from this hospital. The High Dependency Unit is the next natural step from ICU. She will be in good hands there."

But despite having little choice but believe the professor, Dad's lack of trust is obvious in the conversation he has with Mam afterwards. "What if they're only placating us and after a short while they move her from HDU to a ward, Annette? And then on to a nursing home?"

"It's becoming so complicated and difficult," she replies. "Why is every step turning into a fight?"

Chapter 12

Patricia Ingle
July 2009
Bed 6 ICU – MWRH
The bell rings … another fighting round

One Saturday morning, I am convinced I'm in Killaloe walking Cody.

"Tricia, what's wrong?" Dad is at my side, a worried look on his face.

"I can't get out of this dream, Dad. My legs won't work. I can't walk. It's a dream. I need to get out of it. I want to wake up. Help me, Dad."

Dad's face falls. The nurse at his side has a similar expression.

"You are awake, Tricia."

"But I should be walking Cody in Killaloe …"

I look at the nurse. Why is she so upset?

Dad takes my hand, tears in his eyes. "Killaloe is the dream, Tricia. This is reality."

I look away. I don't want to live like this.

I hear the door close gently behind Dad. He's too upset to stay.

*

My care continues in ICU in the days and weeks that follow. My family maintain their bedside vigil.

Dad is a permanent fixture at my side, terrified something else will happen if he leaves.

Mam remains her usual encouraging self.

Melissa stays upbeat and positive.

Kiera is still irritated. "It's as if the doctors don't see Tricia as a person," she says repeatedly. "They're acting as though she's in their way, an inconvenience."

You could be right, Kiera, I say silently in my head.

*

Susie gets to work on my case. From the minimal medical notes made available to her at this early stage, she finds a working diagnosis of Lymphocytic Choriomeningitis Virus (LCMV) recorded. This virus arises from sick rodents and because of this, along with the concerns about the conditions in Petmania, she makes a preliminary view of the Employer's Liability she had suspected. Furthermore, as she pores over my records, she notices that the team at MWRH had noted my exposure to various creatures during the course of my employment.

She requests more medical records from a number of doctors, hospitals and institutions. Naturally my GP, MWRH and CUH were amongst the first round of requisitions. She also adds the National Rehabilitation Hospital and the National Virus Reference Laboratory to the list. She has to issue some reminders to get access to all of the records but, lucky for me, she's persistent.

As well as requesting the medical documents, Susie also makes a start on investigations into the conditions at Petmania, collecting statements from some of the other workers there and quickly confirming that there were little if any health and safety precautions taken during the course of my employment there.

I wonder how they feel about being questioned. I wonder if anything has changed in the last year. Maybe there are some improvements. I hope it doesn't cause any difficulty or awkwardness. I had a good relationship with everyone there. We all got on, were good friends and were mostly around the same age. We sometimes met up outside of work, introducing each other to our other friends and having a laugh. Caitriona and I became particularly close and I enjoy her visits to the hospital now and appreciate her making the time to come and see me.

I looked forward to going to work every day, meeting my friends and doing whatever jobs I was asked.

Mostly I enjoyed the work too. There was a lot more to looking after animals than I thought. Every night after work I went on the internet and researched the different types of animals and birds we had in the shop, finding out as much as I could and learning about them one by one so I could take care of them in the best possible way. My research helped me to do my job better and give better information to the people buying pets.

I was mainly in charge of looking after the birds, feeding them and making sure they had water. I cleaned out their cages and kept an eye on them to make sure they were healthy. I was a very honest worker and did everything I could to advise our customers on the care of their pets. Many customers made repeat visits to the store, some asking for me personally and mentioning how helpful I had been on previous occasions. It came naturally to me to offer as much assistance as I could when I had such a genuine interest in animals and wanted only the best for them in their new homes.

Susie's investigations soon confirm that a lack of personal protective equipment is apparent in Petmania. They were neither in place nor available. Being exposed to an increased risk of infection from the various biological agents being used is another concern of Susie's.

My dream job is suddenly becoming a nightmare and I'm wondering if my passion for animals and birds has cost me dearly!

*

We receive an invitation to attend a meeting on the 12th August 2009 with the professor and a multidisciplinary team. We assume this meeting is to agree a definite discharge plan.

In the lead-up to the meeting, Dad keeps busy. He continues his letter-writing and campaign. Every few days he issues pleading emails, using whatever angle he can think of to get politicians and others to take an interest in our case.

The professor is amongst Dad's letter recipients. In his heart he is still terrified that something will happen to me if I'm transferred from the 24-7 care I've been receiving in ICU and he puts these concerns on paper.

Dear Professor,

We note that a provisional date has been set for a multidisciplinary meeting in relation to Patricia's care for Tuesday next, 4th August 2009, at 12p.m.

As you are aware, questions in relation to Patricia's care have of late raised some difficulty. We believe that it is extremely important that a collaborative rather than a combative approach be maintained in terms of planning and implementing Patricia's care. Unfortunately, it appears of late that we are moving more towards a combative (rather than a collaborative) approach. In particular, you will note that in your absence it was suggested that Patricia be moved to the high dependency unit at extremely short notice. It was only on our invoking the "combative approach" that this train of events was stopped in its tracks. We lost great confidence as a result of this and indeed felt that we may be required to sit in with Patricia on a 24-hour-a-day basis at any point so as to protect her position in relation to the care currently afforded to her.

At the last meeting, we were but minor participants. On one occasion we were told that a meeting was to be started between the relevant disciplines in our absence and that we would come along at a later point to join in the discussions. We did not feel that this was appropriate. If we are to be involved, we would like full involvement. We do not believe that it is appropriate, as Patricia's parents, for us to be excluded at any point during this process. We have not been furnished with the minutes of this meeting to date.

Prior to the next multidisciplinary meeting, we believe that it is proper that we are given an agenda, together with all reports and recommendations to date from all members of the multidisciplinary team. We would also ask for a copy of the minutes of all prior meetings.

We have grave concerns that there isn't a coordinated rehabilitation programme in place to date. Time has been lost in terms of ensuring that Patricia is rehabilitated to the best of her abilities and indeed further time will be lost if these matters are not dealt with now. We would like for proposals to be put forward and an approach to be adopted whereby a collaborative, multidisciplinary approach is taken by all parties, ourselves included, to minimise Patricia's disabilities and maximises her abilities. We trust you agree that this is what she deserves and what is altogether possible.

We would respectfully suggest that the meeting provisionally scheduled for Tuesday, 4th August 2009, be postponed for one week to enable you to circulate papers as outlined above.

Please also let us know if you have any objection to us bringing along an advocate/advisor to assist us in this process as frankly, at this stage, we find these matters quite overwhelming and distressing. We have been dealing with the input of a large number of professionals from the hospital to date and would find it far easier to cope with and address the important issues in relation to Patricia if we had the help of an advisor to assist in the process. We trust there will not be a difficulty with this.

We look forward to hearing from you.

Yours sincerely,

———————————————   ———————————————

Mr. Pat Ingle   *Mrs. Annette Ingle*

On the 29th July 2009, Dad arrives at the hospital earlier than normal to meet the professor and hand-deliver the letter.

"He's doing his rounds at the moment," the professor's secretary tells Dad, "but he will be with Tricia by the end of the morning."

Dad waits around, his patience wearing thin as it approaches lunchtime and still no appearance.

"Would you mind paging the professor, please?" he asks one of the nurses again. He had asked the same nurse to page him earlier but she explained how busy he was and refused to disturb him during rounds.

When Dad asks the second time he's annoyed at her response.

"He's gone to another hospital. He's on the far side of the city by now."

"But I've been kept waiting to see him since early this morning!"

Eventually the registrar who works with the professor takes the letter. "I'll make sure he gets it," he promises.

The following day, Dad meets the professor in the hospital. "I'm wondering if you have had time to read my letter?" he asks.

But the professor's reaction takes Dad by surprise – or shock!

"Your daughter is receiving better care than any other patient that has come through this hospital. What you're suggesting in your letter questions my medical capability."

Dad is dumbstruck. And panicked.

But the professor is far from finished and anything but speechless. "The detail in this letter could potentially be brought to the Medical Council as a letter of complaint against me."

"But we have to represent Tricia's best interests," Dad attempts to explain. "We're her parents."

"We don't have agendas for clinical meetings," he informs my father, "and, in light of your requests, I'm postponing the meeting."

Poor Dad is devastated. The professor's reaction really upsets him. He doesn't need to tell us. It is written all over his face.

"I'm not giving up. He might not like my letter but I don't regret sending it."

To compound Dad's frustration, he also receives disappointing responses from the HSE Care Group and Limerick City Council.

The Council confirms that the Housing Department cannot secure a house until they receive confirmation of my care plan from the HSE.

Meanwhile, the HSE Care Group's response states clearly that without a suitably accessible house, they cannot secure a care plan. One blaming the other, the only loser being me.

Left with no other option, Mam and Dad send both responses to Susie.

"I'll write to both parties," Susie assures us, "and suggest that they take a unified approach to finding a workable solution."

*

My parents' stress is obvious. As the revised date of the meeting gets nearer, Dad approaches the professor. We had seen little of him since the letter incident.

"Would it be okay if our solicitor, Susie Elliott, joins us at the meeting?"

"I'd have grave reservations about this. If your daughter is bringing representation to every meeting, I'd also need a legal representative attending."

Susie advises Dad on this. They agree it's best that she doesn't attend and they work with the professor and his team rather than go against him.

"I'll be available by phone though if you want to leave the meeting and call me for advice," she says.

And, on that basis, preparations for the meeting proceed and Grace helps me write a response to the letter we received from the Disability Services Case Manager. I invite her to attend the next multidisciplinary meeting so that she can discuss my discharge plan face to face with the hospital staff.

But 24 hours before the meeting is due to be held, Grace arrives. I know by her face she hasn't anything good to tell me.

"Disability Services called. She's not attending the multi-d meeting tomorrow."

"Why?" I mouth.

"Because she didn't receive an official letter of invitation from your professor."

This is devastating news. It feels as if the world is working against me. Nothing is straightforward. The HSE has one set of rules, Independent Living Disability Services another and the Council another. And meanwhile I'm stuck.

Chapter 13

Patricia Ingle

11th August 2009

ICU to HDU: Bed 6 to Room Number 6

Bitter-sweet taste …

The multidisciplinary meeting takes place on the 11th August 2009 at the MWRH. To our immense relief it goes well and isn't in any way confrontational. I attend with my family and am pleased to be included in the conversation – particularly as it's about me!

Dad takes the opportunity to thank everyone for helping me. His discomfort is obvious but he continues in a steady voice.

"Annette and I appreciate everything that's being done for Tricia. It hasn't been easy and we understand you all have her best interests at heart."

The professor is the first to respond. "All things considered, Tricia is doing well." He turns to look at me. "Apart from the ventilator dependency, you are in very good shape."

"Thank you," I mouth. There isn't much else I can say. I doubt the professor will lip-read.

"What is the plan for Tricia?" Dad asks.

"You've probably heard that swine flu is an issue in the hospital. Tricia is at high risk if we leave her in ICU surrounded by other critically ill patients. At the very least it would cause her severe problems and worst-case scenario it could potentially have fatal consequences."

"But the move is big and frightening for her and us. Will she honestly be able to manage without the round-the-clock care she has been used to in ICU?"

"She'll have a single room in the High Dependency Unit," the professor explains. "The family can become more involved in her care."

Dad nods and gives in. It's all he can do in the circumstances. The risk of swine flu is greater than the risks associated with the move. The professor is the expert and we have to trust his advice. At least this time, we are part of the conversation as opposed to the shock of being ordered to move without any notice.

"Will she receive the same level of therapy?"

"Nothing will change."

Tom, 'Tilting Tom', intervenes. "You've made very good progress, Tricia, but may well be reaching a plateau. We don't want your hopes dashed."

Dad's quick to jump in on my behalf. "Tricia has surpassed a lot of plateaus already and she will continue to do so. Talking about plateaus isn't going to help. Please don't decide that this is as far as she's going to come. Therapy is working. We have to keep trying everything, keep encouraging, keep setting goals and aiming a little higher."

Tom nodded, clearly not willing to argue against Dad's positivity.

I hope Tom is going to keep encouraging me. Dad's right. No matter how difficult it is to make progress, I refuse to give up. I'd like to be a lot better than now but by no means do I believe this is it. I have lots more fighting left inside me. I'd certainly like to be able to do more for myself. I just need time and help – lots and lots of help.

The dietician then provides an update. Seems a bit comical having a dietician when I'm not allowed any real food. But she manages my intake, making sure I'm getting the nutrients I need.

"I know how unfair it must feel that Tricia isn't allowed to eat or drink. But I'm hearing that you're giving her yogurt to taste. Is this correct?"

"Only Petit Filous, a little treat," Mam explains. "She enjoys it. We were told by the staff to try it."

"I do understand. But even those little tastes are, or could be, quite detrimental. Even the slightest bit of food by mouth will cause her to secrete saliva …"

I look around me, seeing the guilty looks flash on their faces. They mean well. I do enjoy the tiniest taste on my tongue, as Mam said. I tune back in to the dietician's explanation.

"And that is very dangerous for her. Creating saliva compromises her tracheostomy. As tempting as it might seem, it's putting Tricia at serious risk."

"We didn't realise," Mam says. "We'll stop immediately."

"You can be sure it won't happen again," Dad adds, then turns to the professor. "Can I ask about the rehabilitation plans in London?"

"Yes, certainly."

"I suppose firstly we're wondering why plans changed in February. She was all set to go and then it was cancelled."

The professor goes into a bit of detail about the communication between MWRH and London. "The therapists in London were unsure about being able to offer anything substantial to Tricia and felt it a waste of time putting her through the journey unnecessarily."

We look at each other, confusion evident on our faces.

"But we were told it was a funding issue. And we've been hoping all this time that it would come up for review. This is very disappointing."

There are a few murmurs from the others in the room but nothing definite is offered.

"Will you email the London hospital and appeal to them again? Please? We're worried she's missing out. She really needs to get the chance of extra rehabilitation. Surely it's worth asking again? At least once?"

"She is definitely in good enough shape to travel now," the professor confirms, "unless of course she gets an infection which could change or halt any plans even at the last minute because of the high level of risk involved."

*

Mam follows the professor from the meeting to put her mind at ease on a few things. "We are really anxious to get her to London," she repeats.

"We'll have to see if it can be arranged," he promises.

"And her speech and language therapy, her occupational therapy and physio? You're sure they will continue in HDU? They are making a huge difference. If that stops completely or is reduced, it could set her back. We're just afraid she'll lose out when she's moved, Professor."

"Of course you're worried. But there's no need. Her therapists will continue working with her regardless of what ward she is in. That's a given. And she'll be able to personalise the room. Bring in photos. Hang them on the wall. Every little thing helps recovery."

"Thank you." Mam exhales, feeling she's done everything she can to plead my case. "I suppose the move will be a change for her at least. Some of the ICU cases are tough to watch for a young girl like Tricia."

*

The transfer is agreed on the basis of continued therapy.

As I'm moved from ICU, I take a last look around, the sound of a member of yet another family crying reminding me of so many upsetting moments in ICU. The thin curtain between beds was never enough to shield me from the fact that a patient was literally dying beside me. It felt strange to have therapists working with me as coffins covered in white sheets were passing by the end of my bed.

An elderly man took a heart attack one afternoon. A lady doctor ran to help him, jumping on top of him and commencing CPR. Despite a nurse pulling the curtain closed around his bed, I heard every sound and effort to save him. I also heard them announce his time of death.

I remember another specific day. I was working on tongue exercises with the speech and language therapist while a stream of peope paid their final farewells to a man on life support in the bed next to mine. This was one of many dying patients during my stay in ICU. Knowing somebody's life was ending so close to me left me very uneasy. To make matters worse, my family were asked to wait outside to allow the other family some privacy while I was left lying there alone listening to it all going on around me.

"I hate it when people are dying right next to me," I told my parents.

As usual Mam wasted no time doing something about it and thankfully a nurse gave permission for one person to stay with me, providing the curtain was kept closed.

I'm not sorry to leave ICU for that reason. I've seen enough coffins and white sheets and heard too many final farewells.

Hopefully the next people leaving around me will be getting on their feet and walking out alive!

Chapter 14

Patricia Ingle
August 2009
HDU – Room Number 6
A Room with a view …

A few days later, I'm moved upstairs to Room Number 6 in the High Dependency Unit. It's strange, to say the least, after spending a year of my life in the Intensive Care Unit. But it's exciting too.

"We can bring in more of your clothes now," Mam tells me.

"And we're allowed put photos on the walls," Kiera says.

"And some posters would brighten up the place," Melissa adds.

This is good news. Finally, I have a say or choice in something. Though I'm still more or less immobile, it will be nice to have more photos around me. I'm looking forward to Kiera and Melissa adding a bit of colour to the drab walls of Room Number 6!

"You'll be very safe here," the nurses assure me, setting up all the machinery and alarms and settling me into my new space. "We'll be watching you. We are only over there." They point towards the nurses' station. "And we have cameras on you too so you won't be able to get up to any mischief."

It feels like I've moved to a new destination, the sounds unfamiliar, the passersby a distraction. It's a single room cut off from the main High Dependency Unit by a narrow hallway. The high window makes the view non-existent. But, nevertheless, it has a bit more space and hopefully will give us a lot more privacy. It isn't quite the destination I had in mind but I'm here now and I'll do my best to adjust.

The nurses fix my tubes and make sure I'm comfortable. "Some of the ICU nurses will be working with you, Tricia. It'll be nice to see a face you know."

This is reassuring.

Kiera and Melissa waste little time in bringing in photographs and putting them up on the wall.

"Let's make it as homely as possible," they suggest, unpacking more clothes.

Mam makes sure I am dressed in ordinary clothes during the day. Though it's an ordeal for those caring for me and myself, it feels better than wearing pajamas the whole time.

Dad is equally eager to learn the steps in my care, taking this responsibility so seriously that he and Kiera sign up for a course with Acquired Brain Injury Ireland. The course is designed to show how to help and understand a family member who wants to live at home after acquiring a brain injury.

"The hours of the course won't interfere with us visiting," Dad reassures me when he tells me about the course. "It's for eight weeks."

He's also very generous to the nurses and visitors, making sure there's a huge bowl of sweets – every variety you can imagine – on the windowsill of my new room. Every Friday without fail, he arrives with a shopping bag filled to the brim and the sweet bowl is filled as quickly as it empties. He also arrives with a flat-screen TV, an upgrade on the model I had in ICU. The hospital already had another television in the room.

"A picture of a St. Bernard dog would be lovely to cover the screen of the telly we won't be using, Dad," I mouth.

And, as usual, nothing is a problem and he arrives with a huge picture that fits perfectly over the screen. Some of my visitors think I'm watching a nature programme!

When I first move into Room Number 6, the shower is working perfectly. The nurses and carers bring me in on a special shower chair and I enjoy one proper shower. It feels strange at first, the water a shock to my system after months of bed baths.

But just as I'm beginning to relax and enjoy the flow of water on my skin, the shower tray begins to overflow and spill out on to the tiled floor. Within minutes there is water everywhere.

"The bathroom is flooding," the nurse calls, reaching up to turn off the shower, her feet soaking as she maneuveres the shower chair and begins the ordeal of getting me dry and dressed while another nurse hurries to get help.

"The boardroom underneath is like a swimming pool," one of the nurses tells me later.

"Hopefully they'll get it seen to shortly," Mam comments. "Tricia was enjoying it. A nice change for her."

"I'm sure the plumber will be up to take a look at it," the nurse responds.

But despite Mam reminding the hospital staff over and over, they never bother having the shower fixed and since then I've had to do without. I managed to have one proper shower but now I'm back to bed baths I'm sorry to say.

It's humiliating if I'm honest. It makes me feel like a small child getting her face and hands washed! And despite numerous reminders and pleas to have the shower repaired, it doesn't happen.

My daily hygiene routine continues as before.

My parents watch and note everything the nurses are doing for me.

"I'll need to be expert when we bring you home, Tricia," Dad tells me.

There's no formal training being offered to them. However, the nurses are aware of Mam and Dad's hunger to be able to care for me and they take the time to show them some of the techniques required for my care. It's all part of the preparation for my homecoming – if it ever happens. Attending to my daily routine is complicated because of all the tubes still attached. These have to be considered no matter what's being done. Getting dressed is a minefield of dodging wires and finding a way around them to put my arm in a sleeve or get a top over my head. I never thought I'd say this but there's a lot to be said for the freedom of a hospital gown!

It's frustrating I'm not advancing more. Transferring me from the bed to the chair is still a bit of an ordeal. The hoist has been tried. I can't say I like it very much but unlike other patients (who hate it apparently), I'm willing to tolerate it. My next option is a banana board. It sounds more exciting than it is in reality and far from anything floating on the sea. The board rests from the bed to the chair and the idea is to slide along the board to get into a seated position in my chair. Because I have no feeling in my hands, it takes a few people to help me using this method. But nevertheless I'm willing to keep trying.

"I'm taking notes, Tricia," Mam says, her diary filling up rapidly as she watches the staff closely and memorises the techniques being used, writing down a few key words as an aid. And the notes pay off because, in a short space of time, Mam and Dad are putting their learning into practice and the nurses are happy to step back and let them.

My 21st birthday is getting closer, whatever it will bring. For my 20th, I received more Mass cards than birthday cards. At the time my prognosis was poor and 2008 could very well have been my last birthday, but it's a year on now and though I remain in hospital I am still here with my family. I am still alive. They won't get rid of me that easy! Thankfully!

Chapter 15

Patricia Ingle
September 2009
Room Number 6
Turning 21 … but no key and no door!

On the 6th September 2009, I celebrate my 21st birthday in the Mid-Western Regional Hospital. I've been in hospital for 370 days and nights. I'm grateful to be awake and alive. I'm grateful to have come out of locked-in syndrome and be able to communicate. I'm grateful to have my wonderful family around me. I'm grateful to the medical staff for getting me this far, despite them believing and telling my family I wouldn't pull through.

Before I got ill, I had plans for turning 21. The idea of moving out of home had crossed my mind. Mam and Dad should be enjoying their freedom, probably doing some travelling. Who could have predicted how things would turn out? Who could have foreseen that when I 'moved out of home', it was into hospital where my whole family are at my side most of the time?

"Happy birthday, Tricia," Mam, Dad and the girls chorus early in the morning, their delight evident as they spoil me with gifts.

My parents have arranged with the staff to host my party in Room Number 6.

"We're going to move out the bed so we'll have more room for guests," Mam says.

I nod and mouth 'thank you' over and over as I watch them decorate the room with banners and balloons.

Melissa has been shopping. She knows how much I love novelties. She must have bought everything in the shop, I think, watching her unload yet another shopping bag.

Family, friends and numerous hospital staff pop in throughout the day and evening, congratulating me and showering me with gifts.

"Happy birthday, Tricia!" Mam carries in a huge cake and they sing 'Happy Birthday' to me.

It doesn't bother me not being able to taste it. I'm thrilled to see everyone who arrives having a slice and joining in the fun.

"I'm delighted you like your pressie!" Kiera laughs as she places a huge tiger teddy bear she'd bought me on my bed.

I grin back at her. Like Melissa, she knows me so well. Once I have an animal close by, I feel better.

Mam is exhausted when all the guests finally leave. She put so much effort into surprising me and making sure my birthday was the best it could ever be, despite the circumstances.

"Thank you," I mouth to Mam, Dad, Kiera and Melissa when it's just us again.

"We're so lucky to have you with us, Tricia. When you come home, we'll organise a big party to make up for the birthdays you've spent in hospital." Melissa understands I'm feeling cheated, despite the effort they made for today.

I nod my head and smile, too weary to even mouth words now and a little bit sad that the day has ended. I can never repay my family for all they're doing for me and I know they'll do everything in their power to get me home so that one day (soon, hopefully) we will be having that party. I cling to that hope. It is the only thing that keeps me going when things get tough. As they often are.

*

After the excitement of my 21st, the campaign to get me home from hospital resumes. Dad does what he can to secure suitable accommodation.

"I had a row with a girl in Limerick City Council," he tells us on 14th September when he returns from a trip to town.

I raise an eyebrow.

"A row about what?" Mam asks.

I listen, eager to hear the answer to that myself. Having somewhere suitable to live is the key to all the other services coming on board.

Dad sighs. "They've done nothing in the last three weeks. Can you believe that? Nothing!"

Mam shakes her head. There isn't anything to say that hasn't already been said.

"What did you say?" I mouth.

"I was devastated, Tricia. I just stormed out the door."

"What happens now, Pat?" Mam asks.

"As I left, she was stating that the City Council had no obligation under the law to source a property."

"But how can she say that?"

Dad shrugs. He looks exhausted. Hitting one brick wall after another and the lack of support from the housing department is so frustrating.

"Who can we trust?" he asks of nobody in particular.

"Susie and Grace," I mouth.

Mam and Dad nod in agreement.

But his visit does prompt some action and Dad receives an update from Limerick City Council, advising that our housing case is now the responsibility of a specific Case Manager. She will be monitoring progress apparently and has already commissioned a report from my occupational therapist. The report outlines the specific requirements I need in terms of housing so these can be matched to any available properties.

Living at home will only be possible when these needs are fully met. Maybe the OT report will force the Council to act a bit faster. Only time will tell.

*

Susie wades through medical records. Her first task is to sort them out and put them in some sort of workable order. That in itself takes a full two weeks, followed by another three weeks scrutinising the thousands of records in detail. Mary Barry, legal assistant with Cantillons, and all the team are helping Susie with this enormous task. God bless their patience! I'm not sure I'd like their job. Considering all the tests, procedures and medications that I've had since all this began I can't begin to imagine the amount of paperwork!

In the early stages of her investigation, she's concerned about my CT scans taken on 2nd and 3rd September 2008. Both of these showed I had non-communicating hydrocephalus (raised intracranial pressure). What worries Susie now is that something might have been overlooked in the CT scan on September 3rd. It shows I had disimproved significantly. As well as this, the notes show other deteriorations during the same period of time that should have set off alarm bells. Not satisfied to ignore this information, Susie and Ernest decide to engage a consultant neurosurgeon to find out more.

"Once he's had a chance to read the scans and the synopsis I've emailed him, he'll give his expert opinion on whether anything was missed at this early stage."

Susie isn't only poring over medical records. She is also very concerned about the lack of rehabilitation I'm receiving. And she isn't alone. Mam is also worried that the therapy I'm receiving is nowhere near enough.

"I've made it clear that we need an early trial because of the urgency of your case, Tricia," Susie tells us on one of her visits. "Having you incarcerated in a hospital room in need of urgent rehab and a transfer home isn't on."

"What can you do?" I mouth.

"I'm going to apply to court to have your situation case-managed. But first I have to serve court proceedings."

"When?" I mouth.

"As soon as the defence is delivered by the other side."

The legal-speak is difficult to follow but I don't need to understand everything because right from the start I know Susie is a person we can trust completely. She is fully on board with managing my case and it is huge consolation to have her working to get me home.

*

Grace emails the professor to discuss the next multi-d meeting, due to take place on the 5th November. In the email she asks if he will issue an invitation to the Disability Services Case Manager so she can attend.

It feels like a house of Leggo to me, making sure the foundations are set carefully and in the right position so the entire building won't keel over, or in my case that they won't unsettle the fragile tower of decisions and personalities involved in getting me home!

And, speaking of personalities, despite the promises of continued commitment to my therapy before I left ICU, it has quickly fallen to the wayside since my move to HDU. It's as if Room Number 6 is on the periphery of hospital activity and I have been completely forgotten about.

Chapter 16

Patricia Ingle
30 Sep 2009
Lane Fox Unit, London
Up, up and away … Government jet

Though I'm afraid to believe this until it actually happens, plans to send me to the Lane Fox Unit in St Thomas' Hospital, London, are back on the agenda.

"There's a scheme called 'Treatment Abroad' and one of the doctors here is organising to get you over for assessment and rehab," the professor tells us.

"That's great news!"

We're exhilarated.

Dad takes the forms and goes in search of the Patient Welfare Office to have it completed. He's gone for quite a while and tells us about his adventure when he returns.

"I might as well have been going to Timbuktu! It took ages to find out. I've been all over the hospital. Talk about a ridiculous place to have a Patient Welfare Office. It's unlikely they have many visitors. It's right at the far end of the hospital – in the old part where the nurses' residence was long ago."

Mam laughs. "Did you get it signed?"

"No, they were closed. I'll have to make a return journey when they're open – that's if I can find it again!"

He sets off again later that day, this time returning with the completed form and my passport to rehab.

"You'll be travelling in style to London," he tells me.

"How?" I mouth.

"In the Government Jet!"

This brings a smile to my face. Little do I know that it's far from Concorde!

But, despite smiling, I'm quite apprehensive about the journey.

Will it happen this time? I've been built up before.

What about my bed when I come back to Limerick? Will Room Number 6 be here waiting for me? Or will another patient have moved in as soon as I'm out the door? I look around, taking in the photographs and bits and pieces. Regardless of its simplicity and lack of basic bathroom facilities, if I have to stay in hospital it's familiar to me now.

Preparations get underway. My family will travel with me, Mam and Kiera getting ready to fly with me while Dad and Melissa follow on separately. Lots of packing for Mam!

*

The trip itself finally comes about on 30th September 2009 and I'm booked into the Lane Fox Respiratory Unit for five days. They specialise in caring for people like me who are struggling to wean off ventilation.

Leaving the confines of hospital is liberating – even if it is only in the back of an ambulance as I'm transported from MWRH to Shannon Airport!

Unfortunately, I'm not quite travelling in the style I had expected as the Government Jet is busy. Instead I'm being flown in an Air Corps airplane. Mam, Kiera, one of my doctors and a head nurse from HDU all squeeze into the plane once I've been loaded.

"For safety reasons, you'll have to lie down for the entire journey," the doctor explains.

The flight itself isn't very enjoyable but the Air Corps personnel are lovely – and very good looking! They do everything they can to make us comfortable.

I fall asleep after a while and the rest of the journey is a blur until I wake up and we've landed in Norfolk Airport.

Mam and Kiera are very impressed to see a line of Air Corps officers waiting patiently for us to land. It almost makes the bumpy ride – and questionable toilet facilities – worthwhile!

I'm lifted into another ambulance and travel with my doctor and nurse. The others follow in a taxi.

Arriving in St. Thomas' Hospital, I'm brought directly to the Lane Fox Unit where I meet up with the others again.

The ward is massive. I wasn't expecting that!

And all of the patients seem to be on ventilators. I should have been expecting that.

"Clearly I've come to the right place," I mouth to Mam.

"The equipment here is very impressive," my doctor from Limerick comments. "Far better than any I've seen to date."

This is good to hear. Impressive equipment will hopefully work miracles!

My Irish doctors hand over my files, wish us luck and leave.

It's a busy few days for me in St Thomas' and I'm introduced to various members of staff who carry out numerous assessments. We meet a doctor from Limerick who works in the unit.

"Nice to meet people from home," he tells us and stays to chat for a while.

Work begins in earnest on that first day. Not a moment is wasted while I'm here. Assessments, physio, movements, ongoing monitoring during the day and night and that's only for starters. Physio prevents my muscles from stiffening. The teams here are confident and knowledgeable. They aren't afraid to try anything and I can't believe what I'm able to achieve with their help.

The facilities are set up specifically to make things more accessible. The television swivels down in front of me from the ceiling. It's so much easier to see the full screen at this angle.

I do a lot of physio from a plinth.

"Now we're going to work on some head movements," I'm told.

It's difficult and takes a lot out of me but with the physio team's encouragement and support I manage a few movements. Unfortunately, I don't have the same success when I try to move my arms.

"Don't worry, it will all come in time."

Their upbeat encouragement is great for my confidence. Nothing seems to be an issue in this hospital and the amount of time they spend with me makes it possible to reach new limits, however small. In just a couple of days the difference is remarkable. The hospital's attitude towards ventilated patients is completely different to what we have experienced so far.

"Bring Tricia out whenever you can," Mam and Dad are advised. "While you're here in Lane Fox, we'll make sure she gets a chance to get outside the hospital."

Talk about a literal breath of fresh air! For the first time since August 2008, the five of us get outside for a walk. Dad pushes my wheelchair. I'm wrapped up to keep warm and we walk along by the Thames River, close to Westminster Bridge. I enjoy it so much, looking at the boats cruising leisurely through the water and taking in the buildings and sights on the opposite bank of the river. What a difference it makes to see something other than the walls of a hospital room! What a difference it makes to feel like a normal human being! We even fit in a little bit of shopping.

And the best is yet to come from our trip to the Lane Fox Unit.

"I'm going to try and fit you with a speaking valve," the doctor tells me.

"It didn't work when they tried it back in Ireland," Dad says.

"I'm going to look at the breath settings on your ventilator, Tricia," he explains. "Sometimes a few adjustments can make all the difference."

I listen. I hear him. I'm in no doubt he knows what he's talking about. But I'm afraid to hope. I'm afraid to believe it's true.

My family watch. I'm not the only one speechless!

The doctor refers to my notes, working away as we wait. Nobody speaks. He does what he needs. I feel him working on the trachea tube at my throat. I feel a funny sensation as the speaking valve is connected.

"Want to try and say something, Tricia," he encourages.

I look at my family's expectant faces. It's tempting … but I resist playing a practical joke.

Instead I open my mouth to try.

"Finally," is the word I utter, the first word out of my mouth after more than a year, the huskiness in my voice strange but in no way taking away from the magic I've just experienced.

I can talk. I have a voice. I can be heard.

Mam is in tears. She hugs the doctor. "Thank you so much for letting us hear Tricia's voice again," she says through her tears.

Dad also looks a bit wobbly and close to tears. "It's a miracle."

As for me, ironic as it sounds, there are no words to describe this feeling.

I am amazed by the work being done on me and for me while I'm here. The rehabilitation opportunities are unbelievable. But what's just happened is the best of all so far. Finally, I can communicate again. Finally, I can take part in conversations.

Unfortunately, the five days come to an end and I have no choice but return to Limerick, the distance I've travelled in recovery far more significant than the short flight to the UK.

"Thank you all for everything these last few days. Not only for Tricia's speaking valve but for suggesting and allowing us to take her outside." Dad's gratitude is heartfelt.

"We'll send an extensive report to your consultants," the doctor assures us when we are ready to go. "We'll include a large number of recommendations on how to build on the therapy you've received here."

The experience in Lane Fox has been eye-opening. Seeing what's available in a specialist unit like this one makes it harder to accept how little rehab I'm getting at home. Maybe that will change when the doctors in Limerick read the St Thomas' report. Maybe. Mentally I'm crossing my fingers and toes, hoping that the advice from Lane Fox will materialise in MWRH.

*

"We simply don't have the time here to devote special attention to one person," is the excuse I'm given by the nurses when I'm settled back in Room Number 6.

The Lane Fox report is ignored. Another set of broken promises, another brick wall.

My world has shrunk to the dimensions of an isolation hospital room that is smaller than the living room in our house.

My family settle back to their 'shift work' of visits. They attend to my needs from early morning until late at night. Between them they wash and dress me each morning, the entire process sometimes taking almost two hours. I co-operate to the best of my ability, sometimes falling asleep the moment they're done and I'm supposedly ready to face the day. The lack of basic shower facilities makes the process far more difficult. And humiliating.

The shower is still out of action, the shower room now being used as a storage area for my suitcases of clothes! Far from ideal but completely out of necessity, Mam has no choice but to put them in there so there's enough room for people to sit around the bed.

"I'm not sure those suitcases should be in there," one of the staff commented one day. "How will the cleaners get around them? What if the cases are holding any sort of grime that could give Tricia an infection?"

"What option do we have? Tricia's here so long. There's no mention of her getting out. She needs clothes to wear! And there has to be somewhere clean and dry to store them." Mam is insistent and stands and waits for an answer.

The nurses understand how we feel and think of my situation when they spot a single wardrobe on another corridor. They bring it to Room Number 6 and place it in the shower room. Surprisingly it's left there. Even more surprisingly, nobody objects when it has to be moved so cleaners can get in around it. Instead of a shower, I have a wardrobe. Instead of the promised rehab, I get excuses.

It's difficult not to be affected by the anticlimax. Leaving Lane Fox on such a high, hoping it was the beginning of something new, it's not surprising my spirits dip when I realise the therapy won't be continued in Limerick. My family try what they can to motivate me and keep my spirits up. And I try to respond for their sakes. But they know me too well. They can see through the façade. They know I'm faking.

Unlike the attitude in Lane Fox, I rarely get outside of the room in Limerick. It isn't the staff's fault. I understand that. Their time is limited and there's a lot involved in moving me because of all the wires attached. On rare occasions when the nurses can make the time, they wheel my chair to the garden at the back of the hospital. Dad is in charge of the huge oxygen tank behind my chair. But even that little excursion is difficult because of how close it is to the Cancer Unit. Despite my gratitude at getting a change of scenery, the location makes the outing daunting and depressing as I glance toward the unit and wonder about the young and old patients inside.

But I enjoy passing the hospital shop and one day I choose a balloon and a toy rabbit and Mam buys them for me. Dad slips the balloon on my wrist and everyone laughs when I beat Dad with it – playfully of course! They're secretly chuffed that this tiny movement proves I can move my hand a little.

Mam watches my mood closely and mentions her concerns to my doctors that I'm not coping so well.

"It's getting harder for her. She wants to come home and it's upsetting that nothing is happening. To be honest, I'm worried about her state of mind."

Her pleas are considered and a psychiatrist comes to visit, her attempts at help more about medication than anything else.

I mouth a very clear "No, thank you" and wave her away.

I have my speaking valve in later and make sure my family understand. "I don't want her back, Mam. No happy pills."

Mam relays this information to the team. She had already asked them not to give me pills but she had politely but firmly been told that I'm over 18 and able to make that choice for myself.

The psychiatrist doesn't return. I don't accept the offer of anti-depressants. Mam and Dad are relieved I made the same choice they would have made for me. I'm relieved the doctors listen to my wishes. But the darkness remains and I find it harder and harder to hide my despair from my family.

Chapter 17

Patricia Ingle
October 2009
Room Number 6
A mention in the High Court ...

Susie brings us the consultant neurosurgeon's view of the CT scans that were taken on the 2nd and 3rd September 2008. The news is difficult to hear. The neurosurgeon believes that my condition needed urgent neurosurgical expertise and intervention. In his expert opinion I should have been transferred to the CUH at an earlier stage because the required neurological facilities or expertise isn't available in Limerick Hospital.

"I'll be writing to the Injuries Board," Susie tells us, "now that I have this report as well as the one from the consultant in infectious diseases. It will be a very long letter."

"Why do you have to do that?" I want to know.

"Whenever there's an Employer's Liability aspect to a case, Tricia, it's necessary to make a submission to the Injuries Board. There's no way around this. But I'll tell them about your situation, the lack of intensive rehabilitation. I'll plead with them to treat your case as urgent."

In her submission letter, she requests that the matter be rejected by the Injuries Board as soon as possible to have the appropriate authorisation issued.

"I want to get to Court as a matter of urgency. I don't want any more time wasted in getting you the rehab you need. And of course we want to get you home to your family."

"Will the reports from your experts help that?"

"I've decided to base it on the hospital records rather than introducing third-party evidence at this early stage. I'd rather let the hospital records dictate decisions for now. I want to keep our reports fully confidential."

I smile unknown to myself, my story becoming a bit like a CSI Crime Scene Investigation programme!

*

Susie brings an update on her next visit to Room Number 6.

"Step one has worked in our favour. The Injuries Board have done what I asked and rejected the matter of your case. Now we can get on with the next stage."

She gets to work on serving proceedings to my employers Petmania Ltd., as well as their head office, O'Keeffe's of Kilkenny Ltd. She also serves medical negligence proceedings on the Health Service Executive (HSE).

"Are you saying that where I worked caused me to get the disease in the first place?"

"Yes, but I'm not going to base the case too tightly on just one specific disease," she explains. "They've mentioned LCMV – that's lymphocytic choriomeningitis, a rodent-borne viral infectious disease – but the records don't show a formal diagnosis, only a working diagnosis. On that basis, it's safer to keep our options open just in case something else shows up later in the investigation."

*

The first time my name is heard in the High Court is October 2009 when Susie issues an application to have my legal proceedings urgently case-managed – a landmark date in our diary.

Susie is cautious. She takes nothing for granted. She has gone to great effort to support the court application she's submitting with a lengthy and extensive affidavit containing four very important reports from four experts in their fields. In a nutshell, the reports spell out how urgently I need rehabilitation. They don't hold back on the appalling situation I'm currently in, incarcerated (this is one of Susie's great words) in a hospital room, without the appropriate equipment to even have a shower! 'Incarcerated' really paints the picture of being imprisoned – and this is exactly how I feel.

Susie progresses the case to the next step and so far is having good luck.

Mr. Liam Reidy Senior Counsel and Mr. Alan Keating Barrister at Law take Susie's affidavit seriously and promise an early court hearing. Mr. Reidy opens the reports to the Court and the result is that a case-management process is successfully secured on my behalf.

Courts and cases aren't something I know very much about but I've no doubt this case-management process is a good thing.

"My next job," Susie tells us after she shares the good news about this result, "is to request all the CT scans, MRI scans and X-rays from MWRH and CUH."

I tune out and let Mam and Dad carry on the conversation with Susie. Several times they stop to ask for my opinion, determined not to exclude me no matter how long it takes me to mouth a response.

The speaking valve is making a great difference. It's giving me a way of voicing my fears and concerns. But I can only wear it for very short periods. Half an hour is as much as I can manage some days, less if I'm under pressure to breathe. But a little while is better than none at all. And when I have the speaking valve on I have plenty to say!

It grazes against my throat when I'm wearing it but I'm told the sensation will fade in time. But it's worth every bit of discomfort. The sound of my own words will never be something I take for granted again. But there are risks. I'm told this on a daily basis. There's also a fear of infection if I wear it too long. When the speaking valve is in place, the cuff from my ventilator needs to be down. The cuff provides protection. It stops the saliva seeping into my chest. If I have too much saliva in my mouth, I need to be suctioned.

"Suction, Tricia?" is Dad's constant reminder when I'm wearing the speaking valve. The poor man is terrified I'll overdo it. And he is probably right. I am a strongwilled person, always have been. But I'm careful too. I don't want to make myself ill or cause aspiration and infection. I don't want to be back to that place where I can never speak at all.

I'm able to sit out in my chair for a bit longer too. I'm moving my head gently from side to side. This makes it easier seeing around me, getting a better view rather than just straight ahead. I'm happy with these little improvements. If I could get more of the type of neuro-rehabilitation I received in Lane Fox, I know it would make a difference. Being completely weaned off ventilation is my dream. I hope against hope I'm not fooling myself. What I wouldn't give to be able to breathe normally. My recovery chances would multiply I'm sure. I wouldn't need suctioning. I wouldn't have to wear secretion patches behind my ears to control saliva and make sure it isn't seeping into my lungs. Life would be a whole lot easier. And I'm sure the people looking after me would agree. There's no let-up.

*

Susie's patience is tested by the scans and X-ray images she's receiving from MWRH and CUH. Some of the CDs are unreadable and other images missing entirely. She has to get back on to the hospitals to generate new disks, and pay a second time for her trouble!

"Any update on rehab?" Dad enquires.

She shakes her head. "Not unless we can get Tricia to London again, I'm afraid. There's no equivalent here in Ireland."

"Will you contact St. Thomas' again?"

"Of course," Susie promises. "I'll put something in writing to the professor. And if that doesn't work, I'll try and source some independent rehabilitation consultants and have a needs assessment carried out. They should be able to recommend the best place for you to go. If it merits it, we can make it one of our motions for court."

Rehab sounds as far in the distance as ever but at least Susie has a definite plan, more than we could have hoped for a few months ago and certainly more than we could have achieved without having somebody to fight our corner.

Chapter 18

Patricia Ingle
November 2009
Room Number 6
Court appearances and empty promises ...

Hope, though it's difficult to cling to at times, is what keeps me going in my darkest moments. I will never give up hoping that I will get home, that I will improve, that I will get my legs and arms to work again, that I will be able to move without an army of people and gadgets required to get me from lying to sitting to standing.

I try to stay positive. I try not to dwell on the things I can't do anymore, like eating real food or enjoying snacks and ice creams or an ice-cold drink on a warm day. These are impossible for me now. Whether it will ever change, I have no idea. But I continue to hope. There might be a miracle around the very next corner. There has to be something better than this waiting for me. I have a heightened sense of smell. And there is nothing wrong with my taste buds except the sweet or savoury taste of anything could kill me! Instead I'm reliant on the PEG feeding tube and automatically receive 1000mls between 8 o'clock in the evening and 5 o'clock in the morning. Straight after, I get 750mls of water, also 200mls supplement. I don't think about it anymore. Where's the point? I have no choice in this. I prefer to put my health first and if it helps me get better, then I'm happy to do without food. I know my family and other visitors feel sorry for me. They feel uncomfortable eating around me but I reassure them that I'm fine. I love to see them eating and enjoying their food. They should. I would.

Am I happy about this? Of course not! It upsets me at times but I try not to show it. I think about getting better instead. I still love all the different tastes and foods. I dream about them sometimes. I'm still me.

*

Another multi-d meeting is held on the 5th November 2009. I'm happy there's a little progress. At least the guest list is increasing! All of my various therapists arrive with folders of notes on the progress (or not!) that I'm making.

The Case Manager from Disability Services arrives in plenty of time. The Public Health Nurse from our district in Ballinacurra is also here. The conversation is positive when the meeting gets underway.

"What we are suggesting is up to 21 hours nursing care as well as some Personal Assistance hours for Tricia once she is discharged into the care of her family and the Community Care team. Let's face it, she is dependent on others for everything. This has to be taken into account." Disability Services are clear in their request.

This all sounds good. Or should I say, it will be good if it is agreed!

The ward sister from ICU gives an account of my daily requirements. She details the specific tubes that need to be changed at various times throughout the day, the trachea needing cleaning and suctioning and much more. "Cumulatively, there are approximately three hours spent with Tricia each day."

The Community Care nurse joins in at this point. "You'll be lucky to get a nurse to fit in with that schedule, being available at certain times of the day."

Dad isn't impressed. "There will be no risks taken with Tricia. We're lucky she is still alive and her care plan cannot be down to a question of luck."

"Of course if we are in a position to arrange a weekly schedule, whatever nurses are assigned to Patricia will work to a specific timetable and be there to care for your daughter at their designated time," the Community Care nurse clarifies.

The conversation proceeds. I'm amused to hear them suggest baby monitors. Again, my parents have their say about something as unreliable as this.

"That's ridiculous," Mam says. "She'll need a nurse with her. Baby monitors aren't going to tell if Tricia's trachea tube has come off. We will do what we can as a family but we cannot provide 24-hour care. If she isn't given the relevant care, we will have to work around the clock. This means we won't get any sleep. That would be dangerous for Tricia. And for us too."

"I'll follow up on the nursing hours once I've checked with my manager," the Community Care nurse confirms. "But I'll have to get approval before I can commit to the level of service you're suggesting."

The Disability Services Case Manager isn't as convincing about the PA hours, however, and my heart sinks at her response. "I can't guarantee anything at this stage. Resources are already stretched our end. But I'll see what I can do and get back to you."

Grace notes everything. She won't give up easily. But will that be enough? The authorities seem to hold the reins. They're the ones with the power to get systems in place to get me home.

*

Following the meeting, conversations resume and despite the positives floating around about nursing and PA hours, there is nothing definite.

"I've written to Disability Services again," Grace tells us a week later. "If she'll give us a letter confirming the provision of a home care package, the Council will be able to purchase a house for your family on this basis."

But the response – despite arriving within a few days of receiving Grace's correspondence – is another in a long line of delaying tactics. All the letter seems to offer is an explanation around the reasons for not giving us anything in writing guaranteeing a home care package. Grace reads an excerpt.

> *Preliminary discussions are ongoing between Public Health Nursing and the Nursing team here in the hospital but there is so much confusion around your care, Disability Services say it's too soon to give anything definite in writing.*

"Talk about moving chess pieces around a table!" Mam is furious and frustrated.

"Is anyone willing to make a decision for Tricia? One blaming the other, Public Health Nurses waiting for the hospital nurses and vice versa – or so it seems!" Dad's ready to explode.

Meanwhile I'm stuck. Still nowhere nearer getting out of Room Number 6!

At this stage I'm beginning to wonder if the number 6 is becoming my unlucky number. It certainly seems to be following me. I was born on the 6th and so far I've been in Bed 6, Ward 6 and now Room 6. And Melissa laughed when she told me that the Room number in Brú Columbanus – where they stayed in Wilton, Cork – was also number 6!

666 – the code of demons. Is this an omen? Am I doomed to be here for the rest of my days?

"What can we do?" I mouth to Grace.

"I'll keep following your case up with them," she promises. "I will not let them forget about you."

Winter sets in. Natural light is replaced with increasing hours of darkness, inside my heart as well as outside my window. I can report, however, that my family and team of therapists are very pleased with the progress I'm making.

"Well done, Tricia," is a comment I'm hearing more and more. The encouragement is motivating.

"You're making our job much easier," a nurse comments another morning when I manage to make some movements during the sling transfer from bed to chair, which we are now using.

Mam is watching closely. "You'll be out of a job soon," she teases, visibly delighted with this new development.

Dad is quiet as the nurses and carers do their work but the pride on his face is impossible to hide. And only that I'm so exhausted from the effort of moving my body I'd probably be a bit embarrassed that he's so proud of his 21-year-old daughter doing something as basic as moving!

But he isn't only watching with pride. He's watching to learn, as himself and Mam are particularly busy these days. They've had training in everything to do with my feeding, ventilator and suctioning. Kiera and Melissa also learn about suctioning. They're comfortable with most of my equipment and know whether to react to an alarm or not. Perfecting it took some time and lots of false alarms (pardon the pun). Every time they hit against a wire or tube when I was being dressed, it seemed to trigger an alarm.

"My heart is in my mouth. Everything I touch seems to set off a bell," Melissa told me.

But after a few days of beeps, they got used to the various tones and are now adept at distinguishing bad from good.

"We're great students," Dad boasted when they'd accomplished hooking up the PEG feeds.

It needs to be done three times every day and didn't take them too long to figure it out. First they learned how to manage solids and then liquids.

Suctioning is far more complicated.

The suctioning machine itself is a very important part of the whole set-up in terms of equipment. The nurses give it a lot of time, explaining the various attachments and adjustments.

"The machine can be set at different pressures."

"How will we know what the right pressure is?" Mam asks.

"Don't worry, Annette, we're going to help you with that. The state of Tricia's lungs, her oxygen stats and the amount of suctioning required on the day will determine what adjustments are made to the settings."

The nurses don't hide behind the seriousness of this process.

"Suctioning is extremely important and requires extreme care, particularly the one going into her chest. If you get this wrong, you could inadvertently puncture Tricia's lung."

No pressure on my poor parents!

The number of suctions I need depends on how healthy my chest is on a particular day. When I have a chest infection, it can be up to four or five suctionings in just one hour.

"The timing is crucial. It has to be spot on. Take the ventilator off Patricia's neck for about ten seconds and –"

"What if we get mixed up and can't get it done quickly enough?" Mam interrupts.

The nurse understands her fears and takes her time to explain.

"If you make a mistake, put the ventilator back on. Fix whatever has gone wrong and try again."

"It sounds easier than it is," Mam says later.

"We'll practice, practice, practice, Annette," Dad says. "Surely, between us, we'll learn it in time."

"Work carefully but quickly is the advice," the nurse tells them. She takes plenty of time to help Mam and Dad.

The scariest piece of information is the reality that when the ventilator is off I'm not getting any oxygen. In other words, I could die if the suctioning isn't completed within the ten seconds! After surviving so far, I'd really like to stay around for some time longer.

Getting the first part right is only the beginning. Suctioning has a few more streams to it.

The second type of suctioning is through my mouth and down the back of my throat to reach the upper side of a balloon sitting at the back of my neck as part of the tracheostomy set-up. It sounds complicated and it is complicated. And a little uncomfortable too at times. This needs a lot of suctioning. If the balloon goes down, the saliva goes straight into my chest. And then I'm likely to get an infection.

Poor Mam and Dad are weary. And they're still not home and dry with their lessons.

"The trachea itself also needs suctioning."

I've been made to feel quite special because of my 'unique' trachea. It's a new type of trachea I had fitted in the Lane Fox Unit in London. The nurses in Limerick haven't seen this type before.

"What's different about it?" I mouth.

"It has a small-diameter tube sitting in the trachea device. It's collecting saliva all around the balloon all the time."

Oh and what happens then? I don't mouth my question but the nurse is already explaining.

"A syringe is inserted into the tube and takes the saliva from the balloon intermittently. The best part about this is that it's done without taking you off the ventilator, Tricia. Less risk for you."

It wouldn't surprise me if Mam and Dad have nightmares about suctioning. They're certainly uptight about it. There is quite a lot riding on them getting it right.

I have no gag reflex. I can't cough. This is why the suctioning has to be done right. Who can blame Mam and Dad freaking out a little over this? Dealing with ESB wires and lengths of cable all his working life is rather different for Dad than inserting tubes into his daughter's chest and throat!

The learning continues. The progress my parents and sisters make in so many aspects of my care gives great hope that we will actually be able to manage if (I really mean when) I get home. I'd like to think the hospital are noticing this too. Maybe it will help them trust my parents' ability and dedication. I sincerely hope so.

*

Finally Limerick County Council sanction funding for the purchase of a house for us. It's a dream come true. We find out almost by accident when Dad is in contact with a junior politician and he refers to the funding approval in an email. At least one of Dad's emails is fruitful. We are absolutely overjoyed. Once a suitable property is located and it has passed whatever inspections are required, the care plan can be put in place. All the pieces of the triangle are joining together at last.

And though I'm afraid to get too excited, Mam and Dad are doing their utmost to get permission to start taking me out of the hospital during the day. They have been building up very gradually for a number of weeks, taking me for short trips around the hospital and stopping for a quick cup of coffee at the hospital café.

"A bit of shopping would be nice, Tricia," Mam says with a smile. "What about a trip to the Crescent Shopping Centre? It's easy to get around."

I don't need to be asked twice. The prospect of a change of scenery is as exciting as it gets for me right now. I know she'll spoil me – as will Dad and the girls – if they get me in the vicinity of a shop! And it won't matter if we are accompanied by nurses or not, they will encourage me to spend!

Melissa and Kiera are as excited as I am.

But then I get a chest infection. This halts my progress and my shopping! Luckily the IV antibiotics and increased amount of fluids get it under control pretty quickly and within a few days I'm back on track.

"You can't kill a bad thing," I say when I'm allowed put my speaking valve on again.

This is another downside of having any form of infection. I'm not allowed wear the speaking valve because my lungs are exposed. I'm not exactly in the form for chat when I have an infection if I'm honest, but the lack of a speaking valve makes the decision for me regardless of my wishes!

*

One of my proudest moments at the end of 2009 is managing to stand upright. Seeing the world from an upright position is something I thought I'd never experience again. But my persistent physiotherapists keep working with me and now stand either side of me to make sure I don't topple over.

I smile at Mam and Dad. Kiera and Melissa are also sitting there grinning as I sway unsteadily. I have one physio holding my hips, another holding my legs. I stand for a couple of seconds. It mightn't sound much. But for me, this is huge! As for my family, the look of pride on their faces says it all. They have sat watching me for 15 months. They deserve this moment as much as I do. The stress and strain has been showing on their faces. They try to hide it from me in particular, maybe even from themselves. I've heard whispers around my bed that they're attending a counsellor. I'm not surprised with all they've been through, not to mention the fear and responsibility of what's to come when they take me home. I'm determined to do all I can to make it easier but I'm conscious of how limited my options will be.

The professor makes an unexpected announcement shortly before Christmas.

"The Lane Fox Unit have been on requesting you're sent over again. Has anyone told you?"

"First we heard of it," Mam said. "What date?"

"Next week."

I shake my head. I'm still recovering from the chest infection. I know I'm not well enough just now. Therapy is very hard work. And the weather is dreadful. Making the journey in summertime was one thing, but travelling now in the cold when I'm still getting over the infection? I'm not up to it.

"Can it be postponed until the weather is better?" I suggest.

The professor is understanding but realistic. "I'll let them know in Lane Fox," he offers. "But there's no guarantee of when a slot will become available again."

I stick to my decision to defer and, despite it being my own choice, I hit a severe low afterwards.

One week to go to Christmas. Staying positive is becoming impossible. I can't bear this feeling of ultimate despair. I want to go home.

Chapter 19

Patricia Ingle
December 2009
Room Number 6
Deck the halls …

Christmas arrives and with it bags full of presents from my family and friends. Melissa takes great delight in tipping them on to my bed. The array of colour is fascinating. What is actually there a bit of a blur as I try to focus on the huge pile of goodies. I look around the room, the expectant faces waiting for my reaction. I repay their kindness in the only way I can. I smile. Each and every one lets out a breath. They worry constantly.

Yet again my family do everything in their power to make my limited life larger than it actually is. Room Number 6 is decorated to within an inch of its life, thanks to Mam and the girls. We spend Christmas Day together in the confines of the room, other relations and friends making brief appearances and apologising for tiring me out.

Midnight arrives, another Christmas over, a sigh of relief all around. It's as good as it can be. The hospital staff make a big effort this time of year, with twinkling lights and festive aromas and even a visit from Santa Claus himself. It's an improvement on last year but in stark contrast to the celebrations my friends are undoubtedly enjoying – the parties, sleepovers and nights on the town I'm missing with people my own age. Some friends like Caitriona and Bobby are regular visitors but others are seen here less and less. I understand they've moved on. I understand it's difficult for them to see me like this. Who on earth would want to spend their free time in a hospital when all the fun is outside? And they feel bad telling me their news, filling me in on the latest relationships or what concert tickets they got in their stockings this Christmas. I see it in their eyes, the guilt for living their lives when I can't live mine. At least not the way I want to.

*

I'm shattered after the excitement of the day. It does feel like Christmas and if anything this makes me more homesick than I already am.

I'm back in bed and settled, rigged up to food and drink for the night, my NIPPY checked and humming rhythmically in the background, my catheter bag emptied and my family leaning in close to kiss my cheek and promise to be back first thing.

I close my eyes tight and see my reality vividly behind my eyelids. Decorations, no matter how nice they are, cannot camouflage the fact I'm still in a hospital room, in a building full of sick people. And, unlike the majority of patients, there is no certainty whatsoever that I'll ever be discharged.

I crave a proper Christmas at home with my family. I crave normality. I crave the choices and opportunities I once took for granted. I crave a time machine where I can turn back the clock and enjoy good health and active limbs to run, hop and skip.

*

"We have a little surprise for you," Mam announces one morning during the Christmas holidays. "We're taking you out for a breath of air."

"How?" I mouth, looking out the window.

It's a bright day but cold. The temptation to get outside and feel some real air on my face and smell something other than hospital disinfectant is too great to pass up. I'm infection-free. I'll take my chances. The ordeal in wrapping me up warm and attaching me to portable gadgets, tubes and wires seems to take forever. There's as much fuss involved in getting me ready for a trip around the hospital grounds as there was to get me on the plane and over to St. Thomas'! But it's worth it to see something other than the four walls of Room Number 6.

A nurse accompanies us, and Mam and Dad chat as they take turns pushing the wheelchair around, our first taste of normality since the shopping trip near the Thames.

*

But the weather changes and it isn't possible to be brought outside for quite some time again. I'm struggling against the sinking feelings threatening to take hold. It's hopeless.

Grace emails the professor to set a date for another multi-d meeting.

"It will be February," she tells me. "That's the earliest date I can get."

And meanwhile, I'm expected to smile gracefully and be grateful for twenty minutes of physio every day! It doesn't matter how persistent or enthusiastic the physio team are. There's only so much they can do in such a short length of time. I'm working so hard with them, progressing a little but not enough. Everything seems to be caving in around me. Prisoners have a sentence, a release date. They know the duration they're inside for. But me? I don't even have that.

*

"Should auld acquaintance be forgot ..."

We watch the New Year ring in on TV. Fireworks light up the sky in the distance. Limerick welcomes 2010. Whatever it will hold.

It's the year I'm going to turn 22 and I've no idea if I'm ever going to live in the outside world again. Or will the people in power discreetly slip me into some form of home or infirmary where I will be forgotten about it in time?

"Come on, Tricia," my therapists and family encourage on a daily – if not hourly – basis.

I feel guilty that I'm worrying them. But every morning I wake up here, every night I have to stay here, I feel myself slipping deeper and deeper into depression.

"What's wrong, Tricia?" Dad asks gently. "I want to help."

"I'm sorry, Dad. It's just being here. It's like prison. No way out." I don't actually say all these words. It would take forever. I'm still slow with the speaking valve. But by now Dad's almost a mind-reader, never mind a lip-reader! And when I'm annoyed and irritable as I am right now, I click my tongue when I'm trying to interrupt or get attention.

"But maybe the next meeting will get us results, Tricia. Why don't you think about what you want? We'll make sure they listen. And Grace will help. And Susie too."

I close my eyes to hide the misery and frustration. Everyone is trying their best, except those that really can help. They are just fobbing me and my family off with platitudes. They tell us what we want to hear and then nothing at all happens. Such a waste of time.

One of the anaesthetist nurses in MWRH chats to my parents. They bring her up to speed on what's being offered in the line of nursing and personal assistant hours as part of my discharge.

"That's far too little," she states. "Patricia wouldn't be safe with that meagre support."

Though it's good that she agrees with us and her expert opinion gives us the confidence to keep fighting for a realistic number of hours, it still takes weeks to even get another multi-d meeting.

My parents bring me any news they can to keep me stimulated, using every little distraction to keep me interested and focused.

Dad shares his news. "I've made some enquiries into retirement, Tricia."

Poor Dad. Is there anything he won't do to be available for me?

"But you enjoy your job?" I mouth, looking around at the others.

"But I like spending time with you more," he says with a smile. "Mam and myself will be able to work together to take care of you when you come home."

Despite the darkness enveloping me, he's neither giving in or giving up it seems.

My stock response: I smile.

"I'll probably be allowed retire on compassionate grounds," he explains, "even though I'm still only a young fellow!"

*

"We're going to take another serum sample," the doctor tells me when things return to some form of normality in the New Year.

I nod my head, too fed up to care. It's not as if these tests are making much difference to my day.

If only there was a serum sample, fluid sample, blood test, X-ray or scan that would wave a magic wand and give me my life back. If only. The two words dictating most of my thoughts at the moment. If only this hadn't happened. If only I could walk. If only I could talk. If only I could eat. If only I could drink a glass of water. If only I could taste the foods I enjoyed. If only I could jump out of bed or swim with dolphins like I did in Florida. If only I could breathe without a ventilator. If only my tongue wasn't over to one side. If only I wasn't incontinent. If only I could remember half the things I forget. If only I could meet my friends, drive my car, play with Cody. If only I still had my dog. If only I could still take care of him. If only I had the power in my legs to run up a hill with him. If only I could follow my dreams and set up my own pet-grooming business. If only I had the power in my arms to give my family a proper hug. If only I could grab a pen and write down everything I want to say. Actually, scrap that last statement. If only I could undo all the damage done to my vocal chords and open my mouth to speak and laugh and sing out loud, maybe out of tune but out loud nonetheless. If only.

*

137

Susie's progress is slow but constant as she prepares to issue letters of claim to my employers and the HSE. The expert advice being received from a number of consultants gives concerning results. Apparently the CT scans taken back in those first horrific three days were without contrast, which made it extremely difficult for the doctors to see the full extent of what was going on. And the lumbar puncture, where my mam listened in horror outside the door to my screaming, should not have been done.

"Are you saying the lumbar puncture caused this?"

Mam voices the question on all of our lips. Am I in the state I'm in because the hospital messed up?

"The neurosurgery consultants are definitely seeing evidence that indicates negligence. It looks like the staff in Limerick Hospital failed to realise the extensive intracranial abnormalities. Medically speaking, if there's a blockage in the plumbing network of a person's brain and it's causing various pressures to arise, a lumbar puncture shouldn't be carried out under any circumstances."

"But they had all the X-rays, her scans and everything else. How did they miss it? You're a solicitor. They're doctors. Why didn't they look at Tricia in the way you've just described?"

Susie doesn't withhold information. But her discomfort is obvious. And who can blame her? Telling someone that the reason their life has been changed forever is because somebody made a mistake, didn't take enough care or call in the experts soon enough, is far from easy.

"We need to go through every line of every record before we can prove a case of negligence," Susie tells us in one of her briefing sessions. "It's very important that we have our experts analyse and critique every symptom and sign recorded in your medical notes in those first three days of September 2008. Even if the Court conclude that the CT scan findings were appropriately in line with the treatment that followed, there are still other contraindications for lumbar puncture."

Susie's knowledge is impressive and as always she explains it in a way that's easy to understand.

"Are there many records to go through?" My question is out of curiosity.

"Thousands, Tricia! And it isn't making my job any easier. We've already found a few inconsistencies in the records we've gone through, so there's lots of reading to be done by ourselves and the consultants. We suspect there are notes missing too. We have little choice but pore over every line of every note and record on your file."

What can I say? She's doing everything she can. But it makes difficult hearing. Imagining how things could have been if only … if only, if only, if only.

"I'm working on having a rehab assessment done on you."

"What will this achieve that the hospital hasn't managed already?" I ask. I'm tired of hearing that something will be done when nothing happens in reality.

"I want to have every one of your needs identified for the court hearing."

"Will the Court make the doctors organise rehab?"

"That's the intention," Susie confirms.

She has already written to the professor about this on a number of occasions, discussing the correspondence with us each time – with Mam and Dad more than me if I'm honest. But despite numerous requests, still no rehab.

True to her word, a doctor comes to assess my rehab needs.

"Stoke Mandeville is what I'd recommend to help Patricia," the expert decides after an intense assessment. "This hospital is in Aylesbury in England and has one of the largest spinal units in the world."

"I'll look into it as a matter of urgency," Susie offers.

"Thank you," I mouth to Susie, once again filled with hope.

And as is becoming habit, my hopes are dashed soon afterwards when Susie makes enquiries and comes back to us with the outcome.

"I'm afraid the rehabilitation consultant's suggestion isn't going to happen as –"

"Why not?" Dad's first to jump in before Susie gets a chance to explain.

"I've been on to a consultant in Rehab Medicine in the hospital she mentioned, trying to get things in place to arrange a visit for Tricia. But after hours of liaising, he has come back to tell me that Stoke Mandeville isn't suitable."

"But why not?" Mam echoes Dad's question.

"The hospital can only treat people with spinal cord injuries, not brain injuries."

And why didn't the consultant know that in the first place instead of sending us on a wild goose chase, I wonder. I don't waste my energy mouthing the words. My crestfallen expression tells it all. Another heartbreaking disappointment. Another dead end.

It's January 7th 2010. Mam arrives in the morning and sees I still haven't been washed or dressed.

"It's time you were freshened up, Tricia. I'll ring HDU for help," she says, ringing the bell.

I wish I could help Mam by moving even an arm or a leg but it's impossible.

There's no answer to the bell so Mam goes across to the HDU area to ask for help.

Mam is told to do what she can and they'll follow over. It's not easy but she has made a start when a care assistant arrives.

Breathing is difficult this morning. I feel funny. Dizzy. Tight, caught up. What's wrong with me? The ventilator is connected. Isn't that supposed to do all the work? If I could shout, I would call for help. But I'm attached to the trachea, no speaking valve. And probably not nearly enough breath in my lungs to get a word out anyway.

What's going on? Things are going a bit dark. I'm frightened. My head is light. The dizziness worsens. I can barely see. Darkness is folding in around me. I can't grab Mam's arm. She's facing away from me. I can't get her attention. I feel as though I'm sinking. Or drowning. What's going on? I'm going to black out …

"Oh God!" the care assistant shouts. "Look! Her face is going grey. There's something wrong."

"Oh my God, her lips are purple. Help! Get help quick!" Mam is terrified.

The care assistant hurries for help.

The ward sister is with us within seconds. And immediately she's resuscitating me.

"Her stats have dropped. It's not good. There's a blockage in Tricia's lung."

She works quickly, attaching a bag to my trachea and pumping quickly.

Around five pumps later, the blockage is cleared.

Mam is suctioning as soon as the ward sister tells her.

Two minutes' intense activity and, as suddenly as it left, calm resumes.

I'm aware of them around me. I want to sleep. For a long time.

"That was extremely close," the ward sister says, her grave tone speaking multitudes.

"I didn't see it happening," Mam replies. "I didn't know what to do. It happened so fast. You think you're prepared but …"

"Her lips were purple." The ward sister is busy taking readings, watching my levels slowly return to a normal rate.

"Is this my fault because I didn't notice?"

"It's not about whose fault it is, Annette." She gives Mam her full attention. "Tricia's care is complicated and extremely high risk. She's had another apnoea episode. Responding instantly is vital."

Seems like I'm still only a few moments away from disaster! Like a cat, nine lives. How many have I left?

"This is why she has to have full-time care. This is why you can't care for her at home. She's vulnerable. Turn your back for a second and it could be too late to save her."

"Any sign we can watch out for, when they're about to happen?"

"Her face changing colour, her lips turning blue. They're the main signs to the human eye."

"What if it happens when she's sleeping?"

"To be honest, it can happen at any time. Nighttime is the highest risk but, as you saw just now, it can just as easily happen during the day."

"Oh my God!" Mam puts her head in her hands, the responsibility of my care weighing heavily on her.

"This is why her discharge is not being allowed until she has access to enough care to avoid any unnecessary risks or accidents," the sister says.

They continue discussing it. As for me, I'm soon sleeping off the drama, probably in dreamland where life is bright and full of fun.

Part of the problem is that I'm not able to control these episodes. It's the same when my trachea disconnects from the ventilator. I'm unaware. I need someone to be on watch 24-7! I wouldn't like to be minding me!

Dad is at my bedside when I wake up. Melissa is sitting quietly beside him.

Mam isn't there. The events of the morning were too upsetting. She needed to get away from the hospital for a few hours to recover.

Mam and Dad make a decision today. I will never be left alone again.

I make a decision too. I will never put Mam in this position again. There are nurses and care assistants to manage my hygiene and other personal needs. Mam is not my carer.

*

Mam and Dad are on edge. For one, they have to keep looking at me, watching for signs on my lips, a change in my colouring. If I'm dizzy, I have to find a way to tell them. But if they're not facing my direction, it's next to impossible for me to do so. And inside my head I regularly confuse dreaming with reality; it's difficult to differentiate between the two.

They know how to attach the bag to the NIPPY like the ward sister did but they haven't actually done it yet. They missed their chance when I had my 'episode'!

What is just as upsetting is the way the staff are using what happened to hammer home their point about me needing to stay in hospital.

"But you can see how badly she wants to come home," says Dad.

My parents might be nervous but in no way are they quitting.

"But is home the best place for her?" one of the doctors asks. "The patient's safety is priority. When her saturation levels drop, or the tracheostomy blocks, getting to her in the shortest space of time is crucial. And not only reaching her on time but being fully equipped to save her life."

"We'll just keep learning and practising until we're as good as any of the nurses or carers working with Tricia now," Mam says.

And they do. It's almost our version of The X Factor. We've been through the auditions, had a close shave at the judge's house and now we're waiting in the wings for the live shows to begin, as apprehensive as any performer that the judges (doctors and professors in our case) will press the red buzzer before we're even finished the performance.

"There'll have to be two of us with you, Tricia. All the time." Dad's planning ahead. Where he gets his energy, I don't know. He never gives up. No matter what.

Mam agrees. "You're right – one dealing with the bag and the other managing the suctioning. Even with the experts the day of your 'episode'," she reminds us, "one person couldn't manage alone."

And that's where the main issue lies. It takes at least two people to do most things for me. Whether it's transferring me from bed to chair or washing and dressing me, there are two sets of eyes on me at all times. Even the physios arrive in pairs some of the time. And they're with me for around twenty minutes every day.

The trachea and ventilator are extensions of me at this stage, permanent extensions at that if the vibe from the doctors is to be believed, but we've been told at our multi-d meetings that Public Health Nurses aren't trained to manage somebody on full ventilation.

My family are so willing and able but not superhuman. They have to sleep after all. As it is, they're here for close to sixteen hours every day. They sit through all my therapy sessions. Not that there are as many as I should be having but my parents are there no matter what. Speech and language and occupational therapy are haphazard and nowhere near the daily dose that experts believe I need. But I work with what I have. Every little counts.

*

Mam is writing in her diary again. The pages are filling up. She writes in the names of everyone who visits. The movies we watch on the DVD player are also noted, whether I liked the film or not.

"Score out of ten, Tricia?" is the usual question from Kiera at the end of a movie even if I've slept through most of it.

I mouth my answer or point to it on the spell board. Sometimes my opinion starts a family discussion, and other times a debate. And it all goes in Mam's diary.

She closes the book, sets her pen on the table and looks directly at me.

"Once we get the hours from Community Care that Grace is talking about," she says, her hand gripping mine, "and all four of us take our turn with suctioning and the parts of your care we know how to do, we can still manage. We know we can."

"Five of us," Melissa smiles, winking at me.

She had run in with her exciting news to me before telling anyone else, wanting me to be the first to know she's pregnant. She's over the moon. Her secret was safe with me. It's not as if I can shout it from the rooftops. Becoming an aunty for the first time is fantastic. Mam and Dad being grandparents – that's hard to believe. But bitter-sweet too.

Will Mam and Dad have the time they should to give to the little one? Or will they be stuck nursing their twenty-something daughter? Will I be home before my niece or nephew is born? Will I be able to hold a baby?

"An extra pair of hands," Mam teases. "Exactly what we need!"

And just like Dad's determination, Mam's willpower and positivity is as strong now as it was the day she sat outside theatre worrying how I'd react to a half-shaved head when the experts had prepared her for the very worst and told her it was extremely likely her daughter would die.

Chapter 20

Patricia Ingle
9th February 2010
Room Number 6
Out and about …

Another multidisciplinary meeting, another chance to hear whether anybody has been listening these last months. Once again, the only agenda item I am interested in is my discharge and home care package. Listening to the therapists giving their updates delays the real point of the meeting for me.

The consultant anaesthetist is already at the table when we join the group. Mam and Dad brighten a little as she sets out a far more extensive care-requirements request than has previously been discussed. "Patricia remains vulnerable to apnoeic episodes, particularly at night. I'm suggesting 20 hours care per day with the remaining four hours being managed by family."

Equipment is also on the table for discussion. My trachea needs to be changed every month and the catheter tube needs to be changed every 90 days. The PEG tubing is okay to stay in for a few years, as long as it doesn't become infected. All very glamorous!

"Perhaps the family could lobby for funding toward the care package?" she suggests.

Dad instantly rises to the challenge and offers to try. "If the alternative is to keep Tricia in hospital forever, then I'll certainly plead for funding."

The Assistant Director of Public Health Nursing speaks next. "I'll be requesting approval for 24-hour nursing care for Patricia in the immediate period following transition from hospital. At home she'll continue to be ventilator-dependent. She doesn't realise when her trachea disconnects from the vent and therefore this young girl has no idea when she isn't breathing."

She stops and takes a breath, allowing time for comment and question and responding to those who have questions. Then she takes the opportunity to speak up for me again.

"When she moves in bed or is being moved by hoist or any of the sliding transfers to and from the bed to her chair, there's a risk of her trachea disconnecting."

The consultant anaesthetist interrupts. "I'm not sure what you're describing is within the remit of PA hours, at least not based on what I've seen so far. Suctioning and bagging are a little more intricate than the current level of PA services available."

The debate continues, my whole family cringing when a lack of funding is mentioned.

But the professor intervenes on this sensitive issue. "I don't want funding or resources issues to be part of these meetings. It's difficult enough for Tricia as it is."

The Disability Services Manager promises to write to the Hospital Director to request additional funding towards my care package.

The consultant anaesthetist speaks again. "It's unfair to create an expectation for the family based on unrealistic care requirements."

"We'll need further risk assessments. And we'll send on a report to the professor after today's meeting," the Public Health Nursing representative says.

So they all go back to their jobs and I return to Room Number 6, still no nearer to getting home.

*

Dad is quick to notice how low I am after the meeting. I can't help it. I build myself up for these meetings, expecting something to change. And I feel so empty inside when nothing at all is decided.

So he takes on another fight to be allowed take me out again to get me a change of scenery. If only for a few hours during the day. Finally getting permission and organising nurses to accompany us, he surprises me with a trip to the Crescent Shopping Centre.

"I know you were disappointed when your chest infection stopped us previously."

He researches the most suitable wheelchair taxis and organises transport so we can get out. But at the last minute, the ward sister surprises us by organising an ambulance to take me there and back. This is so kind of her. And easier on those travelling with me too.

It feels strange being out and about. The noise. The people. Ordinary life going on around me. It's weird.

Before my illness, I wasn't much of a shopper but now, in the Crescent Shopping Centre after almost a year and a half in hospital, I am suddenly interested in shopping! If a trip around the shops is as good as it gets, I am happy to convert to believing in the benefits of retail therapy.

Melissa joins in my enthusiasm and makes sure we look at baby clothes any chance we can!

People stare at me as I'm wheeled through the shops. I don't meet their eye. I know I am different because of the ventilator. I know I'm different because of the chair. And despite having lost my sense of touch, I still have feelings. I'm not numb. It would make such a difference if people remembered the person behind all the tubes and the wheelchair.

The more often I get out, the more I understand people's curiosity. But why not come up and ask questions? Why not talk to me instead of staring?

*

The weeks pass and soon we are into the early days of spring, the evenings brighter and my trips outside of the hospital becoming more frequent. And more manageable. Mam and Dad are very confident about most aspects of my care now, and it's safe for us to go on short trips without nurses or care staff.

As well as shopping and the cinema, Dad organises a visit to my aunt's house one afternoon. Thank God somebody in the family has a bungalow! Other relations call in to see me while I'm there. Being in somebody's home instead of a public place is magical. I feel different afterwards. It's difficult to explain but returning to Room Number 6 after the visit to my aunt's house, I am filled with new determination and hope. I want to be part of the community again. I want to be me. I want to be home.

Chapter 21

Patricia Ingle
March 2010
Room Number 6
Skyfest …

Limerick City is buzzing in the lead-up to St Patrick's Day. The National Lottery Skyfest is being held in the city as part of the St Patrick's Day celebrations.

"We're all going, Tricia," Mam promises when the festival is announced. "It's going to be a huge event! And I'm not having you miss something so exciting."

It's a focus. It's an outlet. It's exhilarating. I'll be part of something big. I can't wait.

Mam insists I get my hair and make-up done on the day. This is so unusual for me. Getting ready to go out for an evening – for real. My first date with my boyfriend in a very long time, even if my entire family are tagging along as gooseberries!

We have a fantastic view from the courthouse where we were assigned an area suitable for my wheelchair. The atmosphere is electric. The city comes to life like I could never imagine. This is the first time since August 2008 that we are out on a social evening without being chaperoned by medical people. I want this feeling to last forever. Fire dragons, acrobats and guys on stilts perform and entertain the huge crowd. The noise, the squeals of excitement and the biggest display of fireworks Limerick has ever seen! The colours and patterns are beyond anything I could ever imagine. There is a fantastic backing track playing continuously and one song really stands out for me: 'Soul Sister' by Train. I loved this song before I got ill. It's fantastic to hear it here tonight and in a way helps me forget that things have changed. The sky is on fire, King John's Castle is lit up in green and makes a fabulous backdrop as bursts of fireworks explode over our heads, their reflection sparkling on the water of the River Shannon as they shoot toward the stars before descending into oblivion and another amazing display is set off. The fireworks keep going for over an hour and a half. I can't clap my hands like everyone else but inside

I'm singing for joy to be part of this extravaganza, while Katy Perry's track, 'Firework', blares across Limerick City. Her lyrics resonate strongly with me, her words describing exactly how I feel tonight – a plastic bag drifting in the wind. And, yes, I want tonight to be the start of something. I want to start my life again.

The media are as excited as I am. They come to the courthouse and single me out for a photograph, taking some details from Mam and Dad and advising us to get the papers the following day.

And they're not joking – I'm amazed to feature in several newspaper reports in the days and weeks following Skyfest!

'I'm a celebrity, get me out of here' – or maybe I should say 'I'm a celebrity, get me out of hospital'!

The day after Skyfest, Dad brings in the Limerick Leader to show me the photo. He reads out the commentary, his voice filling with pride.

"Being able to attend the event meant more to one young girl than all the money in the world.

Twenty-one-year-old Patricia Ingle, from Ballinacurra Weston, was struck down two years ago with a viral infection that left her suffering from brain damage.

Her father, Pat, said it meant everything to his daughter and the whole family. 'It was just excellent. We had a great time. Patricia really loved it and we hope that this is the start of a new beginning for her. It will all start from tonight,' said Mr Ingle."

"Your name is on a few media sites too," Kiera says, reading them from her laptop. "There were 50,000 people in attendance! And you get a mention! Aren't you a real VIP now! The Glo Ultra Lounge would welcome you in their reserved area now!"

Melissa buys a few copies of the newspapers. "We'll start a scrap book, Tricia," she suggests, taking the scissors and cutting out the photographs and articles.

Dad is right in what he said to the reporter. Getting out to an event as a family is the boost we all needed. And Room Number 6 is a little easier to bear in the days that follow, mostly because I'm so exhausted I sleep a lot but also because the buzz of that evening ignites a different kind of firework inside me.

*

But the excitement is short-lived and another dark cloud wraps itself around us when we receive a memo from the HSE Administrators at the end of March 2010. In a nutshell, it states that it is neither safe or feasible to let me home from hospital.

Dad is on the campaign immediately and meets with the professor in relation to this.

"I'm extremely disappointed to see this," the professor says. "And it isn't for the administrators to state whether or not it's safe for Tricia to go home. That responsibility lies with the clinicians, the medical professionals in charge of her care."

"That's what I thought," Dad agrees.

The professor discusses the risks, assessing them on the basis of how I am now. "It's never going to be completely risk-free in Tricia's situation. But we have to measure the risks against the obvious benefits of your daughter living at home with her family."

"Thanks, professor." Dad is relieved to hear this.

"I'll respond to the memo as the person in charge of Tricia."

*

Mam's writing in her diary again. Dad's smoothing face cream on my cheeks. If anyone had ever told either of us that he'd be doing this for me, we would definitely have thought they were mad!

"Are you okay, Tricia?"

I nod. Dad continues massaging my skin.

Two nurses hurry into the room.

"Her stats are only at 84%."

"We need to suction her. Sorry, Pat, I'll need you to stop while I suction her."

Mam and Dad are annoyed with themselves. But how could they have known? The alarms are heard over in HDU but not necessarily in Room Number 6! I'm not much help as I'm usually the last person to know when I'm about to have an episode.

"We didn't realise. I'm sorry."

"It's all experience," the nurse explains. "Recognising the different alarms takes time. It might well be that her hand is cold. The probe might pick up on this and trigger the alarm."

"Is that what happened just now?"

"No, it was an apnoea episode this time and she needed a much faster reaction."

Another learning experience. Another opportunity for the hospital staff to make my parents doubt themselves. The ward sister tells the professor. Poor Mam and Dad. It must feel like they're in school with every move being monitored.

"We'll do better," Dad says. "We've become so good at checking your stats. We will be more vigilant and react to every beep that alarm makes! We won't let this happen again."

As soon as I possibly can, I want to tell them I think they're great as they are. I hope I remember. I close my eyes and sleep.

Chapter 22

Patricia Ingle
April 2010
Room Number 6
Time to party …

In April 2010, Dad becomes a free man – from his job at least. He has officially retired. A number of key moments brought him to this decision: the number of scares he has had watching and caring for me, his promise to Mam that he'd be there to share my care and his concern that his mind was elsewhere when he was at work. Dad is an exceptionally conscientious worker, whether it's with the ESB or with his family. He makes his choice. He chooses family.

The ESB are sorry to lose Dad under such tragic circumstances and Dad is sorry to leave the company. He has only good memories of his thirty-one years working there, and the support he received from his managers and colleagues is something my family will never forget and never take for granted.

The party is another excuse to have my hair and make-up done as Mam and the girls get me ready for his retirement party.

I really enjoy the evening. Seeing my family and cousins and being in their company is good fun. Dad's colleagues make a fuss of me but the night flies by and soon it's time for me to be brought back to Room Number 6. I feel like Cinderella, leaving before midnight to be whisked back to my dungeon long before the ball is over! But I'm so relieved that for once Mam and Dad get to let their hair down and relax and have fun. If anybody deserves a break, the best parents in the world certainly do.

*

"Post for you, Tricia," Dad announces one morning, showing me an envelope and pointing to the embossed harp on the flap.

He has a devilish glint in his eye. What is he up to?

"It's from the President of Ireland!"

I'm very impressed. But also confused. "How?" I mouth.

"I wrote to President Mary McAleese and asked her to get in touch."

Is there anything my dad doesn't think of, I wonder, as I listen to the very kind words in the letter.

Christy Moore also sends me a note in response to a letter from Dad.

"I'll have to frame these letters!"

My therapists are all very impressed when they see the letter from the president. It's certainly a conversation topic to distract from the tedious work they do with me on a daily basis. Therapy is hard. Frustrating too at times, if I'm honest. But I always feel better after a session, certainly better than if I have none at all.

"You're making slow but steady progress," Mam tells me.

"If you look how far you've come since August 2008, Tricia," Melissa agrees.

Speech and language therapy is only once a week which probably isn't enough but it's better than none at all. Mostly it consists of blowing and sucking exercises as well as trying to say particular words.

The physios get me to stand up for a few moments during each of their sessions. I wobble a lot and my head is dizzy. My balance is a major issue but mostly I manage a few seconds and feel I'm doing well before they put me sitting down once more.

"It's your blood pressure, Tricia," Dad says, explaining the dizziness. "Every time you stand up, your blood pressure falls. The therapists call it 'postural hypotension'."

"I want to keep trying," I insist, despite it being as difficult as it is.

"I hope this little one is as determined as her aunt," Melissa says with a grin, rubbing her tummy.

I return her grin. "I hope so too. I can't wait to meet him or her to find out."

*

May 2010 arrives and Susie is getting a team of specialists on board to help with my case, the latest of these being an Adult Neuro-Rehabilitation Physician to come and assess my condition.

"The physician has sent an email to the professor to arrange a visit with you tomorrow afternoon," Susie explains.

My family and I are happy for anyone to see me, more than willing to have as many tests done or answer any questions they might have. And a second, third or fourth opinion can't do any harm.

But the hospital staff aren't as welcoming to my visitor. The professor's secretary intervenes as soon as my guest makes an appearance. She contacts the ward manager who puts an immediate halt to the visit.

"The risk-management people need to meet to discuss any visits Tricia has in relation to litigation. We can't allow anyone to visit until after that meeting has occurred."

Dad is already making alternate arrangements with Susie and they arrange for the Adult Neuro-Rehabilitation Physician to see me at my aunt's bungalow instead.

The physician is extremely nice and very thorough in her examination. The meeting is constructive. Naturally she can't give any guarantees but is very optimistic that I still have further potential and should continue to progress in numerous areas.

"You've already made huge improvements. In my opinion this will continue if you keep working as you have been." She goes into more detail, her positivity a welcome breath of fresh air.

It's as if she has turned on a light in a very dark room. Her attitude is motivating and hopeful. Her prognosis for me is the best news I've heard in quite some time.

Susie is happy with the outcome too. She's ready to take the next step. "I have enough material gathered. I'll issue proceedings against Petmania, O'Keeffe's of Kilkenny Ltd – the headquarters for Petmania – and the HSE."

"What are we accusing them of exactly?" Dad asks.

"As we know already, the HSE have given a working diagnosis of LCMV. The statements we took from Petmania employees give more than enough evidence to show that Tricia was negligently exposed to a variety of biological agents while she worked there and this exposure naturally increased her risk of contracting infection."

"And that's enough?" Mam asks Susie.

"Enough to issue the proceedings. While we're waiting for a court date, I am lining up other experts to visit the premises where you worked and submit a report to support the proceedings further."

Susie doesn't need us to help her make decisions. It's clear she has it all under control and a clear path set out. She's impressive.

Chapter 23

Patricia Ingle
July 2010
Room Number 6
New address – new hope ...

"Yes! We have at last been allocated a house by the Council!" Dad reveals in July 2010. "It's wheelchair accessible. The rent's a bit high but we'll manage."

You'd think we'd won the lotto if you passed by Room Number 6 when Dad's sharing the good news. We've waited so long. So many other things depended on us having an address and a suitable place to live. And now we have. Dad has fought so hard. It's a relief to see the results of his efforts.

But once again we barely get time to take in the good news when it is followed with a blow, this time by way of a letter from the HSE.

> *I wish to advise you that the discharge of Patricia from the Mid-Western Regional Hospital has been examined. Unfortunately, given the dependency levels and the clinical representation in this case, it has not been possible to facilitate a transfer to community services, mainly on the grounds of maintaining an acceptable level of patient safety.*
>
> *The HSE will continue to monitor this situation but for the present I regret my response cannot be more favourable.*

*

It's devastating. We are gutted.

Dad and Mam speak to the professor.

"Don't give up," is his advice. "Keep fighting and eventually you'll get there."

Dad goes back to his emails and commences a fresh rounds of appeals to TDs and officials.

'Again we are up against a brick wall. Please help,' he pleads.

He also researches the various places of support for people with disabilities and emails them asking for information, advice and assistance.

"It can't do any harm," he tells Mam after he presses the 'send' button.

Rumblings begin amongst the hospital staff.

"Tricia is being considered for a move to a general ward," one of the nurses mentions casually one morning.

I'm sitting upright. If I had the power I'd pull the blankets over my head at this stage. Room Number 6 has become a place where I feel safe. I've a tightness in my throat that has nothing to do with my tracheostomy and everything to do with disappointment and dread.

My family continue to argue about my safety. The hospital continues to defend their reasons for a move.

"Patients are not transferred home directly from the High Dependency Unit. HDU staff are not equipped to make decisions for a complex discharge home. The ward sister in the general ward, Ward 2C, is the expert in this area. But she can't help until Tricia is in her care."

Do they just want to get me out of Room Number 6? Or is it really in my best interests? I don't know who to believe.

Mam makes a practical suggestion. "Why not have both teams work together? We're concerned about her getting infections if she's moved to a general ward."

"But she has been out and about at the cinema and shopping," says the professor.

"That's different to placing her amongst sick people!"

The professor doesn't dispute that. Neither does he offer any guarantee.

Following this latest pressure to vacate Room Number 6, Dad's emails take on a new determination and frequency.

Wednesday 14 July 2010
From: Patrick Ingle
To: Minister for Finance

Hi Minister,
    YES!!!
    We have at last been allocated a tenancy that is wheelchair accessible.

We would like, on behalf of Patricia and our family, to thank you for your help.

We are very grateful for all you have done for us. Patricia is doing well and is looking forward to finally going home to her family. And we also thank you for your time, your efforts and the representations you have made on behalf of Patricia.

As you now may know, another battle has begun. This is for a reasonable primary care package for Patricia. Hopefully we can again call on your help in this matter.

Thanks again,

Pat and Annette Ingle

Thursday 15th July 2010
From: Minister for Finance
To: Patrick Ingle

Dear Pat,

I am very pleased that at long last appropriate accommodation has been provided for Patricia. When you have completed Patricia's application for the primary care package, please let me know and I will pursue it on your behalf.

Yours sincerely

Minister for Finance

Thursday 29 July 2010
From: Patrick Ingle
To: Minister for Finance

Hi Minister,

Again we are up against a brick wall. Please see the attachments. Please help if you can in any way possible.

Attachments: From Kildare North Constituency, Dáil Eireann, Leinster House

---

Dear Pat and Annette,

I enclose herewith correspondence received in response to representations made on your behalf.

If and when further information is to hand, I shall be in touch with you again. But failing further response within a reasonable period, you might remind me so that a satisfactory conclusion can be reached.

Yours sincerely,

Kildare North Constituency, Dail Eireann, Leinster House Enclosure – letter from the Health Service Executive

---

From Local Health Manager

To: Kildare North Constituency, Dail Eireann, Leinster House Re: Mr Patrick Ingle and Mrs Annette Ingle

Dear Deputy,

I wish to refer to your representations dated 7th July 2010 to the Minister for Health & Children, in relation to Patricia Ingle, daughter of the above-named. You will be aware that there has been significant development in community services in order to facilitate earlier discharge from hospital and to facilitate the discharge of complex cases to the community.

I wish to advise you that the discharge of Patricia from the Mid-Western Regional Hospital has been examined in the above context. Unfortunately given the dependency levels and the clinical presentation in this case it has not been possible to facilitate a transfer to community services, mainly on the grounds of maintaining an acceptable level of patient safety.

The HSE will continue to monitor this situation but for the present I regret my response cannot be more favourable.

Yours sincerely
A/Local Health Manager

From: Patrick Ingle
Date: 29 Jul 2010 09:07
Subject: Tricia Ingle
To: "Susie Elliott"
Cc: "Grace Moore"

Hi Susie

I have just received this letter a few minutes ago. We are devastated. We don't know what to do or who to talk to. Why are people doing this to us? Why is this happening to us? We cannot show this letter to Tricia. It will break her heart as it is doing to us. Do these people know what they are doing to us?

You know how dedicated we are to Tricia and we are going to bring her home with or without their help.

Coping with this is hard enough but this is draining us. They are dragging us to the ground. I just don't know what to do next.

Susie, please help us.

Regards

Pat and Annette Ingle (Proud Parents)

From: Patrick Ingle
To: HSE A/Local Health Manager
Date: 30 Jul 2010 10:51
Subject: Patricia Ingle

Good Morning,

This is Patrick Ingle, proud father of Patricia,

Patricia is my daughter who after almost two years in hospital is coming home to her family very shortly. Patricia (19) stopped breathing on the Wednesday 3rd September 2008 and has not taken an unassisted breath since then. Two weeks prior, Tricia had started to complain about headaches, nausea and dizziness which ended with her brain swelling and damaging her brain stem, which has now left her on a ventilator (breathing machine). As well as not being able to breathe, Tricia is unable to speak or swallow and has restricted use of her limbs.

Tricia is now almost 23 months in hospital: three days initially in the ward at Limerick Mid-Western Regional Hospital, then four months in ICU in Cork University Hospital, a further eight months at Limerick ICU and here in the High Dependency Unit eleven months now, under a consultant professor and his team of specialists.

Despite all this Tricia is fully aware and alert and can somehow communicate by mouthing words (no sound) and we, the family, now communicate through lip-reading but have found it difficult at times. After a five-day trip to St Thomas' Hospital in London, they found that changing the setting on her ventilator and fitting Tricia with a speaking valve for one hour three times a day, she can talk with a somewhat croaky voice.

Tricia is well taken care of by the nurses and staff of the HDU but she is so looking forward to going home to her family.

At last we have got a wheelchair accessible house that Limerick County Council is renting to us. We are now in the slow process of moving house and getting ready for Tricia to return to her family. We bring Tricia to the new home every day, some days for over 10 hours. We administer her medicines there. We look after her dressings, trachea, PEG, ventilator tubing and so on. As well as bringing her to the cinema and to the UL Concert Hall, we bring her shopping where she is now picking out furniture and paint for her new home.

I am very disappointed with your conclusion that it is unsafe for Tricia to return to her family. I would be very grateful if you could give me details on what you have based these conclusions on. I would be very grateful if you can tell me if the people who have made out the reports that you have received have seen Tricia. Could you tell me if you have met Tricia or have met her family or talked to her consultant professor?

I am begging you to review Tricia's case. She has become much stronger and is less dependent on people.

I am pleading with you to review her case. She has not committed any crime and she has been damned to spend the rest of her life in one room in an institution. We cannot and will not accept this.

On my knees I plead,

Pat and Annette Ingle (Proud Parents)
Farnane
Murroe
Co Limerick

From: Patrick Ingle
To: A/Local Health Manager
Date: 6 Aug 2010 09:33
Subject: Tricia Ingle

Hi,

Thank you for your email. To help with the review, I would like to know how the conclusion was made that Tricia's safety would be compromised. I would like to know, in preparation of the review, how Tricia's complex case has been examined and in what context. I would also like to know, as Tricia's case is being handed over to a new area, the clinical and medical findings that have helped to come to the conclusion that Tricia's safety would be jeopardised. In preparation of a favourable and positive response to the review, I would like to know the risk assessment which may have been carried out that led to the conclusion it would be unsafe to bring Tricia home.

As you may know my family and I are constantly with Tricia. I have recently given up work to help get Tricia home and to get an early retirement lump sum payment to purchase a special needs vehicle as transport for Tricia. We have acquired a tenancy with Limerick County Council of a home suitable to Tricia's needs. I am sure you would do all this too for your daughter. Anybody would.

Again to help to get a more favourable outcome of the review, I would like to receive answers to the above questions – hopefully without resorting to politicians and without resorting to begging again.

Hope to hear from you soon,

Pat and Annette Ingle (Proud Parents)

_____

From: AWARE
(one of the miscellaneous national disability-related supportive and charity organisations contacted by Pat).
To: Patrick Ingle
SUBJECT: PATRICIA INGLE
DATE: Tuesday 10th August 2010

Dear Patrick,

Thanks for your email and my apologies for the delay responding. I cannot imagine how difficult the last two years must have been for Patricia, yourself and your family. She has obviously come such a long way in that time and that's testament I'm sure to her own strength of character, the love and support of her family and the expertise of her care team.

As an organisation we provide support services for individuals and families who are affected by depression. That support is emotional and by way of information and education. If it is a thing that you or any of your family are experiencing depression or feeling down as a result of the traumatic experience you have all been through, then we may be able to help by way of our helpline (1890 303 302) or support groups. But outside of that we wouldn't have the expertise in terms of Patricia's illness to help in any way with that. Some of the other organisations that you have contacted are more relevant for that. I'm sure that they will be able to help in some way. If any of you do wish to talk to one of our volunteers then please do feel free to contact our helpline in confidence. Family difficulties or illness can mean a person's mood is impacted and of course caring for a loved one who has been through so much can sometimes trigger a depressive episode, so if you think we might be able to provide a listening ear then please do reach out to us.

I'm sorry I can't be of more help, Patrick. You have all come so far and my heart goes out to Patricia and to you all. You should all be so proud of yourselves for having come this far and I wish the very, very best on the journey. I will keep you in all my thoughts.

Take care,

Aware Representative

In the midst of Dad's continued efforts to progress decisions for getting me home, my sisters are constantly working on ways to keep me entertained.

"Jedward are coming to Limerick, Tricia," Kiera tells me one evening. "They're performing in UL."

"Tell her about the surprise, Dad," Melissa says.

Dad is beaming. "I got in contact with the management team and asked if you could have a private audience with them."

"And?"

"They've said yes!"

On the evening in question we're brought into the area close to Jedward's dressing room. We wait a few minutes and then they bounce into the room to see us. There's no awkwardness. They chat non-stop, hugging me and hopping all over the place.

Dad takes loads of different photos. They're happy to pose, attempting to jump on my chair at one point. They're curious about my trachea.

"Do you have a hole in your neck?" John asks.

I nod my head.

"That's so cool!"

"What would happen if you turn off your ventilator?"

We just laugh. As if they don't know the answer to that one!

They sign a hoodie, a scarf, and some Jedward photographs for me.

"I can't believe our Jedward stuff is sold out," they tell me. "We'd give you more!"

"And we're colour matching too!"

I'm wearing blue and so are the boys.

"And your boots are amazing," they squeal when they spot my silver boots with green laces.

"Come on, boys, it's time to go." Their managers are waiting patiently, watching the time and coaxing them to get on stage.

They take their time but after a few reminders by their managers that their audience are waiting patiently outside, they finally say goodbye, give their two-finger victory sign and skip away from me.

It was fun. They weren't one bit shy or uncomfortable around me. In a strange way, it made me feel normal!

"Come on," Dad says, "let's go and watch the show."

Chapter 24

Patricia Ingle
August – September 2010
Room Number 6
New house, new territory, new services …
  and another birthday in hospital!

August 18th is the beginning of a new series of meetings between the various parties involved in my case. Grace meets with the Disability Services from our new area, East Limerick/North Tipperary. A new case manager is assigned.

"The case manager sent me the minutes of the meeting," Grace tells me later, "and she's already preparing the application for 24-7 care."

Staying positive continues to be difficult, particularly when the new case manager from Disability Services reveals to Grace that she's having difficulty getting hospital reports. It's as if we are starting from scratch again.

"I'll meet with the hospital manager. I'll ask him to appoint a hospital case manager to liaise directly with the Primary Community and Continuing Care team," Grace tells us.

Though I know she is doing her very best to speed up the process, unfortunately I've heard it all before. It's feels like one delay after the next, one excuse after the other with ultimately the same outcome – nothing!

*

September 6th 2010 arrives. Another birthday in hospital. My mood isn't good. I feel trapped and alone. I'm bored and frustrated. Friends call by with gifts of DVDs and other nice things. It's a distraction and helps me forget where I am for the briefest time. That in itself is the best gift anyone can give me! But they leave. My boyfriend stays a while longer than the others but he also needs to be somewhere and reality returns. Birthday or not, I'm still stuck here while the others are free to escape and get on with their lives.

Dad is in touch with the Rehabilitation Centre in London but still nothing is secured. He's anxious, Mam's anxious. I'm anxious. The hospital suggest we focus on getting me home first and then worry about rehabilitation. And

I suggest we focus on both! Because right now, neither are moving along. The progress I'm making with movement and development is at a snail's pace without expert intervention.

"Why can't rehab be organised now? It's vital she gets it as soon as possible. We want what's best for our daughter. It's what she deserves," Dad insists each time the discussion is raised with the doctors.

"We'd like if she can stay at home on the night of her birthday. Can it be considered?" Mam asks.

"Unfortunately it isn't safe without the right equipment, particularly a pressure mattress," is the disappointing response.

My 22nd birthday, when I should be worrying about where to have my party and how to get home in the early hours, not a mattress so I don't get pressure sores!

"Can the hospital loan us one?"

"I'm afraid we wouldn't get funding to donate a mattress to your home."

"Don't worry, Tricia," Dad assures me later on. "We'll buy one ourselves. Something like a mattress is certainly not going to prevent us getting you out for a birthday treat."

But getting the correct mattress at such short notice isn't as easy as he thinks and my birthday is a low-key affair. I don't get my wish to wake up at home. The day passes and another year of my life begins in Room Number 6 of the High Dependency Unit in the Mid-Western Regional Hospital.

*

Susie's working non-stop, determined to get my case to court as soon as possible.

"The site visit to Petmania was enlightening," she tells us. "There were a few new Health and Safety signs up that weren't in place while you were working there. Apart from that, the staff are still not provided with personal protective equipment, there were open bins around the place, a dead mouse on the premises and no quarantine area for new animals."

I visualise the scene and feel sorry for the poor animals being housed in such conditions. I also feel sorry for my friends who still work there. I hope they don't get an infection and end up like me! Or am I just unfortunate? One in a million? Why me?

*

Dad resumes his emails as the Dáil returns after their summer break.

Sunday September 12, 2010
From: Patrick Ingle
To: All members of the Dail
SUBJECT: BRAVE DAUGHTER

Hi Deputies,

Welcome back from your summer work in your constituencies. I would like to thank all of you that have taken the time away from your clinics to visit my daughter, Patricia, in HDU in the Mid-Western Regional Hospital, Dooradoyle, Limerick, and I would like to thank all of you who have sent letters of support and good wishes to Patricia and I would specially like to thank the deputies who have made representations on behalf of Patricia.

As you may now be aware there is positive news regarding Patricia in that the Limerick County Council has given us tenancy (albeit at a very high rent) of a home which is suitable for Patricia's needs and I thank the deputies who have helped in this. I have also purchased a special needs vehicle with the lump sum I received when I left work to help look after Tricia. Now we can get Tricia out and about. I have enclosed some photos.

With our new home address, we are living in a new primary care and local health area and have a new primary care team. Patricia and our family have met the new team. They have been extremely positive regarding Patricia's home care package. They have come together and put a home care package together and submitted it to their superiors for funding.

This, Deputies, is where I have again to ask of you to make representations on behalf of my wonderful daughter, Patricia Ingle. The people involved in the granting of funding include of course the Minister for Health and Children.

Others directly involved are:
The Local Health Manager, HSE West, Limerick
Programme Manager, Acute Hospital Services, HSE West, Limerick.

I would be forever grateful if you can again make representation on my Patricia's behalf and after two years in hospital finally get her home to her family and friends.

Please let me know how you get on,

Regards,

Pat Ingle (Proud Parent)

Monday September 13, 2010
From: TD, Wexford
To: Patrick Ingle

Patrick,

Thank you for your email and I will raise the issue with the Minister for Housing and Local Services and ask him to address your concerns.

With best wishes and kindest regards to all,

TD
Enniscorthy
Co Wexford

Tuesday September 14, 2010
From: TD, Kerry
To: Patrick Ingle

Dear Pat,

I have made representations on Patricia's behalf for the homecare package to be expedited. I hope that my efforts are helpful. You are all a very admirable family and if I can help Patricia in any way at all possible, please don't hesitate to contact me from time to time.

Kindest regards

Wednesday September 15, 2010
From: TD, Dublin
To: Patrick Ingle

Dear Patrick,

Thank you for your recent communication. I was pleased to hear from you. I took careful note of your concerns regarding funding and please be assured of my interest and support.

I am pursuing this issue on your behalf and I will do all I can to help.

Please continue to feel free to call on me anytime and may I wish you, Patricia and your family well.

Best regards,

TD, Dublin

Dáil Office

Wednesday September 15, 2010
From TD, Limerick
To Patrick Ingle

Dear Patrick,

I am delighted to hear that Patricia and yourself will be able to begin a new life together. You mention in your email that you need me to make representations on Patricia's behalf.

You might let me know the specifics of the representation you need me to make and I will be delighted to do so. You might also supply me with your postal address.

Many thanks,

Regards,

TD, Limerick

Monday 4th October, 2010
From: Patrick Ingle
To: Ward Sister
SUBJECT: SEVEN HUNDRED AND SIXTY-TWO DAYS IN
HOSPITAL

Good morning,

I have received correspondence from my local TD in a letter he received from the HSE's Area General Manger.

In this letter it states that Patricia is a resident of the MWRH. I don't understand this as Patricia is a patient of the MWRH whose wishes and her family's wishes are that she comes home as soon as possible.

Also it states that liaison between Acute and PCCC and Family are ongoing. This I don't understand as Acute won't talk to the family unless Patricia goes to Ward 2C.

It also goes on to say 'how best to suit her needs in a safe and appropriate setting'. This I find very worrying and upsetting because as you are aware Patricia and her family's wishes are for her to return home. What other settings are 'Acute and PCCC and Family liaising about'?

This I need explained to us as Tricia wants to go to a Home Setting to her Family Home to be with her Family.

Life for us in the last two years has been completely and utterly changed. To help look after Tricia I have left my job where I worked for thirty years. With my lump sum payment I have bought a special needs vehicle so that we can get Patricia around. We have moved house to a tenancy that suits Patricia's needs. My wife and family have made changes to their lives so that we can get Patricia back home to her family and not to any appropriate setting. All this we are happy and proud to do.

I would like you to come and visit our home in Farnane, Murroe, to see for yourself how we are making this family setting suitable to Patricia's needs. Come and see her bedroom and presses and sliderobes, her wet room, medical storage room, her oxygen concentrator and spare compressed oxygen bottles for emergency use, her nebuliser and so on. Come and see where we are going to put the generator in case of power supply interruptions. Come and visit when Patricia is there – this is almost every day. And if the other staff involved are available, ask them to come out too to see Tricia in our family setting.

I know there is a lot to do and a lot of things to be purchased and a lot of learning and training to be done. We also know how vulnerable Tricia is, and how her stats can drop suddenly and how there can be accidental disconnects of the tubing and actual trachea. We as a family are aware of the severe consequences of these disconnections and have been trained to recognise and swiftly respond to them.

We are just an ordinary family who want our Patricia home.

Just an ordinary family who have seen our Tricia at one week short of her twentieth birthday suffer an illness that has left her unable to breathe, unable to eat, unable to talk, unable to walk, unable to use her hands, unable to cough, unable to cry tears.

Just an ordinary family who have for the last eighteen months been trying to get our brave Tricia home.

Just an ordinary family who see when we bring Tricia to shopping centres and cinemas how children stare and point at her and parents take a wild berth.

Just an ordinary family who see our Tricia tethered by plastic hosing to a breathing machine and who still can smile so broadly and keep us all going.

Just an ordinary family who see our Tricia wake each morning facing another day like she is.

Just an ordinary family who prepare a feeding pump and medicine and who change our 22-year-old daughter, Tricia.

Just an ordinary family who see the disappointment and frustration and sadness in our Tricia as we prepare her for the journey back to the hospital each evening.

Just an ordinary family that sees our young Tricia, once back to the hospital, with nothing to do but go to bed.

We are just an ordinary family who are crying out for help, to help our Tricia, to help ourselves to get back to normality as soon as possible.

At the end of the letter it says, 'I trust this clarifies'. To me it does not. Maybe you will clarify this to me and our wonderful and brave client and her family.

To finish, myself and my family as we said at the meeting on Wednesday 18th August 2010, we don't want Patricia in any other setting other than the family home setting.

Again we are just an ordinary family looking for help.

Best Regards,

Pat and Annette Ingle (Proud Parents)

It's October 6th 2010 and we attend yet another multidisciplinary meeting. I try my best to be part of the meetings now, getting Grace's help to list the things I want discussed and making sure they're included. But other than round table discussions, and provisional dates for more meetings, there's still nothing concrete. I've heard the term 'meetings about meetings' and that's exactly what these feel like.

"We've been asked to keep a timetable of the care we give you each day," Mam says. "Even more specific than the diary I've been writing."

This seems reasonable and every tiny detail is recorded over a period of three days to try and give a realistic picture of how much care I require and how capable Mam and Dad are in each aspect.

New people are introduced as talks of a care package continue.

"This is the bed manager, Tricia. She looks after bed assignment in the hospital and she's also assigned as your hospital case manager."

Grace makes the formal introductions and the case manager outlines her plan.

"For starters, I'll get the hospital reports to Disability Services as quickly as possible," she promises.

"Disability Services seem determined to do whatever is necessary to get you home," Grace assures me when the bed manager has left. "Moving to the new area of Limerick seems to be a positive change. She is in agreement that it is necessary to get you out of hospital and back into the community. She'll organise another meeting once she has the reports and has had a chance to go through all of them."

I nod my head. I need a target, a specific date to aim for. "Halloween?"

Grace crosses her fingers. "Let's hope." She starts an email to the hospital manager, thanking him for appointing the new case manager and asking if he can supply a bed so I can go home for Halloween.

'Trick or treat', I wonder silently, before turning my attention to Dad who is also logged on to his email account, checking for responses and hoping for something positive from at least one of his pleas for help. But he shuts the laptop down too quickly. The Inbox is silent. And so are we.

*

Susie brings us some unexpected news.

"The proceedings against the HSE have made swift progress. What we weren't expecting was their defence."

"What defence have they?"

Dad's impatient – as we all are – and wondering what Susie has to tell.

"Their defence specifically states that Tricia does not have LCMV!"

"But you said it's on her notes. It's what they've been treating her for. How can they change their minds?"

Then what is wrong with me? I think.

Susie, naturally, cannot make a medical diagnosis, but she does give a bit more detail.

"We're surprised by the HSE. It would have made perfect sense if they let the LCMV diagnosis stand and push the full cause of your illness or injury on your employer. Why withdraw a diagnosis, thereby contradicting what is recorded in the notes, and which is supportive of a case against Petmania, the Co-Defendant?"

When she puts it like that, what she says does make sense.

"Is this a setback for us? Is it going to hold up the case?"

"As the law stands," she explains, "the burden of proof lies with us in relation to the liability of Tricia's employer."

"What do you mean?" I mouth.

"We have a few hurdles to overcome to prove the relationship between unsafe work practices and the onset of your illness. Every lead points to Petmania, with the added complication that the hospital didn't relieve the pressure from your brain soon enough. I've been reading up on other cases. I'm confident we're on the right track. We agreed as a legal team to leave open a few more avenues in respect of other potential zoonotic causes in the unlikely event this would arise."

I nod.

Mam and Dad are quick to state how much confidence we all have in what Susie's doing for us.

"With your approval, Tricia, we'd like to have you tested again for the virus – just to be on the safe side and to keep our argument as water-tight as possible. I'm not sure I'll trust anything other than concrete proof either way."

As always, I'm happy to co-operate with anything that will help.

"I'll make the arrangements so it's done in private. I'll send the sample to London for analysis, not only for LCMV but also for the other zoonotic pathogens not yet tested for. And then we can proceed with more confidence."

Chapter 25

Patricia Ingle
October 2010
Room Number 6
Aunt Patricia Ingle …

"It's a girl!"

Melissa has her baby on October 19th 2010. The news is fantastic. We are all so excited. And emotional. And filled with wonder. It's a magical time. Not even my illness can cast a cloud over this wonderful news.

"Name?" I ask.

"Layla," Mam says, turning her phone around to give me my first glimpse of my niece.

"We're aunties," Kiera laughs.

Layla is the first grandchild for our family and also for Aaron – Melissa's partner – and his family.

Excitement obliterates all the other drama going on in our lives. Melissa's happiness is contagious. And the arrival of little Layla becomes the focus for a while as we all look forward to enjoying time with the latest addition to the Ingle family.

I'm so happy for Mam and Dad. They need a break from worrying constantly. Even when we are driving home to the new house most days, poor Dad has one eye on me the whole time, often looking through the rear-view mirror more than he is watching the road. I have started ducking sideways so he can't see me. Because of the episodes I take sometimes, he watches in case my lips turn blue. My oximeter alarms for the least thing: there are a lot of false alarms. It beeps for the slightest bump in the road or if my hands are cold. It's difficult to relax. One afternoon we were travelling from the hospital to Murroe and I asked my nurse to put on coloured gloss so Dad couldn't see my lips turn blue. It's my nurse's responsibility to keep an eye on me. It's Dad's responsibility to drive safely, even more important now he's a grandad.

In the same way Dad coached me through Maths when I was in school, he is now taking charge of my medication and readings when we are away from the hospital. Little did Dad know that the adult apprenticeship training he took a few years ago when he was going for promotion in the ESB would benefit him now. At the time he could not put 2 and 2 together, never mind multiplication. Now he is managing medication, mixing micros and milligrammes and checking air pressures in millibars, using various units, monitoring alarms, saturations, heart rates, doing medicine ratios because I'm PEG-fed and can't take solids so all medication needs to be liquidised. Risk assessment and safety planning, reaction to alarms was also part of the apprenticeship training and has never been so important than it is now. Dad found studying hard, even took grinds to improve his Maths to make sure he passed the course. His determination and persistence, maybe traits I have inherited, paid off on the double. His hard work helped him achieve the promotion. And now he is putting his Maths to great use and becoming an expert caregiver.

And Layla is the most precious little parcel we could wish for.

"When can I see her?"

"As soon as Melissa's home, Tricia, we'll take you out to see her."

I can't contain my excitement as we travel the short distance to Melissa's house a few days later. Dad, as usual, improvises in whatever way necessary to make everything possible.

"Very cool ramp, Dad," I say when I see the two planks of wood perched on Melissa's front doorstep.

"It would be a bumpy ride otherwise," he laughs, eager to see my reaction when I meet Layla for the first time.

Kiera is waiting with Melissa and Aaron. Our whole family in the one room, with Layla taking all the attention. It's a nice feeling for a change, not to be the focus of everyone's attention and worry.

"Hello, Layla," I mouth, when Melissa takes her out of her crib and brings her over to sit on my lap. Poor little thing is tiny. I can't believe how little she is. But she is gorgeous. I'm so grateful I'm still alive to welcome her into our family. I refuse to worry about my limitations and the type of relationship I can have with my niece. We're all here in Melissa's house. We're here together. That's all that matters.

I sit back and watch, fascinated by Layla and she fascinated by me – well, maybe not me but the probe's flashing red light that's attached to my finger!

This first visit is wonderful. But it isn't something we will be able do very often I'm sure. And bringing a young baby into a hospital environment isn't wise either.

Mam and Kiera argue over holding Layla, both wanting to cuddle and spoil her.

"I'll be around to see you as much as ever," Melissa assures me. "It's useful living so close to the hospital. I'll leave Aaron to manage the nappy changes."

"Maybe she can come to my Halloween party," I mouth, wanting more than ever now to spend a night at home in the midst of the excitement of having a new baby in the family.

"Let's hope," Dad agrees, starting to pack up my bags and get ready for our return to Room Number 6.

"Grace is working on it so let's hope."

Almost as if we were heard making plans to get me an overnight pass, there's a letter waiting on my bed when we get back that spells out in no uncertain terms why I won't be enjoying Halloween evening and welcoming the 'trick or treaters' with my family.

Mam picks it up and starts to read.

22nd October 2010

Tricia and family,

The Bed Manager called to Tricia – ye had gone out.

The Bed Manager had just spoken with the professor. It is not safe for Tricia to go out at night until ALL community supports are in place. (This includes nurses).

The Bed Manager feels it's unlikely, given the above, that the hospital manager will provide a mattress.

Clinical Nurse Manager

22/10/10

16.20 hours.

My heart sinks as Mam reads the few short lines. I want to scream! And I can't even do that much for myself. The excitement of the day shatters in smithereens, the memory of how lonely I felt listening to fireworks last year as vivid now as it was then.

"I'll give Grace a call, Tricia," Dad suggests. "We still have more than a week to go."

*

"I've emailed the hospital manager again, Tricia," Grace tells me a few days later. "I've told him about the issues regarding a bed and a mattress and the other obstacles being put in your way."

"And?" I mouth, just one word, just one wish.

"Nothing back from him yet."

I shake my head and close my eyes, not wanting to see the pity she has for me on her face. I don't want to be pitied. I want to be helped.

"There are still a few days, Tricia. Let's stay hopeful."

But yet again nothing materialises, despite Grace pleading and appealing right up to the last minute.

Halloween 2010 is another depressing evening in Room Number 6 as bangers and sparklers explode in the distance, the torture of living in a life removed from normality ringing loudly in the night sky.

I stare at the TV screen, MTV playing loudly and Katy Perry's song, 'Firework', the only thing cheering me

This song is inspirational and transports me back to the magnificent night I shared with my family at Skyfest. A normal night. A normal existence. The lyrics seem to speak directly to me. It's as if the song was written for me. At least I certainly think so – and I choose to believe there's still a chance for me!

*

"Is there anything else you want to mention today?" Mam asks as we wait for the multi-d meeting to start.

I shake my head. I'm weary repeating the same request over and over. I want to go home. I want to be free. I want to be with family and friends. I want to have a private conversation with my boyfriend. I want to be back with Cody. I want more than sneaking to the back of the hospital to catch a glimpse of him while my boyfriend holds him up to the window. It's better than the emptiness of not seeing him at all. But only just.

It's the 17th November 2010, a little over a month away from another Christmas. This multidisciplinary meeting seems to have a larger guest list than usual! All of my family are here. Grace is with us. The professor is joined by the Community Care rep, the ward sister and the newly appointed hospital case manager overseeing my discharge.

Community Care take the lead. "I'm making every effort to get Patricia discharged. So far I've attended a few clinical meetings but we still have a bit of a way to go."

"We can't see anything new in place to show progress," Dad says.

"Training nurses to look after Patricia will be the first step. We'll need to bring them into the hospital, make sure they are fully equipped to care for Patricia."

"And then move me home?" I mouth.

The lady from Community Care shakes her head. "We'd prefer a temporary move to an alternate facility so that the nurses can be monitored in that environment. We need to make sure they are fully competent and capable of managing to mind you, Tricia, to expert standards."

Dad's frowning. Mam is shaking her head. Kiera and Melissa are waiting for one or other of our parents to say something – and it's Dad who speaks up first.

"Can I interrupt?" he begins. "Are you talking about a nursing home? Because if you are, we're saying a definite 'no' to that."

"There is no mention of a nursing home. The only person speaking about a nursing home is you, Pat," Community Care confirms.

"What temporary facility are you suggesting then?"

"I can't say for definite right at this moment. I need to make a few phone calls to clarify what unit will be used as a type of 'halfway house'."

"But why not let her come directly home to us and have the nurses monitored in our house?" Dad asks.

"That's too risky. In the first instance, the nurses might not operate at home as they would in a hospital environment. In a hospital, they are assured of back-up if it's required."

If I had proper feeling, I know for sure I'd feel a shiver run right through me. There's something very unsettling about this suggestion. Though her intentions are good, my terror is that I would get out of hospital, find myself in another type of – I'm not sure how to describe it – a halfway house as she said. And then I'd be left there, forgotten about once again. I can't let that happen. I look at my family, watching their darkening expressions and suspect they feel exactly like I do about the options being offered.

The current ward sister has only been involved since September but she seems to be working hard on my behalf.

"My biggest concern is the fact your stats drop extremely low on occasion," she says, "and we have to be sure there's urgent assistance available at all times. Your care is complicated. I know you're tired of hearing that but we have to keep that as priority. You're doing so well but being on a ventilator means you are prone to infection. A serious infection could leave you in a potentially high-risk situation. We cannot leave anything to chance."

"But she is so happy when we take her outside of the hospital. You only have to look at the photos of Tricia with Layla. Look how she's enjoying her little niece. She's contented. She feels like a normal person again. In hospital, she feels imprisoned."

"I'm aware of this. And of course I understand it too. Who wouldn't feel like that?"

Dad is still very concerned. "I don't think we'll agree to moving Tricia to an alternate facility. If the choice is between hospital and the 'halfway house' as you have described, I think we'd choose hospital until her move home is arranged."

"Will you at least think about the option, Tricia? Just while we train the nurses?" The Community Care lady looks directly at me.

I nod, willing to at least think about it and discuss it privately with my family. I don't think our decision will change but at least we will show we are prepared to listen to all suggestions.

Dad brings the conversation back to Dún Laoghaire and the neuro-rehabilitation facility there. "Can you look into organising it for her? I know her application was turned down previously. But she has accomplished so much since then, maybe they will reconsider?"

The response is lukewarm, our hopes of rehab knocked back once more. It seems I am as far away from rehab as I am from home.

*

Following the meeting, we discuss everything suggested by Community Care but our answer is 'no' to the halfway house. The story continues.

My boyfriend's form has dipped too. The situation is draining him. He has been a constant by my side, visiting as often as he can, entertaining me, keeping me up to date, telling me about the cars he's been working on. But it's not the relationship we knew before. How can it be? I'm not surprised when he asks to speak to me alone. I try to understand when he explains how difficult it has become. I don't blame him when he says he has to break up with me.

He has been amazing, sticking with me, visiting week after week right from the start, patiently waiting for me to come out of a coma, learning to lip-read and communicate in whatever way was possible, ignoring the physical change in me. But we've come to the end of the road. He asks me to let him go. Inside I'm clinging on for dear life. But I smile and nod. It's only fair he isn't held back by my illness. It's a cruel blow. I can't deny this as I feel emotion well up inside me and imagine iron gates closing behind him as he walks away, leaving me in the prison of Room Number 6, while he takes his freedom and leaves.

"I knew something was wrong," Dad says later, concern etched in the lines of his face.

"I'll survive, Dad. It's not his fault."

Dad nods. But he's devastated. It's a loss for all of us. He was a friend to them too.

Mam takes up the conversation. "Will he still call up with Cody?"

I shake my head, closing my eyes. This is almost as difficult as losing my boyfriend. "He can't. It's a clean break. And because I've no other choice, custody of Cody goes to him. He has taken such good care of him since I became ill. It's impossible for you to mind him. And Melissa has her hands full with Layla. It's heartbreaking but it's for the best."

Mam shakes her head. She's gutted our relationship – and our friendship – is at an end. She tires to hide it but it's written all over her face. She'll miss him too. He has been in all of our lives for so long.

Dad's expression is difficult to read but easy to imagine.

My parents take our break-up worse than I do. It kills them to witness another disappointment for me.

"I wish him the very best, Mam. I hope everything works out well for him in life." I mean this. But I don't feel it yet.

The days and weeks that follow are difficult, empty and lonely. I try to get used to my boyfriend not being around. My family watch me closer than before if that's possible. I try not to wallow in self-pity. It's difficult not to imagine what if. It's difficult not to wonder whether we would have stayed together and had a family if this hadn't happened. Would we be like Melissa and Aaron? Setting up home together and maybe in time have a baby? Now, we can never know. It isn't to be.

Darkness swoops over me. I feel nothing. I want nothing. I don't care anymore. There's no point in hoping for change. It's not going to happen. Not even a visit from Melissa with my adorable little niece can raise my spirits. I hit my biggest low since this whole ordeal has begun. I feel there is no way out.

Mam and Dad hurry to my side when they come to Room Number 6 on the morning of November 19th.

I can't look at them. I won't look at them. I can't do this anymore. I want to withdraw inside myself – like I was back in the beginning of this horrific nightmare. When I was locked inside myself and oblivious to the world around me, oblivious to what I couldn't have, oblivious to what I'm still being denied – my freedom.

Nurses speak in hushed tones to Mam and Dad.

I close my eyes.

"The physiotherapist would like to talk to you," I'm told. "He has some new exercises to try."

I shake my head. Where's the point? What can he do to change how things are? The facts remain. The hospital is threatening to put me into a nursing home by another name. I no longer get speech and language therapy. The occupational therapist has also discharged herself from my care, obviously believing there's no more she can do for me. Her parting words are frightening.

"They may do something for you in an institution."

An institution? Is that my only option? I feel like damaged goods on a warehouse shelf, the broken toy that nobody buys on Christmas Eve. I'm fighting for equipment so I can go home but, even here in hospital, I can't get the proper cushion to avoid pressure sores. I was given one for a while but it was taken away again, the same way as the special chair I was given to make it easier to transfer from bed. How can I keep going with all this disappointment? Am I unique? Have the hospital ever had to care for someone as long as this before? Is this why they're giving up on me? Have I overstayed my welcome?

My heart rate is worrying the nurses. My readings are not what they should be. The amount of equipment I'm attached to increases.

"It's best we don't take you out today," Dad explains gently. "They're monitoring you a little more closely."

I know my parents are upset. I know they're worried as the monitors are put back on. But I just can't pick up my spirits – not this time.

I wallow in my despair.

"I'd be better off if I was back in a coma, Dad."

His face crumbles as I suggest he ask the doctors to consider this.

"Ask them, Dad. Please." I have my speaking valve in so I'm not misunderstood.

He shakes his head vigorously.

"They can wake me again when they've sorted out my discharge. I can't cope with this any longer."

I'm a 22-year-old woman whose mother and sisters have to wash and change me. I don't want that. It's embarrassing. It's humiliating. It's cruel.

I look into Dad's face. "My life is no longer worth living. I don't want to go on."

Chapter 26

Patricia Ingle

December 2010

Room Number 6

I'm dreaming of a Christmas at home …

Saturday 4 December, 2010
From: Patrick Ingle
To: numerous government TDs and Minister for Defence
Cc: joe@rte.ie
SUBJECT: HOW MANY MORE CHRISTMASES?

Good morning, Deputies and Minister,

Pat Ingle here again regarding my daughter, Patricia, who is in hospital now almost two and a half years and facing her third Christmas in hospital.

After two and a half years of trying to get my daughter home and after getting a tenancy from the County Council with all your help and after leaving work and purchasing a special needs vehicle, all the Primary Care people are mentioning is a home for Tricia in a Nursing Home, an 'alternate care facility'. Regardless of the name they give, it is a Nursing Home!

This is completely unacceptable to Patricia and her family.

I am calling on each of you as Public Representatives to come and meet Patricia and myself and family to find out why they want to do this to my daughter.

I am calling to you to meet and come together to help my daughter return home.

Please let me know. Please give this family and Tricia some hope this Christmas.

Regards,

Pat Ingle

Monday 6 December, 2010
From: Minister for Defence
To: Patrick Ingle
SUBJECT: HOW MANY MORE CHRISTMASES?

Dear Patrick,

Thank you for your email which I will pass to the Minister at the earliest opportunity.

Yours sincerely

Private Secretary
Minister for Defence

Tuesday 7 December, 2010
From: TD, Limerick City
To: Patrick Ingle
SUBJECT: HOW MANY MORE CHRISTMASES?

Hi Pat,

I would be glad to meet you, Annette and Patricia again before Christmas to try and find a resolution. Maybe next Monday or Friday if it suits you. I am in Dublin the other days.

TD, Limerick City

Monday 13 December, 2010
From: TD, Limerick City
To: Patrick Ingle
SUBJECT: HOW MANY MORE CHRISTMASES?

Hi Pat,

I got Annette's message about meeting on Friday and I will ring her to arrange a suitable place.

TD, Limerick City

Tuesday 14th December, 2010
From: Minister for Defence
To: Patrick Ingle
SUBJECT: HOW MANY MORE CHRISTMASES?

Dear Patrick,

I understand that your query is being dealt with by the Limerick TDs who represent your area. I trust that Patricia's case can be progressed and wish you well for Christmas and 2011.

Yours sincerely,

Private Secretary
Minister for Defence

Chapter 27

Patricia Ingle
December 2010
Room Number 6
Money, money, money …

Susie's back with an interesting update.

"Tricia, the results of your most recent LCMV test are back from Dr. Pat Kane in London."

"Do I have the virus?" I mouth.

Susie shakes her head. "It definitely shows that you don't have it and, according to the report I've received, you have never been exposed to that particular virus."

"But why did the hospital give that diagnosis if it isn't true?" Mam asks.

"Interesting question. What's even more interesting – or confusing – is this. When I spoke to the doctor in London after receiving his report, he told me that he had already run these tests on you and returned a negative result to the hospital back in 2009."

We look at each other.

"I've had it checked out and it's true," Susie confirms. "But up until now, the test results hadn't been released to us with your records. Neither LCMV test requests or results showed in any of the records furnished under Freedom of Information."

"So the HSE knew what the result would be? And they said nothing when you put that virus at the centre of the case?"

"Fortunately, I had the foresight not to limit the case to just one virus – a prudent approach now as things have turned out."

"So we can still proceed?"

"Yes. But there's more to this."

"What do you mean?"

"Ernest and I discussed it with our Senior Counsel. We suggested releasing Petmania and O'Keeffe's. They took this up with Senior Counsel and together they agreed a figure of €250,000 to release them from proceedings."

The atmosphere instantly changes in Room Number 6. A quarter of a million euro from Petmania. I can get out of hospital. We could afford to pay nurses, carers, buy equipment and medication. Everything I need. We could even afford to pay for rehab ...

"That's a lot of money," Dad says. "It would make a big difference to transferring Tricia home."

But Susie's expression changes and she raises a hand to interrupt. "I know how you must be feeling. And I hate to say this but ..."

I shake my head. No, no, no! There can't be any 'buts' to this story. They've offered me this money. I am taking it. I click my tongue to get their attention.

"I'm taking Petmania's offer. I need it. It's my only out."

Susie addresses me directly. "I'm sorry, Tricia. But we had to get the HSE's agreement before accepting."

"Why?"

"Under the provisions of the Civil Liability Act, we could not accept Petmania's offer without the agreement of the HSE."

"They've said no? They can't! Why would they stand in our way to get Tricia home?" Mam is furious. Her words echo my thoughts – well, a more polite version!

"They seem determined that your employers are in some way connected and responsible."

"But the test proved otherwise?"

"They're suggesting that a particular animal from an exotic land could have given you the infection."

"That's ridiculous!" I can't believe the HSE are taking away this first opportunity we've been given to afford all the care and equipment I need to go home.

"I'm genuinely sorry," Susie says. "What's even more frustrating is their reliance on our evidence. As far as I know, the HSE haven't even had your place of employment investigated!"

"It's so unfair."

Susie looks from one of us to the other. "We will keep going against all defendants and specifically against the HSE in terms of medical negligence."

"What's next?" Dad asks.

"I'll get back to the infectious disease expert and have your serum tested for other possible viruses. We need to narrow your diagnosis down to specifics."

And how long is that going to take, I think, too fed up to bother mouthing it.

Mam asks the question instead.

"With the weather so bad and the Christmas post already in full swing, I don't want to risk the serum samples getting lost in the post. It's safer to defer the next round of testing until the New Year."

Which New Year, I wonder silently.

*

My fury remains. I am so fed up with everything. Where's the point in believing anything that is suggested anymore?

Grace updates Community Care with my answer in relation to co-operating with a temporary move. She tells her that I'm not willing to accept a transfer to an alternate facility. I'm going to wait it out in Room Number 6 until they eventually allow me home.

Christmas is coming fast and furious, the first for Layla and a very special occasion for her mum, aunts and grandparents.

"I'd like to stay at home Christmas Eve," I tell Mam, Dad and Grace as we approach mid-December. "Can we try?"

All three of them smile broadly. They recognise their Tricia surfacing once more. It lifts them to see my determination reappearing.

"Can you help us, Grace?" I ask.

"Of course."

Grace draws up a plan and presents it to the professor and HDU ward manager. On December 21st we receive a lengthy risk assessment document from the ward sister. As I listen to Grace read the document aloud, hearing each and every risk, all I can think of are the three sleeps left to Christmas Eve and me waking up on Christmas morning with my family around me.

*

To: Patrick Ingle and Tricia (me!)
From: HDU

1. Hypoxia – condition where there is insufficient oxygen in the blood to supply the brain

Caused by:

i. Spontaneous dislodgement of the tracheostomy.

ii. Disconnection from ventilator tubing which does happen due to sudden head movement, particularly prone to happening at night.

iii. Build-up of secretions.

iv. Failure to detect early clinical signs of hypoxia.

Management:

Always hand ventilate using C-Circuit with 15 litres of oxygen when/if:

- Disconnection occurs or problem with Nippy.
- If there are signs of hypoxia, i.e. lips turning blue.
- If saturations drop.
- Until saturations are back up to 100% then suction to clear secretions if necessary.
- Ensure the tracheostomy is always well secured.
- Ensure the cuff is inflated.
- Suctioning as required, check inner cannula is patent.
- Immediate reconnection to ventilator tubing should disconnection occur and then check ventilator ensuring desired pressures are being achieved.
- Monitoring of oxygen saturations – dependent on probe.
- Clinical expertise to detect clinical signs of hypoxia early.
- Person available to instantly respond to and manage dislodgement of tracheostomy.

Main Risks:

Failure to recognise the problem and address appropriately due to lack of necessary clinical skills and experience.

Rated: High

2. Airway Management Failure

Caused by:

i.   Dislodgement of tracheostomy during moving and handling/ following a fall.

ii. Disconnection from ventilator tubing.

Management:

More than two persons to be present when moving and ability to monitor the airway throughout.

Immediate reconnection to ventilator tubing should disconnection occur, then check ventilator ensuring desired pressures are being achieved.

Main Risk:

Inability to manage the airway – hypoxia.

Rated: High.

3. Skin Breakdown and Pressure Sore development

Caused by:

i.   Being incontinent of faeces.

ii. Unsuitable seating, infrequent position change.

Management:

i.   Immediate attention to hygiene if bowels open.

ii. Half hourly repositioning and tilting on chair as recommended by O.T.

iii. 2-4 hourly minimum pressure care relief on recliner chair depending on pressure area.

Main Risk:

Pressure sore developing and subsequently become infected.

Rated: High.

4. Spontaneous Blood Pressure Drop

Caused by:

i.   Moving to upright position.

Management:

Awareness and recognising Blood Pressure drop by change in Tricia's colour and lying back down.

Main Risk:

Fall.

Patricia becomes unaware of her surrounding (fainting).

5. Medical Back Up

Medical assistance not available immediately if required.

Main Risk:

Potential delay in administering appropriate treatment in correct setting.

6. Equipment Issues – mechanical failure

NIPPY Ventilator

i.   Tubing becoming kinked.

ii. Power or ventilator failure and inadequate back up (i.e. second nippy not available).

iii. Water in circuit.

Suction Machine

i.   Problems with the seal.

ii. Problems with assembly.

Oxygen

i.   Access to oxygen and having a backup supply.

Oxygen Saturation Probe:

Probe failure – not having a second one available.

No supply of batteries to power unit.

Main Risk

i.   Not being able to identify the problem in the event of failure of equipment.

ii. No clinical engineering expertise on site to fix the equipment and no back up of second units.

*

Grace places the document on the bed, takes a deep breath and a sip of water before continuing.

"Still happy to go home, despite the risks set out in the report?"

She gives me every chance to opt out. But there is no out. Not this time. I see a glimmer of light. I see a chance and I am grabbing it (mentally, seeing as I can't do it for real) before anyone takes it from me.

"I'm going home for Christmas!"

*

"You've received a letter from Community Care," Mam tells me on December 22nd. "Will I read it to you?"

"Please, Mam. I hope it's good news."

> *22 December 2010*
>
> *HEALTH SERVICE EXECUTIVE,*
> *LOCAL HEALTH MANAGERS DEPT, NORTH TIPPERARY/*
> *EAST LIMERICK HSE*
> *Strictly Private & Confidential*
>
> *Dear Ms Ingle,*
>
> *I understand that you are going to leave the hospital overnight on the 24th December, 2010, despite the fact that the optimal care plan as proposed by the clinical team is not in place.*
>
> *I understand that discussions have taken place with you and your family regarding a discharge plan and you do not agree with this plan and have not accepted same. This plan requires a very significant investment in our Community Services, in manpower, and additional developments in skills and competencies of our staff, and we are not in a position to put this in place immediately but rather it can be put in place over a period of time.*
>
> *I realise and appreciate your wish to go home directly to Murroe. However, given the Community and Acute Services assessment of your needs the Community Services are not at this point in time able to provide staff with the skills and competencies required to provide you with safe care in your home to allow for your safe direct discharge to Murroe.*

I understand that the professor in charge and the Clinical Team at the HDU have met you and your family and have informed you of the risks involved if you decide to proceed with taking your own discharge against medical advice to your home without accepting transitional care as outlined in the Acute and Community Discharge Plan. It has been indicated to you that the HSE will consider putting the necessary arrangements in place over time to support you to live at home. However, we will not accept responsibility for any decision you may take which is contrary to the medical advice already to the advice given to you.

I would urge you to reconsider your decision and to work with us to ensure you can be safely discharged home into the future.

Yours sincerely

A/General Manager

North Tipperary/East Limerick

Chapter 28

Patricia Ingle

Christmas 2010 – Christmas Number 3

Room Number 6 … Murroe, Co. Limerick

Driving home for Christmas …

It's Christmas Eve. I'm going home. I'm going home. I'm going home for Christmas! I can't believe it. I'm scared something will go wrong at the very last minute, that somebody will call or insist I have to go back to the hospital.

Mam and Dad have everything ready. They've even bought a pressure mattress that we can keep at home so the hospital can't use that as an excuse as they did at Halloween. Despite them saying they couldn't loan us one, there was a storeroom full of them along the corridor. It seems so mean but we have our own mattress now and it's one less thing to cause an issue at the last minute.

It's the coldest December on record but not even sub-zero temperatures can hold me back.

I'm so excited, I'm almost impatient. But I have to wait for Mam and Dad to get here. They travel slowly in the frosty weather. It's snowing heavily and there's still snow on the sides of the road. They're filled with terror as well as excitement. They're getting their daughter home. Home for real. Home to stay for the entire night. Our whole family would be together in the one house, under our roof. They could check on us while we're sleeping and there wouldn't be one daughter in hospital as has been the case for the last two years.

As well as fear and excitement, Mam and Dad are filled with determination to prove, not only to the hospital, but also to me that coming home is going to be okay. It's going to be safe. We will manage. We will be fine.

Mam and Dad take the stairs, hurrying to the second floor with pounding hearts. It's a big day for them. The walk seems longer than normal. It's not as if they haven't done the same trip hundreds of times already. But oh, is it worth it! When they see my face. When they see how happy I am. When they see that all I want in my life is what today is about to bring. That I can come home. That I can properly join my family again.

"Your smile is brighter than the snow we've just driven through, Tricia," Dad says, his own smile broader than I've seen in a very long time. "You're beaming. We won't need any electricity. There's enough power in your smile for all of us."

Dad is in a powerful mood himself, so proud to be taking me home.

"Even if they put up iron bars and have armed guards and walls sky high around the hospital, you are coming home today. No obstacle will stand in our way. No obstacle will prevent this dream coming true for you."

"I can't wait. Let's go. Are you nervous?"

"Not now. We were, a little earlier, but the closer we got to the hospital, the more confident we became on our way here. Today is an extension on the day releases we have had already. You'll be safe. We have been putting preparations in place for months. This is your day, Tricia. And it's a very special occasion for all of us."

A private nurse has been booked to come and stay with me through the night. But the afternoon and evening is going to be just us. Our family.

"The nurse has ICU training. She will be well able to look after you, Tricia," Mam insists. "We're not taking any risks with you."

My private nurse arrives to the hospital and Mam brings her in to introduce us. She seems lovely and she also seems very conscientious. While she's with me, she takes the time to go and chat with my HDU nurses.

"I'm Tricia's nurse while she's at home tonight," she tells them. "I was wondering if I can get a full account of anything unusual or anything that should be avoided."

The nurses are extremely helpful. They give her a full rundown on my care and she's smiling when she returns to Room Number 6.

"The nurses have been great. We are good to go. I have all the info I need for tonight."

It's really happening. I'm so excited. And scared too – but not scared of anything going wrong. Scared this magical moment will be cruelly taken away from me. Scared it will be all too much for me. Scared of the thought of having to return to Room Number 6.

The excitement is overwhelming. How could the hospital refuse and put obstacles in my way? How could they refuse me this happiness? I can't remember the last time I felt like this – my heart feels like it will burst with happiness.

*

Dad has decorations up, more than I can ever remember seeing in our old house.

"I don't think you'll find a room in this house that doesn't look like Christmas."

"The house looks fabulous, Dad." If I could pinch myself, I would, just to test I'm awake. This feeling inside me right now is something I will never forget. Being surrounded by normal sounds. Savouring the brightness of our new home, the freshly painted walls hidden behind so many family photographs, the gust of fresh air when anyone comes through the back door, the bright glow from the fire, the bright glow from my parents' eyes when they see how happy I am. And the delicious smells of Christmas familiar and inviting. In a strange way, the smells make it easier for me to cope with the repetition of being fed through a tube, the rich aromas reminding me of the numerous Christmases in our old house when I took every single thing for granted and assumed they'd be available to me for the rest of my life.

*

It's 2 p.m. The afternoon stretches ahead. We are all looking forward to it.

A Christmas movie comes on TV.

"We'll get you from your wheelchair to the couch," Dad offers. "Then you can relax and enjoy the movie.

"That's great. Thanks," I mouth to Dad.

And then the lights go out. The television screen goes black. The hum of the oven stops. My NIPPY starts to beep. Candle flames glow on the table, casting shadows on the walls.

Dad jumps to attention. "Don't panic," he says. "I have a generator outside just in case this happened. It has limited power outlets but should tide us over."

We look around at each other, nobody mentioning that it is more bad luck. Or asking what we'll do if the power stays out.

Dad's back to the living room. He has the generator up and running and it's giving us enough power for one electric light and my NIPPY.

As quickly as he returns, he disappears into the attic.

"What is he doing?" I ask, but I don't really get an answer.

"Is every other house out too?" Kiera asks.

"Yes," Mam says after she's taken a look outside. "The road is in darkness. The housing estate is also in darkness."

"Hook up the Christmas tree to the socket," I suggest. "Then our house will be like a bright star shining in the darkness."

Even brighter than the moon ... once again the lyrics from 'Firework' find their way into our excitement.

We relax and chat. The others enjoy the Christmas nibbles and Mam is up and down from her seat, keeping the festive atmosphere alive as well as tending to my suctionings and making sure all my medication is given bang on time.

The doorbell rings. We look at each other. We weren't expecting anybody.

"I couldn't resist checking in to see how you're doing." It's one of the nurses from HDU.

"Come in," Mam invites her, proceeding to explain about the power cut and the standby generator.

An hour has passed already. Dad's worrying the generator won't have enough power.

"I'll call the controller of networks in the ESB and ask how long the fault will take," he decides, searching through his list of work colleagues and dialling his number.

The HDU nurse says she needs to get on home and leaves.

"The controller says an hour," Dad tells us as soon as she's gone. He's getting anxious. "The generator will only last eight hours."

He doesn't need to say anymore. It's obvious what's going through his mind. If the electricity doesn't come back on, my NIPPY won't work. My night home for Christmas is back in jeopardy. Or could be.

"What do you think?" Dad looks at me.

I close my eyes. Please don't send me back.

Mam catches my hand. "Tricia?"

I open my eyes. All five of us know there is only one option. "I'll have to go back."

"We'll wait the hour and see what the controller says then."

Dad phones after an hour.

"There are a few faults causing the outage," he tells us when he hangs up. "And it could take three and a half hours to fix the major fault."

"Dad, we'll wait. I'm okay. It's warm from the gas heater." I plead for more time.

The standby emergencies are all in use.

"Yes!" Kiera and Melissa squeal together when the lights flick on around the house and the oven kickstarts again, the fridge shuddering to life.

"Thank God it's –" but before Mam even finishes the sentence, the power outs again.

We all shake our heads. This can't be happening.

"Don't worry. This could be a good sign," says Dad. "They're probably isolating faults."

The power returns, fails, returns, fails and finally returns and stays a little longer. But just when we think it's back to stay, it cuts out again.

"What are we going to do, Pat?" Mam asks.

"I'll phone again," he offers, "but it's getting serious now. It's not only the lights. There's no heating either. I can't have you getting cold. I'm sorry, Tricia, but you'll have to go back if they can't guarantee the power is going to stay back for the full night."

I can see he is annoyed this has happened. It's more than disappointment. There is so much depending on tonight being a success. It's our chance to prove home is an option, that with the right home care package I am as safe here as in hospital.

"We're not waiting any later than eight. With the weather the way it is, I can't risk the roads either."

At around 7 p.m. the room is flooded with light.

"I'll phone the controller."

Dad grabs his phone straight away and dials.

"The lights are on. Is this a permanent fix?" he asks.

I watch his expression. He seems to be relaxing a little.

'The faults are repaired," he tells us.

"Will it be okay?" he asks the controller, putting the call on speaker so we can all hear the response.

"You know I can't guarantee a full supply. But I can tell you that it's no different than a normal day. It's as reliable as it can be."

Dad thanks him and ends the call.

"You're staying at home – but only by the skin of our teeth."

Christmas starts for real. The atmosphere is literally 'electric'.

Dad disappears into the attic again, this time taking a hair-dryer of all things.

"What were you doing? Drying your hair in the attic?" I ask him when he comes back down.

"I was thawing the water tank to make sure the heating works."

Poor Dad. It's probably the busiest he has ever been on Christmas Eve. But he has got things in hand at last. He looks shattered but relieved as he turns to ask Mam how he can help.

The whole family eventually get to sit down. The heating is on; the house is cosy and warm. The Christmas tree is twinkling. Everyone is smiling as we toast this special occasion.

"Merry Christmas!"

There's a knock at the door. "That will be the night nurse," Dad says, going to let her in.

"You all look nice and relaxed. Obviously you had a nice peaceful day?" she comments when she enters the room.

"If you only knew!" Dad laughs as he sits back down on the couch.

What an eventful day.

*

Though I've lost my sense of touch and my ability to feel with my fingers, one thing I can feel stronger than anything I have ever experienced in my life are the feelings of love, excitement, nervousness and disbelief when I open my eyes Christmas morning and realise I haven't been dreaming. I'm at home. At last.

My family hover around me, their excitement as evident as mine.

"You slept really well, Tricia," Mam says.

"The bed was so cosy," I mouth to her.

Being able to watch my family is such a novelty first thing this morning. I don't have to wait for them to arrive as I do in hospital. They don't have to travel to see me, getting up really early and facing out into the cold. It is better for them too.

Our day begins, the process of getting me dressed and ready to celebrate Christmas already underway. I savour every second at home.

*

The only problem is the speed at which the time flies by until the dreaded 10 p.m. comes around.

This is it, the day is over and I'm on my way back to the hospital.

This is horrible, my hopes and dreams ripped away from me as Dad parks outside the MWRH and I'm returned to Room Number 6 once more. I don't even get until midnight on this occasion. I don't even get a Cinderella experience.

Chapter 29

Patricia Ingle

January 2011

Room Number 6 with a taste of home

Dreams really do come true – but they also come to an end …

I get to experience the joy all over again when I'm allowed sleep at home again on New Year's Eve and I'm delighted to ring in 2011 in the comfort of home.

New Year's Eve is a perfect trip. The electricity stays on. The water doesn't need defrosting. Dad isn't disappearing into the attic. Things run so much smoother second time around.

The private nurse is lovely. She's glad to see Mam and Dad have reorganised a few things on my second visit, based on her advice from Christmas Eve.

"This bigger room is far better for Tricia," she says. "It's important her bed is in the middle of the floor so that staff can access her from all sides. Ideally she needs an automatic bed. But this will do for now."

Mam and Dad are constantly learning. Without them, where would I be? I shudder to think, a vision of nursing homes first to rush into my mind.

But for now, I'm in a different room with a different view and a whole two days to look forward to.

*

Christmas and the New Year feel like a glorious dream. The magical feeling of staying at home, staying up late, being part of normal family squabbles and bickering when board games are produced. I wasn't excluded from anything, everyone happy to help me in any way they could.

Nothing could dampen the feeling I experienced those two nights at home – not even the power-cut disaster.

But January 2011 is harder than any other month I've been in Room Number 6. The crash following the euphoria of staying at home is devastating.

Being a patient in hospital is even more depressing now than it was.

I look at the shower room – or the make-shift wardrobe as it is now – and want to throw something at the door! Of course that's impossible as I wouldn't be able to pick something up or lift my hand high enough to even do that. The shower is still out of order. And nothing at all is being done to remedy the situation. I don't have a shower chair so I haven't had a bath or a shower for a number of years. If the equipment was working, I'd have to remain tied up to my machinery but it could be done and it would be far less embarrassing than the situation now.

Still getting bed baths. Still hating them. Still mortified. At the very least if I had independent carers doing it, somehow this would feel less embarrassing.

*

The routine continues, my parents arriving early each morning to dress me and sit me upright. I'm usually dizzy for a while and it can take up to five or six minutes before it settles down. And then they connect me up and get me into Dad's van. It has a special lift to get my chair in and out, making life much easier for my parents but still requiring both of them to manage the move. It feels so bright when we're travelling towards home but dark as we load up again in the evening to make the return journey to Room Number 6.

There's so much I still hope to achieve, despite what has happened to me.

I want to access proper neuro-rehabilitation in the best facility available. I am extremely anxious to come off my ventilator. It's extremely cumbersome and I hate to have a tube coming out of my neck. I cover it with a scarf whenever I am out in public. I know there's nothing here in Ireland but I will travel anywhere just to get every opportunity to improve.

I want to regain bladder and bowel awareness and control (if possible). If I cannot regain bowel awareness, I certainly want to have a proper formal bowel program put in place so that my bowel movements can be managed properly. At the moment, the situation is undignified.

I would absolutely love to be able to eat again. The PEG is unpleasant and cumbersome. Eating is an activity for all human beings and animals in fact. It's something we enjoy.

I can't wait to have a shower again. It's something else human beings enjoy and benefit from.

I want to keep moving with my rehabilitative exercises on my legs and my arms. I know that I can continue to make progress because my progress to date has been slow but steady. However, I need far more time with proper neuro-physiotherapists who are equipped to deal with injuries like mine. I remember at one multidisciplinary meeting being told by the physio that I had plateaued. I didn't accept it then. I never will.

I have an enormous party planned for when I am finally discharged.

I want my family to go back to being my family. My carers should be nurses that are hired. I don't want my family to be changing me. I want them just to be there to relax and chat with me and live as a normal family would. My carers would look after my bodily functions. My family shouldn't be burdened with this. They are exhausted already.

I have retained my absolute love for animals. I have every intention of getting a dog when I do come home for good.

In the future, I would like to live independently of my parents. I appreciate all they have done for me but it has been extremely difficult for me to be in their presence all day every day for the last number of years. That isn't normal for a 22-year-old girl. They need to be allowed to get on with their own lives because I can see what sort of effect my illness has had on them. They also need to get back to being a married couple and doing other things together for fun including socialising with their friends. I want to get back to socialising with mine.

I love the home we have in Murroe. But I would like to live in my own house. I appreciate I'll require a house that's wheelchair accessible and has sufficient space to allow me to socialise with my friends, separately from the carers who will also be required to live there. I appreciate that it will be some time before I will be in a position to live independently with my carers.

But I would like to live independently in my own home and keep my animals with me. I'd like to be able to control my environment, in so far as I possibly can, through environment-control equipment. Little things like leaving visitors in or out, matters that are so normal for so many people, would mean the world to me.

I always wanted to have my own dog-grooming business some day. That was always my intention. My plan was to work with Petmania for a number of years, undertake a dog-grooming course in the UK (which I had been researching at the time I became unwell) and get some experience in that area. Working with animals is my absolute passion in life. I am never giving up on that dream.

I want to be able to speak or else communicate in a far more satisfactory manner than I can at the moment. When I don't have my speaking valve in, I have to mouth words and spell out words that my family cannot understand when I mouth them. I click with my tongue when I'm trying to get attention to participate in a conversation. However, this is all extremely frustrating because it takes so long for me to say one sentence where everyone else just natters away. It can often be hard for me to keep up with the conversation because I am trying to formulate my own sentence to participate. But, I do have a lot to say and I want to be able to say it.

The consultation with an assistive technology expert was extremely valuable. I learned about all of the various technologies that are out there for people like me so that I can communicate and engage with the world on a far more satisfactory level than I can at the moment. I'm looking forward to seeing what environmental-control equipment is available for me.

I have a laptop computer which is touch screen which my parents got me for Christmas. I can use this but I have difficulties in hitting the right button because of my dexterity problems. I would like to have a gaze-tracking computer.

I would like to go on holidays in the future.

I would love start a new relationship in the future. I have a lot to give.

*

Unfortunately, my future plans fail to prevent darkness from wrapping itself tightly around me, sticking to me like clingfilm until my parents arrive the next morning and the routine starts again.

I have to make the hospital hear me. I have to try and explain how it is for me. I think it's time they listen to me now.

"Grace, can you help me write a letter, please?"

> TO: A/General Manager,
> North Tipperary/East Limerick HSE West
> FROM: Patricia Ingle (Me!)
> 19 January 2011

> Dear Manager,
>
> I am writing this letter with the help of my independent advocate, Grace Moore, in response to the letter you sent me just before Christmas 2010. As you know I have been in hospital now for two and a half years. I decided to write this letter because when I go to meetings or meet people involved in my case I find it hard to speak up. While I do find it hard to speak physically I can do it with my speaking valve – however,

the reason I stay quiet is because I don't want to disagree with anyone or hurt anyone's feelings. I think it's because of the way my mam and dad raised me to have respect for other people and always be polite. In this letter I am going to let people know how I am feeling inside.

Every morning I am woken at 6 a.m. I get very lonely waiting for my family to come into see me at 8 a.m. I don't want to wake up in this room; I want to wake up in my bedroom at home. My advocate and my family organised for an accessible house to be bought for me and my family; Limerick County Council let us move into the house last July. This was a great achievement because it meant I could live with my family again. I was so excited picking out furniture for my room and picking the paint colours. I have been home to the house lots of times. I usually go home every day or every second day. When I am at home with my family and friends I can be normal.

I am very sad and disappointed that I am still waiting to move home. I don't like the way people have to come to visit me in HDU. I think it's taking them away from other things in their lives they could be doing. If I was at home, visits would be more normal and my family would have a more normal life. This situation is very hard on them too. My family are with me every day from 8 a.m. to 11.30 p.m. When they go home I get very lonely and sad.

I have spent three birthdays and two Christmases in hospital. This Christmas (December 2010) my advocate and family organised for me to stay at home for the night on Christmas Eve. I was afraid to get excited about this. I didn't believe it would actually happen until Christmas Eve came. I stayed up until 1.30 a.m. watching movies and playing games with my family. It was a fantastic night! We hired a nurse with experience working with fully ventilated patients from TLC Nursing Services. She looked after me during the evening and while my family and I slept. The next day I didn't go back to HDU until 10 p.m. Because things worked out so well for Christmas Eve I went home for the night again on New Year's Eve. It cost us €1,000 for the nurse for the two nights but we had to pay it or I would have been in hospital for Christmas and New Year again.

I hate going back to HDU. I get very low when I come back here; the walls in my room are covered with pictures of my family, friends and pets. I look at them and it reminds me of what it was like to be normal. When I am in HDU I feel trapped, like I am in prison. My first niece was born recently. I only get to see her when I go home as it wouldn't be a good idea to bring her to the hospital. I want to get to know her and not just see her once a week. Anyone who knows me knows I love animals. I am worried my three cats won't know me when I get home. One of my cats, Rachel, is 14 years old and I'm worried that something will happen to her when I am not there. I miss them a lot. I have not seen them a lot since I came to hospital. I saw them from the car when we went back to our old house.

My consultant professor said that I was ready to be discharged from hospital in March 2009. I met with the Disabilities Team in August 2010 to discuss a home care package that will allow me to join my family at home. At the last meeting I had, the Disabilities Case Manager said that the HSE would hire HDU nurses who would be trained to look after me by the staff in HDU. She also said that it was necessary to move me to an 'alternate care facility' with my nurses after they were trained. She said that when the HSE are confident the nurses are competent then I will move from the alternate care facility to home. She would not give any commitment on how long I would be in the alternate care facility.

I do not want to move to an alternate care facility. I want to move home. I have been away from my family for too long already. It took a lot of courage for me to say no to this plan. After reading your letter, I am afraid now that I will be left in HDU until I agree with this plan. I believe that what I want should be taken into consideration. I believe there must be an alternative that will be acceptable to all of us.

The Case Manager's plan is based around my nurses having backup for a period of time from nurses based in the alternate care facility. However, the nurses who will be

*looking after me will be much more specialised and highly
trained than those in any alternate care facility I know of. I
don't understand how they will be of benefit if something was
to happen.*

*I have a suggestion to make which I would agree to and
which I feel is a compromise. I suggest that when my nurses
have been trained by the HDU staff to look after me I am
moved off the HDU ward to a room on the ward down the
corridor which has been closed for some time now. When this
happens I will be cared for exclusively by my team of nurses
and PAs and my family. If any of my nurses were to get into
difficulty then they will be able to call on the HDU staff for
back-up. However, I feel that this will not happen based on the
two nights I spent at home with a nurse without any incident.
Following a short period where the competence of the nurses
working with me can be assessed I will then move home.*

*Every day that goes by I get lower and lower. I desperately
need to go home. I ask that you all agree to this suggestion.
I'd be happy to meet with you, supported by my advocate to
discuss this further. If you want more information you can
call my advocate, Grace Moore.*

Kind regards,

Patricia Ingle

*

"Grace, can you change the wording of my letter a bit so we can send it to Dad's list of TDs and Ministers to see if they will make a case for me with the HSE. Maybe it will appeal to their sympathies a little more!"

Grace as always is happy to help.

"I'll go through my photos and send them a collage with the letter. And I'll see if I can get in touch with the hospital manager to see if he can arrange the competency test of nurses in one of the closed hospital wards."

*

Dad's worried about my form being so low. He watches me closely, doing everything in his power to try and cheer me up. He makes sure to get in early in the morning so I can have as many hours as possible at home. Between himself and Mam they are expert carers now and do almost everything for me.

"The professor is worried about you, Tricia," he tells me. "He knows how much you enjoyed staying at home those two nights at Christmas. But he's also noticing how hard it has been for you since, despite getting out of the hospital most days for a number of hours."

"Why doesn't he make it permanent then?"

"He is trying, Tricia. Somebody will help us. They have to eventually. Because I won't stop asking until they do."

And he takes out his laptop, opens his email account and gets to work.

Tuesday 8 February, 2011

From: Patrick Ingle
To: Minister for Health
SUBJECT: PATRICIA INGLE

Hi,

    Thanks for your call yesterday. Sorry I missed it. I was with Tricia. I got your message and you can call this afternoon before three if that's possible. I have sent numerous emails over the last two years to you and all politicians. If you go back on the history of those emails, it will give you an insight into Patricia's position and how she is still in hospital two years after her consultant said not only can Tricia go home but she would benefit from being at home with her family. If you can't retrieve these emails I would gladly forward them again to you.

Thanks again for your email and calls,

Pat Ingle

Chapter 30

Patricia Ingle
March 2011
Room Number 6
What could have been …

In March 2011 the professor surprises us when he mentions contacting the National Rehabilitation Centre in Dún Laoghaire as a possibility once more.

"It can't hurt to try again, Tricia," he states. "I'll argue for a place on the basis that you require it urgently."

"But I'm still ventilated?" I mouth the obvious.

"What I'm going to suggest is that you stay in the Mater Hospital at night and be transferred by taxi or ambulance during the day."

"Will they attempt to wean her off the ventilator?" Mam asks.

The professor shakes his head. "They don't have the facilities to do that."

"But her dependency is a big issue for her. It should form part of her rehab."

"I can't say that the centre will be able to meet all the rehab needs." The professor is hesitant.

Another brick wall. Is funding the issue? Is the professor's suggestion going to lead to anything?

I won't hold my breath – even if I could!

*

Susie is making significant progress, however, and her investigation is coming up with interesting results. We listen eagerly as she updates us with the latest, cringing as she shares some graphic findings by the experts she has hired to look into all the detail.

"I had an A&E expert analyse your case notes. In his report he states very clearly that when you went to the hospital on 19th August 2008 with headaches and vomiting, your symptoms suggested raised intracranial pressure and not tonsillitis. They should have sent you for an urgent CT scan at that point."

Oh my God! The very first time I went to A&E they should have seen the problem. I look at my parents, Mam's expression grave, Dad's fists clenched.

Susie pauses a moment to let that bit of news sink in properly. "Though there was probably some damage done before 1st September, he's confident that up to the 2nd September all was not lost and the damage could have been remedied. Even up until the morning of September 3rd, they missed a valuable opportunity to insert an external drain and relieve some of the pressure. This intervention could have avoided some of your more severe complications."

"So it's true?" I mouth. "This should not have happened to me?"

Susie nods. "He's an expert in his field. His report clearly states that your brain was denied oxygen for at least 24 to 48 hours longer than necessary. You should have been transferred to the CUH on the 1st September and not the 3rd. And they should never have carried out a lumbar puncture. I'm sorry, this must be so difficult to hear."

"It is," Mam replies. "And the reason she became ill in the first place, are you any further on with that?"

"As I told you already, all the tests for the LCMV virus came back negative. I went back to the expert in infectious diseases and discussed your case with him again in great detail."

"Thanks, Susie," I mouth.

"What does he advise to do next?" Mam asks.

Susie smiles as she continues. "Already on it, Annette. He scrutinised your case notes again and came back with four specific viruses. The first, LCMV, has already been ruled out. The second and third, although serum was taken in November 2010 and sent on for testing, could not be identified because of an inappropriately timed sample."

"Oh! Is this a problem?"

Susie shakes her head. "Not specifically as it turns out. There is nowhere, as far as I could identify, in either the UK or in Europe where Listeria and Cryptococcus testing can be carried out anyway. Therefore, even with a timely sample, testing would have been close to impossible."

We look at each other. For me, it's as if Susie is talking about somebody else. For my parents, I can't imagine what's going on in their minds with these latest revelations. Susie's voice interrupts my thoughts.

"This leaves us with the fourth virus, Chlamydia psittacci. The expert I contacted is particularly interested in this specific disease as it's contracted from birds and is a very well-known and highly recognised risk associated with the pet-store industry."

Oh, this is promising! Maybe the results will give Susie the evidence she has been looking for. "What now?" I mouth.

"We already sent your serum sample to the Health Protection Agency in Porton Down in the UK."

"And the results? Are they back yet?" Dad asks.

"A consultant virologist carried out his test and we've been waiting for weeks to receive his report. I phoned him on St. Patrick's Day and went through the background of the case with him over the phone."

As I listen to Susie, I see how dedicated she is, even going as far as working on the day when everybody else is focused on parades, fun and celebrating one of Ireland's favourite holidays.

"The virologist gave me the results."

If I could swallow, I know I'd be swallowing hard at this moment. Can Susie finally tell what caused this?

"The tests proved positive for Chlamydia psittacci antibodies. Because the sample being tested was only taken in November last year – 2010 – the virologist believes the link to your illness in 2008 would be strengthened if an earlier sample was available to test."

"Why didn't they test for it in the hospital at the time? Why did it take your intervention?" Mam demands.

Susie nods her understanding. "We'll be asking that question. Don't worry. But for now, I am focusing on getting the best evidence in place to support this."

"Thanks, Susie," Mam says.

"I've been in touch with the HSE asking for access to a serum sample taken in January 2009 so we can have the same test carried out and ultimately prove the antibodies were in existence when you were taken ill originally. If the results prove positive, it's incontestable and proves a direct link between your illness and your place of work."

"Will they allow you test the sample?" I mouth.

"Technically, yes, seeing as I requested details and access to all samples when I started work on your case."

That's a relief. It's interesting hearing Susie's account of her investigation, even if it is about me!

"Maybe we should get some coffee before I tell you the next bit. I have a feeling it's going make irritating listening."

"I'll skip the coffee," I mouth with a smirk.

Poor Susie. She is mortified.

"Sorry, Tricia! I didn't mean to exclude you."

"She's just teasing," Mam laughs. "She does it to us all the time. But that's our Tricia, always has a sense of humour, no matter what."

My joke seems to lighten the mood and, deciding against the coffee break for now, we encourage Susie to keep going.

Taking a deep breath, she launches into the next part of her story. "The archived serum sample kept by the HSE is dated January 2009 and kept at the hospital in an external unit."

"Is that normal?" Dad interrupts.

"In some cases," Susie responds. "In Tricia's case, there was also a Cerebro Spinal Fluid sample dated September 2009 that had also been retained. It took a lot of time and correspondence to get this information from the hospital but eventually I did. So I've confirmed that the January 2009 sample we are interested in testing has been retained by the hospital and stored at -20 degrees Celsius in an external freezing facility."

It's strange imagining the samples they took from me over two years ago are still in existence in some sort of freezer unit.

"When I asked for the January 2009 sample," Susie continues, "the HSE indicated, via their solicitors, that they wish to retain half of it for their purposes. I need your permission, Tricia, to consent to this."

I look around the room to my parents and sisters and then back to Susie. "Whatever you think is best," I mouth.

"I think it is okay to consent to this, but I'll be sending it with the strict and unequivocal instruction that the serum is not to be thawed and refrozen without contacting me first."

"Why?" I mouth.

"The sample is really important to your case and every time you thaw and refreeze a serum sample the antibodies will denature and degenerate. Simply put, it weakens the content and makes it less reliable."

I'm confused.

Susie goes into more detail. "Repeated thawing and refreezing the sample could potentially lose us the opportunity to prove you had Chlamydia psittacci in your system when you first attended the hospital."

I agree to the HSE's request on Susie's terms, assuming they will respect the conditions of my consent.

*

But assuming anything isn't a good idea and Susie is furious when she visits with the latest news on proceedings.

"Picking up where we left off the last time, I gave the HSE your consent to splitting the sample and I didn't hear anything from them after that. The virologist was still waiting to receive our portion of the sample to carry out his tests. I made contact again with the HSE for your half of the archived serum sample." She inhales deeply. "Can you believe the HSE ignored your clear instruction not to tamper with the sample? I couldn't have been more direct in my message."

"We can believe it," Mam says.

"Until such time as I was contacted," Susie continues, "the sample was not to be touched. They were under strict instruction not to thaw the frozen serum sample."

We nod our heads in unison. Yes, we can believe it. Our anger bubbles. Disappointment and frustration have become par for the course in our experiences so far.

"Is there anything you can do? Is this another roadblock for Tricia?" Dad finds his voice.

"I've written to them complaining. I've received a letter of apology from their solicitors in response, as well as one from the Clinical Science Lab in MWRH."

"A fat lot of good apologies are," Mam mutters.

"You're right, Annette. Our job is more difficult now. We were relying heavily on that serum sample."

"This is so unfair," I cry. "How can they get away with this? What can you do?"

"We have already started researching the effect the thaw-freeze-thaw-refreeze process has on the sample and the integrity of the antibodies."

"Did you send the sample to the virologist?" Dad asks.

"Yes, but unfortunately while it showed an increase in the level of antibodies present, it didn't show anything significant. So we need to support it with the result of our research on the thawing and refreezing."

"Do you think you'll still be able to use this evidence?" Mam says.

"I hope so," Susie insists. "There are two different types of antibodies in the serum, the "fight or flight" antibodies that the body produces after a recent exposure to the virus, and then the long-term antibodies the body holds on to in the future to identify a particular pathogen in case it comes into contact with it again."

I'm a bit lost with the level of detail. But Susie is great at explaining.

"Both of your serum samples showed the long-term antibodies, but the 'fight or flight' antibodies were missing from the January 2009 serum sample."

"And there's no way to prove otherwise?" Dad asks.

"That's why we're doing such extensive research and getting expert advice to see if the thaw-refreezing process can eliminate the 'fight or flight' element."

"And if the research proves something? Will it be enough?"

"We'll put an argument together to show that we would have found the 'fight or flight' antibodies in the January 2009 sample, had it not been for the interference of the HSE. And despite the difficulties with the sample, we are getting closer to proving a link with your exposure to Chlamydia psittacci while you were working in Petmania and your illness in September 2008."

"What kind of a disease is it? Do you know much about it?" I don't even try to pronounce the name!

"Chlamydia psittacci is an unusual disease and one major difficulty is that it can feature in serological testing of a good deal of the population through exposure in normal daily activities," Susie begins.

"Isn't that risky then? Surely the Court will say this and throw out our argument?" Mam has a valid point.

"That's true but we'll make a strong case to prove that you were at far greater risk of contracting infection at work as the disease arises from the inhalation of feather dust, faecal dust and respiratory secretions from infected psittacine birds."

"What are they?" I mouth. Susie gives us so much information, it's difficult to keep up!

"Sorry – they're perching birds and could include cockatiels, canaries, budgies, parakeets, lovebirds, African greys and many more."

I visualise all of those birds in the shop when I worked there, perched in their cages, looking so innocent when all along they were spreading infection and I was unlucky enough to catch it!

"From the research we've done I already know these birds were stocked by Petmania."

I nod my head. "Other shops would have them too?" I suggest.

"But the difference, Tricia, is you've been infected by the disease and others haven't. And we need to keep drilling into the evidence to find out why this happened."

"Thank you," I mouth.

"We're also looking at the difference between negligent and non-negligent exposure. It's vital we're correct in associating your job with your illness. Technically, from what we've found so far, it all depends on the hygiene standards and the importance of wearing gloves and masks."

Dad puts his face in his hands.

I can almost read his mind. He had done his best by getting me gloves. If only I had got a face mask too.

"But how come the others didn't get the infection too?" Mam asks.

"It all depends on how vulnerable we are to infection at a particular time. You've been so unfortunate."

"Did the HSE use their half of the sample for testing? Or did they thaw it as a way to damage ours?" Dad asks Susie.

"They used it alright but not to any great findings. Even though they knew the LCMV had come back negative, they actually used it to test for this again. It doesn't make sense when the investigation points heavily towards employer negligence. I would have thought the HSE would be making every effort to prove that to abdicate liability."

"So you're doing all the work to pin liability on Petmania. And the HSE are letting it to you."

"It seems that way," Susie admits. "But we won't let that fact distract us. Let's keep working."

"What's your plan?" Dad asks.

"We've had experts make site visits and take photos. We have their reports as evidence. Ultimately we need the best outcome for you, Tricia. We're nearly there now. And we'll have a sound case to present to your employers as well as the HSE. We'll leave nothing to chance. I promise you that."

*

"A bit of good news," Dad announces when the sale of our house is finalised.

I try to cheer up at this news but instead all I can think of is another loss. I haven't been in our old house since that fateful morning I staggered out of it, barely able to hold my head up. The fun and happiness we had in that house! The horrific circumstances that forced my parents to sell it and move to an accessible house to accommodate my needs!

This causes upset and emotion. I can't even cry real tears. Even that simple release that others take for granted, I'm denied. Just another reason to be fed up. It doesn't take much these days. I can't stop. It's as if I've crossed an invisible threshold where acceptance no longer exists. Every time Mam and Dad come in now, I'm upset. They can see it in my expression. I've no tears but it doesn't stop me trying to wipe them away. I'm breaking their hearts. I'm upsetting and scaring my sisters. But I have no control over it. I'm stuck in a time warp. I haven't moved on from being 19. Forever 19 is how it feels. Though I'm 22 now, it's as if the last three years have been static. It hit home hard recently. I saw some girls from school when we were out shopping. Their style, make-up, confidence – all so much different to how it was when we were 19, to how it was in 2008. But for me, I've had no life since then. I haven't been able to socialise or meet my friends. I don't even know what is on trend now. I spend most of the time with my parents. And while I'm very grateful to them, it isn't right. It isn't normal. I haven't developed. I haven't matured. I'm little more than a Case Number, a file in a hospital records system.

More efforts, more letters, more pleading.

Same lack of response, same lack of progress apart from one positive – if we can believe it.

"I've set 21st April 2011 as Patricia's discharge date," the professor tells Mam.

"Will everything be in place by then? Will the Community Care team and the hospital have everything ready? Can we go back to being her parents? Can she get on with living her life, albeit with a lot of care?"

"I'm hoping so."

A new manager is appointed to the hospital. I see it as an opportunity to introduce myself and my issues and, with Grace's help, I send her a letter and ask for a meeting. Maybe because she is new, she'll be enthusiastic about my discharge and help make it happen.

The letter is sent but we don't receive a response. Grace follows up with an email on 11th April. As well as sending it to the hospital manager, Grace contacts Community Care requesting much the same thing – a meeting to discuss progress and the issue of equipment required when I'm at home during the day.

The Community Care response is frustrating and disappointing and another 'chicken and egg' situation. Until I'm living at home, I'm not entitled to equipment. And until this is resolved, Community Care are unable to proceed any further.

We've reached deadlock.

The Community Care team won't act until I'm discharged. The hospital won't act until the Community Care package is in place.

Still silence from the hospital manager who it appears is on holiday. The professor's discharge date of April 21st has come and gone. Grace is peeved our correspondence is completely ignored by all the people supposedly representing my case. It doesn't breed much confidence.

Dad is taking a high-profile approach to his politician campaign and has found a way to seek a brief audience with Enda Kenny. Hearing that Enda is due to visit the Rathkeale Constituency Office, he finds out the date and time and makes a point of being there.

The queue to meet Enda trailed along a street and Dad, though he was at the back of the queue, made a beeline for him when he stepped down from the campaign bus. The crowd jeer as Dad skips the line but Dad's oblivious. He's on a mission and is very appreciative when Enda silences the crowd and listens to what Dad has to say.

"I only want help to get a Primary Care package for my daughter," he explains to Enda, handing him an envelope. "All the details are here. We would appreciate any help you can offer."

If the people in power would take a leaf out of Dad's book and find a way to put my case to the top of the queue, maybe my family wouldn't be forced to plead for help.

Chapter 31

Patricia Ingle
May 2011
Room Number 6
Fatal disclosure …

---

5 May 2011
From: Grace Moore Advocate
To: Disability Services
Disabilities and Mental Health Case Manager
Consultant Professor
SUBJECT: Patricia Ingle – 1000 days in hospital

Hello Everyone,

On the 29th May 2011, Patricia Ingle will have been in hospital for 1,000 days, as of today she has been in hospital 977 days. Patricia hasn't had an official update on her discharge or met with anyone to discuss her discharge since November of last year.

To the Disabilities and Mental Health Case Manager, Patricia would like to meet with you to hear what the hospital have done to date to assist with her discharge.

Patricia would like to meet with the Primary Care team to hear what Community Services have done to date to assist with her discharge.

Patricia can meet with you both together or separately. She can travel to wherever suits you both. We would like this meeting to happen asap. Can you both get back to me with dates and times that suit to meet?

Grace Moore

Advocate

11th May 2011
From: Tricia Ingle (Me!)
To: Minister for Finance
SUBJECT: MWRH Dooradoyle – 1000 days in hospital.

Hi Minister,

   I am Patricia Ingle.

   *I am Annette and Pat Ingle's daughter. My father has
been emailing you now for over two years about me in
hospital trying to get home. Myself and my family are very
disappointed even after the elections that only one local
politician has enquired or phoned or sent a text or email to
see how I was, or ask if I was still in hospital. I am!*

   *Every time Mam phones or sends a text to the Primary
Care people they choose to ignore her and not reply which
is cruel to myself and my family. I feel forgotten about and
abandoned. My consultant says there is no medical reason
for me to be still in hospital. Every night I go to sleep crying in
this lonely Room Number 6. Thank God my parents take me
home each day. Otherwise I would go insane.*

   *I voted so that I can email you (see photo) and I thought
I could be helped. Dad say that the Primary Care people are
sending you a standard letter saying that they are in talks
with us. They are not talking to us. This is a lie. They have not
talked to us since October.*

   *Dad says a country is judged on how it cares for its most
vulnerable and there is no care for me.*

   *On Sunday May 29th I will be in hospital one thousand
days. I want to mark this day, not celebrate but to mark it by
asking you to sponsor a visit to Dáil Eireann by myself and
family. Maybe I might get to meet the Minister for Health or
the Taoiseach.*

   *I have enough of this. 1,000 days in hospital is sheer
horror. A citizen of this country should not go through what I
am going through. An animal would not be treated this way.*

I just feel like a prisoner but even a prisoner would have a release date.

I hope you like the photo of me helping you so you can help me. Or did I waste my time? My dad said asking you to make representations on my behalf to the Primary Care people is a waste of time as you will only send back a standard letter of reply, saying they are in talks with the family, a letter of lies.

Can you find out why I am stuck here in Room Number 6 after 1,000 days of hell?

I just want to go home and not cry every night and every morning. I want to sleep and wake up in my own bed, in my own room, in my own home, with my family where I belong.

Thank you for taking the time to read this,

Patricia Ingle

16th May 2011
From: Minister for Finance
To: Patricia Ingle (Me!)
SUBJECT: MWRH Dooradoyle – 1000 days in hospital.

Dear Patricia,

I refer to your email below. Can you email me your home address in order to process your query?

Many thanks,

Minister for Finance

16th May 2011
From: Patricia Ingle (Me!)
To: Minister for Finance
SUBJECT: MWRH Dooradoyle – 1000 days in hospital.

Patricia Ingle,
Room Number 6
High Dependency Unit
MWRH

Dooradoyle,
Limerick.

Patricia Ingle,
Farnane
Murroe
Co. Limerick

Formerly
Patricia Ingle,
Ballinacurra
Weston
Limerick

Grace receives an invitation to a meeting with the MWRH hospital manager, Community Care and a few others. Following a detailed discussion, they conclude that Acute Services and Community Care still have some work to do.

There's nothing new in that conclusion.

Grace tells them it's taking far too long and that I'll be making an official complaint about the management of my discharge.

After the meeting, she helps me write the letter to Consumer Affairs, HSE.

24th May 2011
To Consumer Affairs Area Officer
HSE West
Limerick

Re: Complaint on how my discharge from hospital is being handled

My name is Patricia Ingle. I am writing this letter with the assistance of my advocate, Grace Moore. On the 29th of May 2011 I will have been in hospital for 1,000 days. I really want to get home to my family but it seems to be taking a very long time for this to happen. I want to complain about how long it is taking for me to be discharged from hospital and I also want to complain about the lack of communication from the Hospital and the Primary Care Team in the Community about what is happening with my discharge plan. They aren't telling us anything. I feel like I'm in limbo.

My consultant professor said that I was ready to be discharged from hospital in March 2009. When we contacted Disability Services – HSE West, they wouldn't do anything for me until I had an address. You see my old home in Ballinacurra Weston was no longer accessible to me so we had to get a different house. We went to the County Council and after a lot of work lobbying they bought us an accessible house which we are renting. We moved into this house in July 2010. After getting the house I thought everything would fall into place but it hasn't.

We met the Disability Services Manager for HSE West and his team in August 2010 and they started working on my discharge plan. Since then it seems to me very little has happened. In November the Case Manager met me, my family and my advocate to outline their plan. She said that they would hire some nurses to look after me at home but they wanted me to agree to move to an 'Alternate Care Facility' with my nurses after they had been trained by the HDU staff. She said when they were confident the nurses were competent then I would be moved from the 'Alternate Care Facility' to home. I did not want to move to an 'Alternate Care Facility', I wanted to move home. I suggested that when my nurses had been trained by the HDU staff to look after me then I could be moved off the HDU ward to a room on the ward down the corridor which has been closed from some time now. When that happened I would be cared for exclusively by my team of nurses and Personal Assistants and my family. If any of my nurses were to get into difficulty, then they would be able to call on the HDU staff for back up. This idea was taken on board and I was told through my advocate that it would be an acceptable option.

Since the meeting in November no one has met with me or contacted me or my family to give us an update on what is happening. My advocate gets small pieces of information but no one comes to talk to me. My advocate has been told that someone needs to take over the responsibility of the governance of my care package at home. This is what needs *to be sorted out now. It seems like as soon as one obstacle is overcome another appears.*

It has been six months since anyone has come to see me about my discharge plan. My advocate has asked the Area Manager of HSE East Limerick/North Tipperary and the General Manager of Mid-Western Regional Hospital to come and meet me and my family to give us some news but they haven't. The General Manager of the Hospital introduced herself to me on the corridor of the hospital. I was on my way home for the day. We chatted for a while about things but I felt it wasn't very professional to have the conversation on the corridor. I would have preferred to have a proper meeting and be informed that way.

I would like you to look into what is taking so long. Can you please find out if everyone is doing their jobs correctly and effectively? Why isn't anyone talking to me? I am also wondering why this issue with the governance couldn't have been dealt with sooner? Why couldn't more work like that have been done while I was getting my house sorted? Was it really necessary to wait a year until I had a house to get this work started?

I go home every day but my family don't get any help looking after me and we have to buy equipment I need like a stats probe and suctioning machine. I need a power chair. I had the assessment with the CRC but no one will pay for it. I need a bed so that I can be freshened up at home but again no one will pay for that either. Because I am not discharged the Primary Care Team won't buy me anything I need and the hospital won't buy me things I need in my home. It makes a hard situation much harder on all of us. I've been home overnight a few times. I paid for the nurse to stay with me overnight myself. I went home Christmas Eve, New Year's Eve and for three nights over Easter. I am suffering every day and night. I want to go to sleep happy for once but this won't happen until I am at home.

I have lots of questions and so do my parents. I would like you to come and talk to me and to them so we can tell you how we have been treated. I have enclosed some of the letters I have been sending. They describe how I am feeling.

Please read them. I would like to meet you to talk about my complaint. You can ring my advocate, Grace Moore, to arrange this.

Thank you,

Patricia Ingle

CC: Regional Director of Operations, HSE West
Area Manager, HSE Mid-West
Area Manager, HSE East Limerick
Case Manager, Disabilities North Tipperary/East Limerick
A/Manager, Disabilities & Mental Health, HSE West
General Manager, Mid-Western Regional Hospital, Limerick
Consultant Professor, Mid-Western Regional Hosptial
General Practitioner, Limerick City

*

It's a day for correspondence it seems as on the very same day I receive an email from Minister Noonan. If nothing else, the letters and emails keep me going and I feel I'm doing something, regardless of how small, to help myself.

———————————————————————————————————————

24th May 2011
From: Minister for Finance
To: Patricia Ingle (Me!)
SUBJECT: MWRH – Visit to Leinster House.

Dear Patricia

Thank you very much for your email.

Visits to Leinster House are usually arranged by a TD representing your area. As you have now moved to the constituency of Limerick West, I would advise you to contact one of the TDs who are the Fine Gael representatives for your area.

I have no doubt either of them would be happy to make the necessary arrangements.

If you feel I can be of further assistance to you on the matter, please do not hesitate to contact me.

Your sincerely,

Minister for Finance

We decide against Leinster House, unconvinced it will make any difference considering the runaround we're being given to organise it.

"What about getting public support through Facebook?" my sisters suggest in the absence of anything real from the authorities.

"We could title it 'Get Tricia Home'," Melissa says.

I nod in agreement. What is there to lose? Nothing at all. "Let's do it."

We get to work on putting the wording together, finally agreeing on giving an honest account on how it has been for me.

We read and edit it several times before finally clicking the 'publish' button and letting it go live.

29TH MAY 2011 WILL MARK MY 1,000 DAYS IN HOSPITAL …

My name is Patricia Ingle & this is my story. I've been in hospital (prison) for two and a half years & really want to go home. I have set up this page "Get Tricia Home" in the hope that people all over will help me do that by joining this group & showing your support. I got sick in August 2008. I was rushed from ICU in Limerick Regional to ICU in Cork University Hospital. I was in a coma for a couple of weeks & my family were given no hope. Slowly I woke from my coma but was still very critical. As a result, my recovery was very minimal. At the beginning my family were given minute by minute then hour by hour hope. Until Jan 09 I remained in ICU Cork where my family stayed by my side 24/7. I was then brought back to Limerick Regional in Jan 09 where I now remain as a patient two and a half years onwards. As a result of what happened to me I am restricted in having a normal life.

I have a wheelchair but I'm getting help with assisted walking. I don't eat or drink as I cannot swallow. I can talk with the help of a speaking valve. The main result of what damage has been done is been fully dependent on a portable life support machine, i.e. a ventilator. This may sound worse than it is. I have done a lot of positive things in hospital. Small things like listening to music, watching movies, reading magazines, playing word games with my sisters then progressing to such things as day trips to the shopping centre, going to the cinema with my family, meeting Jedward "Yes, THE Jedward", receiving a personal letter from the President of Ireland Mary McAleese &

singing legend Christy Moore, going to dog shows, going out to watch Skyfest firework display, having my story & photo in numerous national newspapers, been invited by a top London hospital for a week where I was escorted by hunky Air Corps officers but unfortunately slept through the journey. The biggest positive thing that has happened to my family & I was the night I stayed over for both Christmas Eve & New Year's Eve. Which is now the lead up to getting myself home to my family permanently. So this is the reason why I have set up this page to let everyone know what I went through & what I am still going through just to get home. So please invite your family & friends to join this page, leaving your comments, suggestions & support in the "Get Tricia Home" fight. I have been in hospital a long time & now I feel enough is enough. I do get sad, frustrated & angry which isn't me. I am going to use this page daily to express my feelings & use as a blog, please feel free to send your support.

Love Tricia xxx

Please help get me home.

Chapter 32

Patricia Ingle
June 2011
Room Number 6
Day of reckoning fast approaching …

Susie's frustration increases as the court-case date approaches. Working flat out to investigate every detail of medical negligence as well as employer liability, she leaves no stone unturned.

In turn we have provided every scrap of information we can think of about Petmania, my health and the weeks leading up to September 2008.

Susie has gathered statements from Mam, Dad, Melissa, Kiera and myself. Though our details are overlapping, Susie doesn't mind. "It's important to have all perspectives and let the Court see there are no glaring holes in our testimony."

"Thanks, Susie. You know our story better than us at this stage."

"But you'll be the person taking the stand, Tricia," she says. "You'll be the most important person speaking throughout the entire process."

"I don't mind. It's my story to tell."

"And I have new information for you today. Can you believe it at this late stage?"

We look at each other, all in agreement. We are beyond surprise.

Susie brings us up to date. "Considering there are approximately 18,000 pages of records and over 100 boxes of documentation to be taken to Dublin for your trial, I'm furious to find new evidence at this late stage."

"We know you've done everything you possibly can," I say slowly. I have my speaking valve on today, building up the time I am able to wear it so I'll be able to take the stand in court and finally have my voice heard and my views taken seriously.

"Thanks, Tricia," she says with a sigh, clearly exhausted from the intensity of her research and investigation. "What has come to light is an inappropriate amendment to one of your medical records."

Dad speaks up before the rest of us have a chance. "What do you mean? What kind of an amendment?"

"When Tricia was transferred to the CUH, a set of photocopied records was sent with her in the ambulance. Since then, however, the original records have been amended. But it wasn't documented that it was a retrospective note."

Mam is furious. "Surely that's against hospital policy?"

"What change was made?" My words are slow but clear.

Susie sighs heavily. "A note was added stating radiology had been consulted about the lumbar puncture prior to the procedure being carried out. This amendment says it was agreed with radiology that there was no contraindication to lumbar puncture."

"I can't believe this," Dad spits.

"There's more," Susie explains. "The amendment to the record also indicates that a fundoscopy – a particular test on Tricia's eyes – was carried out. This test wasn't carried out at all."

"This is so unfair."

Susie nods in agreement. "These amendments are in the original set of records in Limerick but not in the photocopied set that were sent with Tricia in the ambulance. Clearly the records have been 'doctored'! Pardon the pun."

"Clearly," Dad repeats. "And what about all the other thousands of records? Could the same have happened with them?"

"I've gone through each and every page of each and every single record between the set in CUH and MWRH and indeed as between the sets furnished in discovery and the sets furnished during the FOI procedure."

With my current difficulty in focusing for the shortest time I can't imagine how exhausting this procedure has been for Susie. It's no wonder she's frustrated.

"And did you find anything else of concern?" Mam asks.

"No, but to be on the safe side, we spent an entire day at the MWRH records department. We went through each and every ICU chart. These were never photocopied and didn't form part of the file. We checked everything to make sure no further amendments or unusual entries could be found."

"And?" I repeat Mam's question.

"Nothing. Hopefully we're not going to be surprised by anything else at this late stage. As it stands, we're satisfied we have all the information we need for trial."

*

We ask again for an update in relation to my discharge. There's nothing coming from any of the relevant parties.

On June 15th, a week before our trial date, our local Health Centre tell Mam and Dad they're not allowed give us any supplies to assist in my homecoming.

Tension and strain increases.

I see how exhausted my parents look. How on earth will they cope when I go home if we don't win this case and afford help? I know they're able to attend to almost every aspect of my care. They've been doing it for the last number of months when I've spent most days at home. But at least they get a night's rest when I'm back in Room Number 6.

On June 17th, I receive a letter from the HSE Mid-West Area Manager. My complaint to Consumer Affairs seems to have resulted in a response.

> *Area Manager*
> *HSE Mid-West*
> *Limerick*
> *17th June 2011*
>
> > *Dear Patricia,*
> >
> > *I refer to your recent correspondence to Consumer Affairs in relation to your care in the Mid-Western Regional Hospital Dooradoyle.*
> >
> > *I have today appointed two senior officers to review the matters raised in your letter and to bring forward the most appropriate solution to your care. The first is the General Manager and the second is the Director of Nursing Mid-Western Regional Hospital. Both will be in contact with you shortly with a view to meeting with you and your advocate as soon as possible.*
> >
> > *I would like to take this opportunity to apologise on behalf of our service for the position you find yourself in and to assure you that every endeavor will be made to find a resolution as soon as possible.*
> >
> > *Yours sincerely,*
> > *Area Manager*
> > *HSE Mid-West.*

Early one morning, a cameraman arrives to Room Number 6.

Susi is arranging to have video footage in court, a true account of what it takes to care for me on a daily basis. She wants as much reality as possible recorded – from the moment I open my eyes in the morning, the difficulties and complexities of washing and dressing me, the ordeal taking me out of bed and getting me into my chair, arranging my NIPPY, managing my feeding regime and everything else I need in between that and doing it all over again at bedtime.

"Excuse me," the ward sister says when she spots the cameraman setting up his gear.

She isn't a nurse I've seen previously. She appears to be standing in for the usual person in charge.

"Where do you think you're going with that camera? This is a hospital room."

"Our solicitor has permission for him to be here," Mam tells her while the cameraman continues his filming.

"It's the first I've heard of it," the sister says. "I'd advise you to speak with your solicitor again."

While this conversation goes on, the cameraman is filming the shower room (or make-shift wardrobe or storeroom as it has become).

"I'll give Susie a call," Dad offers, leaving the room to make the call.

He's back within moments.

"Sorry, if you give us time to get Tricia organised, we can continue filming at home."

The sister in charge leaves us to it, the cameraman leaves but not before filming a little from his vantage point in the shower room!

Chapter 33

Patricia Ingle
June 2011
Room Number 6/Dublin High Court
Trial – Day 1 – Black capes, White wigs …

Susie wasn't joking about the amount of records and documentation she had to go through.

"They're all being taken to Dublin for trial, Tricia," she tells me. "Approximately 18,000 pages of records and 100 banker boxes of documentation! Any room in your van?" she teases.

I'm nervous and excited, as is my entire family. The experience of court is a first for us, a daunting experience. We have never even sat in a courtroom, never mind appear as part of a trial. The three weeks leading up to the case are busy with a variety of people coming and going and arranging medical, nursing and therapy assessments. I co-operate willingly, knowing it is all part of the fight we are taking on in court.

Mam takes charge as usual, making lists and getting everything organised for our trip to Dublin's High Court.

"I'm going to fight for you, Tricia, in every way I can," Mam promises. "Nobody with a black cape and white wig will dictate where you spend the rest of your life, particularly when you've agreed to give evidence and put yourself through the exhausting ordeal."

"Tricia's barristers are top class, Annette. They won't allow that happen. How many times has Susie assured us?" Dad is a calming influence and though it's obvious he is nervous and terrified of what's before us, he has full faith in our legal team. As we all have.

But Susie is realistic and already she has insisted we give some thought to a negative outcome.

Mam accepts Susie's advice but is quick to qualify there's no turning back. "Either way, Tricia, this courtcase is going to end your imprisonment in hospital. You're coming home once this is over. We'll find a way to cope together. We'll get help. We need you with us as much as you need to be with us."

"Your mother's right," Dad adds. "We've already bought a lot of the equipment you need. And if we have to buy a wheelchair, we'll do that too. We'll find a way to employ nurses and carers. You don't worry about anything. All we need you to do is focus on the days ahead and get through the trial. What's to be will be after that."

In Room Number 6, my family gathers around me once more. I realise for the umpteenth time how fortunate I am to have their strength and support. Despite all that's happened, their determination has never wavered. They're literally unstoppable.

I smile and open my mouth, shaping the words and allowing them time to lip-read. My message is clear. "I have done nothing wrong. I'm going to tell the judge that."

Maybe, I think, that's why the HSE don't really want me going to Dublin. Sitting in my wheelchair before the judge, attached to the ventilator, seeing me in reality – are they afraid that when they see me like this, it will speak for itself?

From the start when Susie took on our case, she'd told us not to mention anything to the hospital staff. And we didn't. But now the case is upon us, obviously word has filtered out and some of the staff are aware of us taking a case against the HSE. But it hasn't changed anything as such, apart from the ward sister suggesting I avail of a free counselling service available through the HSE. This is the first real offer after three years.

She isn't as willing to help us with equipment for the journey, however.

"I can't guarantee that the hospital will be able to release a ventilator for you, Tricia," she says.

"But I can't travel without one!" I mouth. Surely she isn't serious. Without a NIPPY, I can't breathe.

"I don't see why you need to travel to Dublin. It's a big upheaval. Surely Skype is an option?"

I shake my head. This is my chance to have my opinion heard. Anything could go wrong with Skype. I've been through too much already to give in now.

This doubt over whether or not I'll be allowed the NIPPY hangs over us in the weeks leading up to the courtcase. But Dad, as ever, is on top of things and not leaving it to chance that it will halt us in our tracks.

I wasn't happy with his first suggestion to buy a used one on eBay. "It's the same model as yours, Tricia," he says.

"But, Dad, if it's used and it's for sale, this can only mean one thing – the owner has passed away. I don't want a dead person's NIPPY!"

It doesn't take him long to come up with another plan and he's on the phone to Respicare, the company that supplies the particular model I need.

"There's no need to worry, Tricia," he tells me after his conversation. "Once I explained our situation, they couldn't have been more helpful. They have one on standby for you."

"Do we have to buy it?"

Dad shakes his head. "I doubt it! They cost €14,000! Luckily they also rent them out. They're holding one for us just in case the hospital dig their heels in. They aren't even asking for a deposit to hold it."

I sigh with relief. "Thanks, Dad."

"We're ready for your road trip, Tricia, just waiting for the day to dawn," he assures me. "Sat probes to check your oxygen levels, a suction machine, and of course the most important piece – we've hired a private nurse to accompany us."

"Ready for take-off then," I respond.

Mam shares her one concern. "I hope there won't be an issue with your bed when you come back in the evenings."

Hopefully once the trial is over I won't have to come back, I think. Hopefully I will be able to go home.

"We can't control that, Mam. We can only hope."

At the last minute, the hospital allows me to take the NIPPY and we're saved the trouble of renting.

I receive a lot of good wishes as I'm wheeled out of Room Number 6, wondering what's in store as we set out on our journey to the High Court and put my fate in the hands of our legal experts.

*

The journey to Dublin is quiet, each of us deep in thought. They wanted us there for around eleven in the morning. I have to be back in hospital tonight. Back to Room Number 6. We have reserved a hotel room nearby and we call there first so I can be freshened up. The nurse sets up my PEG-feed and medication and we set off again.

Ernest and Susie are waiting patiently when we arrive at the High Court on Day 1 of the trial, Wednesday 22nd June 2011.

Dad drops us off inside the Main Gates of the Four Courts. The building is being renovated and is a little like a building site. Susie has arranged a parking permit so Dad goes to park the van.

"I've advised the photographers not to take photos," Susie says.

"There's a better parking space over there," a guy says to Dad when he'd manoeuvered the van into the designated space.

"It's fine here," Dad says, switching off the engine.

Mam is pushing my chair and notices the same guy with a camera as she wheels me towards the door.

"He's getting himself ready to take a photo of you going into the courthouse, Tricia," she tells me.

"I'm a celebrity," I mouth.

Although I don't feel very famous as we try find our way around. Access is limited for the wheelchair because of the building works. My entourage follow patiently, carrying my suction machine and other bits and pieces. I don't travel lightly! Unlike Florida where Kiera and I could manage without our luggage, I can't survive without it now. As we try to find our way to the court room, we have to split up as the lifts are tiny and can't accommodate us all at once. We're not taking any risks and make sure my suction machine and I aren't separated!

Ernest has news. "They've made an offer on the steps but I'm not accepting it. They're to come back to me by 12 o'clock if they're going to make a higher offer."

Twelve o'clock arrives. No further offer. My case is going to court.

"There's nothing to be afraid of when you take the stand, Tricia," Susie offers reassuringly once we have a bit of privacy to chat. "We have fast-tracked your case to court in nine months. That's a record in itself!"

"Thank you." How many times will I thank Susie for all she is doing? Without her … I'm afraid to think about that.

She waves away my gratitude. "We've briefed 24 experts. We've engaged a consultant engineer, a neurosurgeon, virologist, microbiologist, neuroradiologist, rehabilitation physician, care expert and an A&E expert from the UK to advise us. Together they have formed a view that the working conditions in Petmania and the care you got in Limerick hospital were both substandard.

It's unified evidence now. We will go to court and argue that. I'm happy that we're fully equipped to do so. Ready?"

"Let's go," I say to the little group gathered around my chair. And together we troop inside the High Court.

"It's a miracle you're even alive, Tricia," Susie adds. "The medics have said so."

I nod and smile, grateful to be alive and well enough to be present in court to hear what's said about me.

Kiera is pushing my chair. I look ahead as we enter the courtroom, taking in the setting with interest, noticing the judge's podium, the witness stand, the jury dock, everything that up to now I've only seen on TV. I'm excited when I should probably be nervous. I'm eager for the show to begin as Susie leads us to our position. All I'm waiting for is someone to call 'Action, Take1!' It feels as though we're getting into character on a film set.

The courtroom fills with barristers and solicitors; the gallery is also running out of seats.

"Who are all these people?"

Susie is quick to explain. "It's a public viewing gallery so anybody can come and watch proceedings."

I hadn't realised this. Seems rather an unusual way to pass the time but I don't mind who watches.

And then the moment arrives where the infamous words are announced, "All rise", and everyone in the court room – except for me naturally – get to their feet.

The High Court Judge, Mr. Justice O' Neill, is introduced. He takes his seat and within moments proceedings get underway.

Our side opens with Mr. Gleeson, our barrister, introducing himself as appearing for the plaintiff ... me! He also names the others appearing on my behalf.

The other sides follow suit and name the people representing Petmania, O'Keeffe's Kilkenny and the HSE.

I enjoy watching the formalities, probably more than hearing the next section where Mr. Gleeson opens the case with a background to my life and the events leading to where I am now.

"She is wheelchair-bound and ventilator-dependent. On a practical matter, she is attended by a nurse all the time. She is intellectually intact and anxious to attend her trial and will give evidence, but from time to time there may be a low level of noise from some of the machinery that the nurse needs to use. Just to warn people of that."

Understandably this is a cue for the majority of those present to look in my direction. But I've become used to people staring at me now and am not disturbed by this.

Mr. Gleeson continues in detail, describing the claim I am taking in plain language. "The claim relates to a serious infection which the plaintiff contracted in the course of her work at the pet store in Ennis in Limerick. It also relates to the negligent mismanagement of her condition when she attended at the Mid-Western Regional Hospital."

He goes on to talk about my illness and how I have gone from being "a healthy, fit, active 19-year-old woman" to being "tetraplegic, voiceless, suffering major irreversible brain damage, suffering from blurred vision, unable to move any limb, having difficulty swallowing, unable to breathe without assistance and requiring a ventilator, is unable to eat anything or take any nourishment and is fed constantly through a tube in her stomach."

Listening to it is difficult. It's as if he's talking about somebody else and not me.

Dad and Mam find this part particularly upsetting. Kiera too. But I remain strong. I'm waiting my turn to talk, waiting to let everyone in the courtroom, including those in the public gallery, hear what life has been like for me since August 2008.

Mr. Gleeson's opening speech is lengthy. He goes into graphic detail of the symptoms that were missed by the medical team in Limerick hospital.

Though Susie has kept us very informed, I still learn things for the first time as I listen in court. And I'm sure it's the same for my family. In fact, the vast amount of information being relayed by Mr. Gleeson is beyond anyone's comprehension.

"For many months after, the view of even the rehabilitation experts was that Patricia was 'locked-in', that she had something called 'locked-in syndrome' and would live a life without ever communicating with the outside world."

I shudder inside. Thank God I'm not like that anymore! It has been difficult enough being locked in hospital, never mind being locked inside myself! I tune back in to Mr. Gleeson.

"She can now communicate, which she does in various ways: by signs, by mouthing words and also by limited use of a voice tube which is attached to her throat and which allows her to speak in a slightly artificial voice for perhaps an hour or two a day."

I stare at the floor when he mentions the more embarrassing aspects.

"Although intellectually intact, she has difficulties with concentration. She is doubly incontinent. She wears nappies and has an indwelling catheter for the urinary incontinence. She requires assistance for all activities for daily living and is urgently in need of neuro-rehabilitation, almost certainly of a type and quality that is not available in Ireland but certainly available in the United Kingdom. She will benefit from speech and language therapy and various other therapies – and specialist advisers from the United Kingdom will be able to tell you, as well as indeed rehabilitation doctors from Ireland, what can and might be done for Patricia."

I hear his words and sense the tension and pity around the courtroom. I retain my resolve to stay strong and have my say.

Mr. Gleeson talks about my job and training (or lack of it) in Petmania. He summarises specifics about diseases crossing from animals and birds to humans.

"The experts on health and safety will say that the most conspicuous, important and significant risk of working in a pet shop is contracting infections from the creatures that are kept there. She was involved in the care of animals, so-called animal husbandry, cleaning out of the cages and so on. It is important, Judge, to understand that the birds and animals (and we are particularly interested in the birds in this case) in the pet shop are not screened. And while screening is recommended, I think we would have to concede that screening is not normal for pet shops."

Finally, after trawling through reams of detail, he gets to the main point.

"Occasionally staff bought their own gloves but there were no masks."

Oh God, I think, something as simple and inexpensive as a face mask could have made such a difference … I tune back in to Mr. Gleeson.

"Petmania had a system for inspecting their premises about every three or four months … you may take it that on the 7th August inspection, in the very month when Patricia became sick, the bird cages were found to be very dirty and the fronts of them smeared. The precise words in the report from the internal assessor are: 'Cage fronts are filthy, cages seem very dirty'."

Mr. Gleeson continues his description of the premises. "Presentationally it was well run but on the point of hygiene, maintenance, husbandry and management, the conditions were very poor and conditions were allowed to subsist in which dangerous infective biological agents developed and were not controlled, which in truth make it overwhelmingly likely that this is where Patricia picked up the condition."

And there it is, the cruel evidence.

The judge becomes uncomfortable and offers to rise when my nurse and Kiera set about suctioning me. But Mr. Gleeson assures him there's no need and continues his opening address explaining that specific instruction had been given by me not to thaw and refreeze my portion of the serum sample from January 2009 which was being tested to prove the disease I had contracted was Chlamydia psittacosis.

"It should have been defrosted and dispatched through a special courier that we had arranged for testing in England. Instead, due to a series of accidents for which, to be fair, the HSE and the laboratory manager both apologised, it was thawed and refrozen. The quality of testing that results from it was possibly impacted."

It's difficult to hear while I'm being suctioned but I catch a snippet of Mr. Gleeson announcing he's coming to the end of his summary on Petmania.

"I think the case at its heart against Petmania is very simple: a known risk of zoonosis, a specifically statutory advertised risk in relation to Chlamydia psittacosis, widespread knowledge that would be understood by a school child that the wearing of masks was useful and has been scientifically proven to cut down the risk of infection, and the unnecessary exposure by the employer and occupier of the workers, including the plaintiff, to biological agents know to be dangerous to humans."

The judge interrupts at this point. "Do I take it then that the method of ingesting was inhaling?"

Mr. Gleeson replies. "Yes, that's believed to be it: inhaling from the air. The three common modes are dust from dried faeces, dust from the feathers, which may include some of the former for all I know, and what are called respiratory secretions, in other words the breathing out of an infected bird. To inhale that breath could be a way of catching it as well."

"But that goes beyond cleaning, doesn't it?" the judge questions.

"It does indeed. We have to accept that. The first two are related to cleaning ..."

I wonder if this is bad for us. The judge is very sharp. I'm relieved to hear Mr. Gleeson continue his response and support his argument with lots of technical detail gathered from experts. He talks about books of evidence and stocks of documents being presented to the Court.

His mention of the letter I received from Petmania offering me the job takes me back to such a happy time. I was over the moon. The handbook I received is also outlined, in particular it's lack of mention of animals apart from an attractive cartoon graphic on the first page!

Petmania's housekeeping standards are lacking according to some handwritten comments in the engineer's report.

"All bins emptied? No. Are shelves and fixtures clean and dust free? No. Toilets not clean. No towels or soap. Canteen dirty."

There are some positives for the birds in later inspections so some things did actually improve. I'm relieved for the poor pets. It upsets me when they're mistreated. Almost as much as when humans are mistreated.

The Court is briefly interrupted when a lady enters wearing a long black cloak and white wig. She approaches the judge and has a quick word, scaring Mam and Dad when she mentions 'life expectancy', their relief palpable when they realise that whatever or whoever she is speaking about has nothing to do with me. As I keep proving to them, they won't get rid of me that easy!

I can't believe it's lunchtime already and we are still only at the introduction to the trial. At this rate, if they've to go through three years of detail, we'll be here for days.

During the breaks, Susie, Ernest and our barristers gather in huddles in deep discussion and then move to speak with the other side, whispering negotiation tactics no doubt.

"I love watching them," Mam says, catching my eye.

I agree. "It's exciting. But I can't really believe they are talking about me all this time."

Dad looks upset, no doubt the level of detail being brought up difficult to hear. Poor Dad is so protective and feels as though it's his job to take care of all of us, me in particular since this happened.

*

The hearing resumes with Mr. Gleeson taking up his account of Petmania conditions and some of the birds purchased in July and August 2008.

"There were significant cash purchases of animals, and birds in particular … you will find that one cockatiel was bought for €20, a bird of the very class which are implicated in Chlamydia psittacosis. The plaintiff's engagement with these creatures was of course cleaning the cages, but also of handling them to get them out of the cages when they were being cleaned, to show them to customers and so on."

The judge interrupts again. "Is it in dispute that the plaintiff has contracted the ailment that is contended for? And is it in dispute as to whether or not she acquired that ailment as a result of her exposure to these creatures?"

Mr. Gleeson confirmed that his argument suggested I contracted the disease in the course of my employment.

The HSE representative spoke up at this stage and confirmed that they agreed.

This makes sense to me and is exactly what Susie had predicted.

Mr. Gleeson lists other birds purchased around this time and then reverts to detail on Petmania's Safety Statement and the fact it had been revised in April 2009, following my illness, and was twice as long as the one dated April 2008.

"This is a 50-page document, but even though it's twice the length it still doesn't mention the word 'animal'. The word 'bird' doesn't appear. And there is no reference, I need hardly say, to the risk of infection from exotic creatures. There isn't even a cartoon of an animal on this one, so you wouldn't know it had, apart from the name of the company, anything to do with animals at all."

I'm enjoying hearing all this detail, surprised I never noticed any of it myself at the time. Amazing the level of detail the legal experts find to argue a case.

More information from the Safety Statement follows, in particular about the responsibility of the employer. Naturally, he explores the sections about personal protective equipment in great detail as he does with ventilation, hygiene standards, biological agents, staff training and required risk assessments. This takes up to an hour to describe.

Again, the Judge is quick to question some of his theories.

I'm relieved when Mr. Gleeson is able to respond confidently and carry on.

Once he is finished his argument against Petmania, Mr. Gleeson moves on to the HSE and starts all over again with a similar level of detail to prove medical negligence.

"Before I attempt to guide the Court through the critical events that occurred, let me just make two points of general importance. It is no part of the case against the HSE that they were in default by failing to identify Chlamydia psittaci in the three or four critical days. That is not part of the case. What they were dealing with was headaches, vomiting, and as you will see, early evidence of increased intracranial pressure, commonly described as hydrocephalus, and because that is important I am going to say a little bit about that."

I need to be suctioned again and am nearly grateful for the distraction.

Mr. Gleeson is in full flow. "But it is the generic hydrocephalus that was being dealt with. It would not be realistic to expect that the precise bacterial or viral agent which was causative would be tracked down in that timescale, but it is perfectly sufficient for the hospital to have known that they were dealing with hydrocephalus, pressure on the brain, which some very early investigations demonstrated was probably not bacterial meningitis."

I'm reminded of the numerous times Dad checked if I had a stiff neck or a rash.

"Bacterial meningitis is the condition which is the subject of public health warnings. It is an infection of the brain that comes on. It can kill people very quickly, but you get warnings like a rash or stiff neck. You will see in the course of the medical records that it was early on determined that this wasn't a rash and a stiff neck case."

If I could turn around, I'd smile at Dad. I wasn't lying when I denied having a stiff neck.

"Furthermore, it is a case where there had been headaches and vomiting for two weeks. You don't have meningitis for two weeks and survive. Meningitis, by which I mean common meningitis, as it were. Now, the brain sits within the skull cavity surrounded by cerebrospinal fluid. But the cerebrospinal fluid doesn't just surround the brain. It is also found in vessels or chambers called the 'ventricles' within the brain. It circulates and brings nutrition to the brain. It takes away waste and acts as a cushion within the skull. If you bang your head, the brain may be moved but it is protected from being bruised by the side of the head. But there are a range of conditions which can cause the supply of cerebrospinal fluid to become excessive. Invasion by an infective agent is only one of them ..."

His opening statement continues, a lot of the detail exceptionally technical.

"That pressure can be extremely damaging. It can damage the brain itself. And it can lead to brain damage and death. But one of the ways in which you can discover whether there is increased intracranial pressure is by doing a CT scan. One of the things you can tell from the scan is if these chambers, these ventricles, are distended, dilated, expanded or larger than is customary."

He could be describing the engine of a car. So many parts inside our heads.

"Another useful piece of information is to see if that is true of all four of the ventricles, or only one, or two, or three? Because in the normal state of brain plumbing, the cerebrospinal fluid flows naturally … but when you have obstruction of one of the ventricles, you may find that it is not distended, and obstruction can be caused, for instance, by infective material. So an alarming thing to find is (a) dilated ventricles and, (b) ventricles not all four of which are dilated, because then there is proof that the characteristic and normal workings of the plumbing of the brain is not functioning."

Mr. Gleeson stops to take a well-deserved deep breath. And then he starts off again, describing my admission to hospital and the various exams and tests carried out, as well as decisions made in those crucial moments. He clearly emphasises the important signs that were missed, building tension until he hits the heart of why I've been damaged so badly.

"Now the next event, and it is an even more central event, is the lumbar puncture. Our experts will be more eloquent I think on this than on anything else. It was, in their view, entirely contraindicated. If you have in mind a lumbar puncture, the thing is to do a scan to make sure you have increased pressure. The information on the scan was that there was increased intracranial pressure. And the risk is this: if there is increased pressure then you have the fluid bursting to get out. And if you release that pressure in the vertical pipe running up to the skull cavity, the risk is that the downward flow or sucking movement created by the vacuum through which you extract will cause the brain stem to be pulled down and descend into the spinal canal. This is a well-known and appallingly dangerous risk known as 'coning'. One of our experts is so exercised about this that he will say that no specialist knowledge should be needed to know that raised intracranial pressure is a bad thing to do a lumbar puncture for. Now, would you ever do a lumbar puncture with raised intracranial pressure? Well, if someone was at risk of death you might take this terrible risk if there was no other option. But remember, this patient was not dangerously ill at this stage. She wasn't inclined to die or anything like that. She had a mysterious troubling illness, but there was no suggestion that her life was imperiled …"

Mr. Justice O'Neill interrupts Mr. Gleeson. "Do I take that if this, as it were, disaster occurs it does not self correct?"

Mr. Gleeson is quick to respond. "No. Well I suppose there is some regeneration of the sort that there can be and there has been in Patricia's case in the sense that she was locked in and has come out of it. But for instance the damage to her swallowing and voice capacity can be specifically traced to control centres at the bottom of the brain, which is the very point that would descend into the spinal canal with a release of pressure lower down drawing a portion of the brain downwards. Again, one of our experts would say that it's not necessary to be neurologically literate to know this; that doctors of ordinary competence, non-specialists who understand the simple dynamics of this system should know, if they were never told, just by their intuition that drawing fluid out lower down could have this effect. One of them goes so far as to say that he would not expect an undergraduate medical student to make this error. Not all of them say that but one of them does."

He supports every theory with an amount of reference to medical notes, research and expert opinion, concluding for the day with reference to my tracheostomy consent form.

When questioned about one of the HSE's experts carrying out a further assessment on me, he confirms that I'm available for the next five days in Limerick. He's firm about not imposing unnecessary strains on me and I'm grateful to him for that.

The judge adjourns the hearing to Tuesday 28th June – six days from now – at 11.00 a.m.

*

We're exhausted travelling back to Limerick.

"Wow, Mr. Gleeson is tough," I mouth to Kiera. "He is not sparing the bullets on this one."

"And the brain is so complicated," Mam adds.

"The courtroom is an interesting place though," Melissa says.

I'm deep in thought as the others continue their chat.

The more information Mr. Gleeson gave today, the more I see how helpless I have been throughout. Yet I've been left to cope in hospital at the mercy of others making decisions for me.

Well, not any more. When I get my turn to speak I will not waste a word or a breath. I have to take my chance to be heard.

Chapter 34

Patricia Ingle
28th June 2011
High Court Dublin
Trial – Day 2 – The story so far ...

Another early morning and long journey from Limerick to Dublin's High Court. Yet again, Susie is waiting to escort us inside and chaperone us through the second day of our trial.

Mr. Gleeson pretty much picks up where he left off last week, with a brief reminder of the story so far. As I listen to him advise the Court that I'd been found unsuitable for a bed in the National Rehabilitation Centre, Dún Laoghaire, and need somebody with me at all times because I'm not aware if the tube in my throat slips out, it sounds as if he's telling a story. And I have to remind myself that I'm the main character in this story. God, I hope it ends well!

The morning continues with a long – and pretty boring – medical account of all the tests, results and treatments I received. Each stage is supported by expert information and he's really thorough in the information he calls out. He reads some of the letters sent on my behalf. He stresses how badly I need neuro-rehabilitation.

I sit and listen, noticing the serious expressions around me.

"One of the most urgent features of Patricia's case, and her life, is the need to get her to a specialist facility in Oxford, which the HSE can't afford, which she can't afford, where it is anticipated she would spend nine months with the best in the world, getting her up to what she can be."

He relays the reality, letting the broken promises and disappointments ring loud and clear as he continues his account from the Book of Records. He uses polite language as he lets the Court know that the HSE wasted Susie's time by allowing her to believe LCMV was a possible root cause when all along they had already tested me for LCMV and the result had come back negative. He tells the Court about the rat bite and the fact my father had to leave his job to bring me to the hospital for a tetanus. He leaves nothing out.

Over and over he argues why I shouldn't have had a lumbar puncture, listing the risks associated with it.

I'm transported back to August 2008 when he reminds the Court that I had been able to go for a walk the day before being admitted to hospital, was able to stagger into A&E on my own steam with a bit of help and yet my life had irretrievably changed in the space of three days, leaving me in the sad way he is now describing.

He lists the number of times my deterioration was missed, the consequences of the delayed CT and MRI scanning, critical decisions being deferred and my brain starved of oxygen for an additional 48 hours.

Hearing him graphically describe my current state is upsetting: my catastrophic injury, that I require skilled care 24 hours every day, a high level of nursing training and a second person there as carer at all times.

"One of the things that is important is the fact that she is intellectually intact, that she understands all these matters, and that if you give her time she can tell you about them and how she feels about them. Biographical details can be provided by her sisters and her mother … but there are certain matters about which only she can speak."

I'm not sure if I'm excited or nervous now. But I know I'm ready.

Mr. Gleeson explains to the Court that I am entitled to tell my story, that I want to tell my story, that I want to live alone in my own house with privacy to prevent becoming an exhibit every time I need to get into a car, van or ambulance.

Mr. Gleeson gives a very positive account of my schooldays and the promise of a strong future that is probably no longer an option – his opinion, not mine!

He talks about my visit to the Lane Fox Unit in St Thomas' Hospital, remarking on the significant progress I made in just five days and how important it is for me to get to a longer term version in Oxford. 'A number of windows were opened in that unit' is how he describes the benefits for me in Lane Fox. He produces excerpts from hospital records about my future care and rehabilitation. He mentions the video to show a day in my life, the same video that got the filmmaker thrown out of Room Number 6!

He leaves nobody in doubt as he states I've been in the control of the HSE for the last three years and their lack of effort to provide me with rehab or improve my bladder and bowel awareness. When he tells them I haven't had access to a bath or shower for a number of years, I think I see people turning quickly to look at me.

I'm not dirty, I want to scream. But I don't. I can't. I don't even mouth the words.

He briefly summarises one day in my life, talks about my requirements and argues for 24-hour care with a minimum of two, and sometimes three, carers.

Discussion goes on around care. It's starting to feel like a multidisci-plinary meeting. Details, details, details, the accounts of the two nights I stayed at home, the lack of all sorts of therapy by anyone's standards, the urgency of the need for a chair and power wheelchair.

He must be coming towards an end because he's explaining that the length of his opening statement is required to disclose the last few years of my life to the Court. He swoops in with further claims for costs for special damages, both past and future. Included is my parents' contribution to my care, the number of hours they spend with me, the items they have purchased with their own money to make it possible for me to come home every day. It's all delivered in a calm but clear manner.

Hearing all the things my parents and sisters do – and the time they have sacrificed – fills me with guilt. They don't have a moment for themselves, being with me day in and day out, reading to me, working with me, entertaining me and taking me out in the new van (with a built-in lift) as often as possible.

He puts a figure out there for the first year. Sounds little when you say it quickly.

"Thereafter it would be slightly less at current rates," he clarifies.

He continues listing equipment and essentials from the occupational therapist's report, breaking down the costs to explain where the money is needed. From there he adds the future specialised therapy and assistive technology I'll require.

"Assistive techonology is the most modern equipment that allows her to have some sort of communication, access to some sort of entertainment systems ..."

This is interesting. I'm visualising a hi-tech cinema screen and lots of gadgets that might give me some independence.

While I'm imagining my in-house cinema, Mr. Gleeson is talking about a specially built house and housework assistance, including adapted clothing – now that would be useful instead of disturbing my tubes every time I have to put on or off a sweatshirt! He has even included gardening and decorating costs, and future transport. He makes me sound a bit unique, explaining the costs were done by experts mostly from the UK.

"... because the condition of her disability, in its complexity, is obviously pretty unusual ... and in her youthfulness and her intact intellectual condition, which is quite distinctive in that she is a person who understands what I'm saying but has difficulty responding because of the mechanical reasons, but can give sophisticated answers to questions when required. Her concentration is not what it used to be."

I will do my best to give sophisticated answers when my turn comes – seeing as Mr. Gleeson has such faith in me. I'm rather impressed by his description of me. And he's spot on about my concentration. I tune back in and realise he has moved on to my future loss of earnings. My humour dips slightly when he mentions the dog-grooming business I had been looking into, the courses I never got to do, the sense of achievement I never got to experience. Not yet at least.

Mr. Gleeson reverts to what he is calling 'pleadings', reading first from the Personal Injuries summons. A lot of this he has spoken about already – negligence, Petmania conditions, negligence, lumbar puncture, negligence – and then he's back to the hospital's undisclosed negative test for LCMV which came to light when Susie sent the sample for testing to the UK and the consultants said, "You must be the same people we negatively tested for years ago. We have your stuff here."

He leaves nothing out. He provides proof of everything. Yet again he refers to meningitis. Yet again, I wish I could swivel around to look at Dad.

"Clinical signs were once again negative for meningitis. That is an important admission by the HSE, that whatever else it was, they were chasing some strange thing that was making her brain fluid block, increasing the pressure inside her head but probably was not standard meningitis ..."

I'm relieved when he calls for a break and we get to leave the intensity of information. Again, we're fascinated with the conversations held between both sides outside of the courtroom. We can only guess what it's about. Another offer of settlement, Mam thinks.

"There's a lot of information coming out. They might not want to hear more," Dad comments.

*

After the break, Mr. Gleeson speaks about costs and care. It isn't so much that I'm not concentrating but it feels like I've heard some of it already. I look around me again, tempted to smile when Mr. Gleeson refers to the judge and other barristers as 'my friends'. I wonder are they? I wonder whether it's possible to be up against each other in court and then be friends?

Chapter 35

Patricia Ingle
28th June 2011
Dublin High Court
Trial – Day 2 continues – Taking the stand …

After some debate between Mr. Gleeson and the counsel for the other sides relating to the excessive number of witnesses and how long the case could actually take, they get back to business. And to me in particular.

Mr. Gleeson introduces the video. "It comprises about four parts. The first is a number of stills from Patricia's past life, getting awards, and one movie from her past life when she was on her holidays in Florida and swam with a dolphin."

I love that video, such a different time, such a different life, such a different me.

"Then the video moves to a day in her life, starting with her day in the hospital in the company of her parents, getting her ready."

I'm a little shy at the thought of the whole courtroom watching this.

"Then the video shows Patricia going in her wheelchair in the van, going home, being moved, put in position and having things changed."

The video is played and takes just under half an hour. The courtroom is silent the entire time.

As my speaking valve is fitted to get me ready to take the stand, Mr. Gleeson suggests a break.

"If you could rise for five minutes, Judge, that would be very helpful. Thank you."

*

I take the oath. Kiera is also sworn in. She also has to swear on the bible in case I'm not using my speaking valve and she needs to interpret on my behalf. In other words, she will be my voice in that instance. But I'm determined that this is my chance to speak. And I'm going to use it. I'm to be questioned by Ms. McCrann. Poor Mr. Gleeson must need a break after all the talking he has done so far.

"Do you mind if I call you Patricia?" is Ms. McCrann's opening question.

And so it begins. A recap on my life, split into two distinguishable parts – before and after September 2008.

"Did you have an idea as to what you might like to do in the future?"

"Yeah."

"What was that, Patricia?"

"Grooming."

"Grooming animals?"

"Yes."

"Where did you get the interest in grooming animals?"

"We had a grooming parlour in Petmania."

She repeats this back to me, surprised it seems to hear this.

"I helped out a lot."

"Had you investigated any courses in terms of grooming?"

"Yeah."

"Where were these courses?"

"In England."

"But I don't think you had taken any steps to actually go to England to start them?"

"No."

"But you were investigating them?"

"Yes."

"Were you excited about getting the job in Petmania?"

"Yes, because it was what I liked."

"Working with animals?"

"Yes."

Our ping-pong style of questions and answers continue. She explores how I got the job in Petmania, training in Waterford, starting out in the Limerick shop, my uniform and instructions on hygiene and the like. I see the direction it's taking.

"What were you expected to do in the normal day?"

"From nine o'clock to half nine every morning, clean and feed the animals."

"What kind of animals are we talking about?"

"There were hamsters, reptiles, fish and birds."

"Can you explain to the judge what the cleaning entailed?"

"Sawdust."

"Sawdust?"

"Sawdust had to be thrown away and fresh sawdust put there."

"Okay. That was in the animals' cages?"

"Yes."

"What was in the sawdust in the animals' cages?"

"They would go to the toilet." This is a little embarrassing.

"So there were droppings?"

"Yes."

"How many bird cages were there? Can you remember?"

"Twelve."

"Can you remember how many birds in each? Roughly?"

"Around twenty. It varied from week to week."

She asks for more description.

I tell her about the birds getting scared and flying around everywhere, creating dust. I describe the steps I took to clean out the cages, removing the tray once the birds were out of the cages.

"Did you notice any physical effect on you personally?" she asks.

"Yes."

"Can you tell the judge what that was?"

"The dust was inhaled and it made me cough."

Her questions go on to discuss the buying and selling process.

"If I came in and said, 'I am tired of this budgie or parrot or cockatiel,' would you buy it from me?"

"Yes."

"And what happened the bird then?"

"It went straight for sale."

"Where was this bird put?"

"On show."

"Were there any systems you were aware of or you were told about in terms of checking the health of birds that were offered for sale to the shop?"

"No, we just bought them."

Then the conversation moves to my personal interest in animal welfare.

"Can you tell the judge how you knew if a bird was sick?"

"It wouldn't be able to chirp."

"How did you find that out, Patricia?"

"At home on the computer."

"So you researched it yourself?"

"Yes."

"How often did you come across a bird in that condition in Petmania?"

"Loads. And I would take care of the bird."

"How?"

"Put it into a cage on its own."

"How?"

"Take him and put him in."

"So you would take the sick bird in your hand and put it in a cage on its own?"

"Yes."

She asks if I had any contact with exotic birds other than those I dealt with at work?

"No."

"Was there a room where the staff had lunch?"

"Yes, the kitchen."

"Was that room used for any other purpose?"

"If there was an animal pregnant or an animal had babies."

"An animal with babies was put in the kitchen?"

"Yes."

"Would that be hamsters and rabbits?"

"Yes."

"What about birds?"

"Yes, the parrot."

"I didn't ask about parrots. How many parrots were in the shop?"

"Two at a time."

"Never any more?"

"No."

"Why would the parrots be in the kitchen?"

"We didn't want to stress them out."

"Why would they get stressed out?"

"If kids were annoying them."

"How would you bring them in?"

"In the cage."

"What happened sick animals? Where were they put?"

"In the grooming room."

"What were the animals in the kitchen put in?"

"Boxes."

"What kind of boxes?"

"Cardboard."

"I see. Was there any other place where you could have your food or your break?"

"No."

I answer every question. And there are lots and lots of questions, particularly about the procedures we used for sick animals.

"Did the cages of sick animals have to be cleaned out?"

"Yes, every day."

"Can you give the judge an idea of approximately how many sick birds might be there at any one time?"

"Maybe three or four."

"Did you have any other reason to do anything with the cages?"

"To sell the birds."

"And what happened then?"

"We put the cage in a box. It took a while."

The judge asks a question now. "I'm wondering would there be a big flap when that happened?"

"Yes," I tell him. "The birds would be scared. They would fly around and fly into the window of the cage. Sometimes they would bleed."

"Was there dust?"

"Yes."

I say a lot during this question and answer phase, more than I have said at any one time since August 2008!

"What formal system was there within the shop structure to check for the health of animals?"

"Just how they looked."

"So you made a judgement yourself?"

"Yes."

"You know that an engineer went to the shop on your behalf after you became ill?"

"Yes."

"He took photographs. I want to show you those photographs now."

She holds the photographs in front of me, pointing to the signs in the shop. "Were those signs there when you were working in the shop, Patricia?"

"No."

This goes on a while and I give the same answer when she points out a number of signs I had never seen before. These included: Wash your Hands, Tetanus Shots, Safety Consultation, Safety Processes, Animal Quarantine Area, Staff Only. No members of the public allowed. And more. I hope this is a sign (pardon the pun) that conditions are better for staff there now.

After signs, the questions move on to masks, gloves and aprons. And then on to the rat-bite incident where my supervisor paid no attention to the fact it had broken the skin on my finger and I had no choice but ring my dad to take me for a tetanus injection.

I'm weary by now. Thankfully the judge is considerate.

"We have got through an amount of evidence in a very short period of time," he says, adjourning for the day.

We make the long journey back to Room Number 6.

Chapter 36

Patricia Ingle
29th June 2011
Dublin High Court
Trial – Day 3 – A game of ping-pong …

Ms. McCrann opens Day 3 with a brief apology. "Patricia was just a little delayed in getting to court this morning." She also asks the judge's permission to continue beyond one o'clock so I don't have to refit my speaking valve after lunch.

The judge is fine with this.

And so the ping-pong question and answer session commences once more. Every minute detail relating to the gloves I wore after being bitten by the rat and the exact way I cleaned out the cages was discussed. Then it moved on to the detergents we used to clean the cages and the floor. And then she brings me back to the type of birds being sold in the shop when I worked there.

"Were there other types of small birds?"

"Ringneck and lovebirds."

The judge interrupts now. "Lovebirds? Do they have another name?"

"I'm sure they do," Ms. McCrann says, having a little joke with the judge. "Not too many of them around here, I suspect at the moment – of the non-feathered variety!"

Lots more questions on health and safety are added in here and then we move on to rehabilitation in Lane Fox.

"Can you explain to the Court how you felt when they were able to let you talk?"

"I was very excited. I could talk and express how I felt."

"It's obvious from the video the judge was shown that your life has changed significantly since August 2008. If you had money of your own, what would your wish list be?"

"I would thank everyone who came to visit."

"But what would your wish list be for yourself?"

"To walk and eat."

"Is that a big thing?"

"It would be, but at the moment it's okay."

"Is there anything else?"

"Breathe normally and talk normally."

"What is your ambition in terms of available treatment?"

"To learn how to eat, and walk and use my legs."

"To use your legs?"

"Yes. And swim."

"I know your family are very good to you but you accept that you need care?"

"Yeah."

"How do you feel about your parents providing that care for you at the moment?"

"It's embarrassing. They are my parents, not carers."

"If you don't want your parents providing your care, who would you like to provide your care?"

"People who are trained for the service."

She drills into more detail about who does what and any particular difficulties.

"I would prefer to have privacy and hopefully learn to use the toilet," I tell her.

"You were making great progress in London?"

"Yeah."

"Where do you want to live in the future, Patricia? I know you are living in the hospital at night at the moment and at home with your parents during the day."

"I want my own house. Obviously with carers."

"Can you explain to the judge what happened with your social life?"

"Friends visit me. They're more comfortable visiting me at home when they can."

"It's going to be a big day for you when you can finally manage to be discharged from hospital, isn't it?"

"Yeah."

"Can you tell us your number one plan?"

"A big party so I can say thanks to everyone for supporting me!"

Ms. McCrann pauses as she is handed a note.

"Judge, 'lovebird' is the correct name for a type of parrot. The experts can elaborate because I can't pronounce it!"

And that concludes Ms. McCrann's questioning – but not mine! I'm to be cross-examined now by Mr. McCullough acting for Petmania.

He starts back at the start again and once more I find myself recalling August 2008 and the stages of my illness.

"You were seen by a doctor who specialised in infectious diseases. Do you remember that? He saw you on 4th September."

"No." Surely they know I was in a coma at this stage. I wonder if they've done all their homework!

Mr. Gleeson intervenes on my behalf. "It's hard to see what purpose this serves other than tiring out the plaintiff."

"I don't concede she knows nothing about some of the matters I want to put to her, Judge. There is one point in particular I think is relevant. Perhaps I should go directly to that."

The judge urges him to be mindful of my condition at the time and whether I can offer any useful evidence as to what happened in those critical weeks.

Mr. McCullough messes up again when he confuses the doctors in CUH and MWRH. Now I (and everyone else in the courtroom) know for sure he hasn't done his homework properly! And then he pulls an unexpected question out of the hat.

"There is a note here, Ms. Ingle, that two of your aunts had TB – tuberculosis. Is this correct?"

"Yes."

"Do you know that while you were in Cork University Hospital you were treated for tuberculous meningitis? Do you recall that?"

"No."

"Thank you."

That wasn't too bad, I think, as Mr. McCullough takes a seat.

Ms. Egan is next to cross-examine me.

"I just have one question for you. I want to know whether, to your knowledge, while you worked in Petmania there was any person designated as being in charge of the health and safety?"

"No."

"Thank you."

Ms. McCrann is back with some more questions.

"The cats that lived at home with you – they weren't allowed into the house?"

"That's correct."

"In terms of your two aunts, are they still alive?"

"One isn't."

"Do you know when she died?"

"No."

"Do you know when your aunts had TB?"

"No."

"Your father and mother will give us this evidence. Did you have contact with them growing up?"

"No."

"Thank you."

I'm tired after a long morning but proud to have been able to speak up for myself. The truth will set you free is the only thought in my head. I hope I'm right.

*

Ms. McCrann and the judge arrange to reconvene at three o'clock in the afternoon.

The consultant engineer is called as a witness and once more the story reverts to Petmania and the lack of health and safety standards in place. More photographs are introduced, ranging from overflowing bins to inadequate air-handling units and the cleaning rota. The detail gets technical as he discusses the obligation on employers to ensure compliance.

"If the plaintiff is right," he says, "she received no training or instruction. So there is clear breach of that regulation."

At four o'clock that afternoon, the court ends for the third day. Once more we make the journey back to Room Number 6 in MWRH where I get a night's sleep before doing it all over again on Day 4!

Chapter 37

Patricia Ingle
30th June 2011
Dublin High Court
Trial Day 4 - Case concludes …

The conversations between our barristers and those acting on behalf of Petmania and the HSE get louder. They stop talking when they notice us approach, obviously conscious we're in earshot.

"They must be making an offer," Mam says.

It's difficult to know.

Mr. Reidy asks the judge for a short adjournment.

"I can assure the Court that matters are being narrowed and it is almost coming to conclusion. It is very complex. In these circumstances, I would ask for another twenty minutes."

"Yes, that's fine," the judge agrees.

*

"All rise."

Court resumes and Mr. Gleeson makes an important announcement.

"I'm happy to say that the case has settled as between the Plaintiff and the Third Named Defendant, the HSE, on an interim basis. The form of the settlement, Judge, provides for a substantial payment now and then the adjournment of the case by agreement for two years with a view to availing, if possible, of intended legislation that will facilitate the payment of the balance of Ms. Ingle's damages via the mechanism of periodic payment orders. We have reduced our agreement (which deals with various contingencies within that broad framework) to writing and we ask that the writing may be received and made a Rule of Court."

Susie smiles across at me. Her hard work has paid off. "The case is over," she mouths to me. She smiles again.

I'm stunned – not only because I'm lip-reading Susie's words! But the case is over. I find it difficult to believe. I've won. I'm free. Oh my God. After three years in hospital! Does this mean I get to go home? What does it mean? Am I free?

"The orders that I'm asking are as follows. Firstly, that the interim settlement be received and made a Rule of Court. Secondly, an order adjourning the plaintiff's claim. I would advise a particular date, if that's okay – Tuesday 2nd July 2013. I'm not sure what Your Lordship's power in relation to date fixing two years out are, but could I ask for that maybe pro tem?"

The judge agrees to fix it for that date.

Mr. Gleeson also files to have my costs paid by the HSE. And then he reverts to Petmania and O'Keefe's Ltd.

"The plaintiff has assigned her cause of action as part of this settlement to the Third Named Defendant (HSE) and has been indemnified in respect of all matters by the Third Named Defendant. So the dispute, as I understand it, between the Third Named Defendant and the First (Petmania) and Second (O'Keefe's Ltd.) Named Defendants still subsist and are unresolved and the contribution claim under the Civil Liability Act remains. At this stage, I think, I'm out of the matter and it is a matter for my friends, Judge."

Mr. Hanratty, acting for the HSE, consents to Mr. Gleeson's orders.

"We have a major issue between ourselves and the First and Second Named Defendants as to who is liable but we were anxious to get the plaintiff out of this case because, in reality, she shouldn't have been in it and in truth it is a dispute between the medical defendants and the employer."

He goes into a long explanation about the HSE moving to seek complete indemnity in respect of liability.

Mr. McCullough says how pleased they are my case is settled and asks for an adjournment until the afternoon to proceed.

And what is a most interesting conclusion is that Petmania and the HSE strike out their claims against each other and possibly live happily ever after … !

*

"Congratulations," Susie says with a smile when we leave the courtroom together. "Your award will be recorded as a landmark case in history. It's the largest interim settlement ever reached to date. And it's well-deserved, Tricia. You've had a long hard journey to get to this point."

It's impossible to believe. But what does it mean exactly? I raise an eyebrow as a means of asking for more information, hiding a smile as I remember the time my eyebrows remained fixed in that position. It seems so long ago now.

"We settled on an interim basis for an interim lump sum payment to be paid immediately," Susie explains. "Further payments will be made to you every two years."

"Will it be enough for all my care?"

"This is the important part, Tricia. They'll do an assessment every two years and base the amount awarded on your needs at the time."

"More tests?"

She nods. "Yes, but you have a choice. You can halt the interim structure and take a final lump sum at any time if that's what you want. That's the more traditional type of award."

We all turn to look at her, relying on her for advice.

"What do you think?" I mouth.

"The interim basis allows for changes to your circumstances as well as future advances in medical and assistive technology. But today isn't the time to be even thinking about it. You've won your case. You're free to leave the hospital and return home."

"Come on, let's get going!" Dad ushers us out.

As we leave the High Court, I think about the trial and the barristers questioning me. They were kind, despite the tough and sometimes tricky questions.

Photographers follow us as we leave court. Dad has left through a different door, going to get the van and have it close by for our getaway.

It's exciting in a way having the media crowding around us. We don't mind. We don't find them intrusive. We are proud. We are happy. I have the financial means now to be cared for at home. The journalists hover around us at the courthouse gates. I don't mind who's waiting. I don't mind who wants to speak to me. I have one thing to say, one thing to shout out loud if my voice would allow it.

Susie has my prepared statement.

STATEMENT OF PATRICIA INGLE

I am so grateful for the legal assistance. Only for it I would still be imprisoned in a hospital room through no fault of my own. NOW I AM FREE.

I would like to thank my family, my friends and all who have supported me throughout the last three years and especially all at Cantillons Solicitors, particularly Susie Elliott, for their work on my behalf.

Dated 30th June 2011

Melissa and Kiera wheel my chair through the gates. Microphones are held close to me. My speaking valve is in. I have my answer ready when they bring the microphone to my mouth.

"Only for this award, I would be imprisoned in a hospital room through no fault of my own. I Am Free!"

Melissa stands protectively behind me.

Kiera's asked if she has something to say. "We're delighted for Tricia. She deserves everything she got. We hope she has a good future ahead of her."

I've a smile on my face and a familiar song in my heart as we make our way to Dad. Just like the lyrics in Katy Perry's 'Firework', I look up to the sky and hope for a rainbow after my hurricane. I wonder what my future holds.

*

Today's journey home is far from quiet, every one of us feeling a million times lighter than we have in almost three years.

"Turn up that song," KIera says, when 'People are Strange' by The Doors comes on.

It seems like music is our universal language today.

Mam, Dad, Kiera and Melissa sing along to the radio. We all burst out laughing for absolutely no reason. The High Court award is starting to sink in as we leave Dublin behind, the reality of what it will mean for me a dream come true as I return to Room Number 6 to be discharged.

Chapter 38

Patricia Ingle
July 2011
MWRH – Room Number 6
It's time to leave ...

After the courtcase, it feels strange. We're not sure what to do.

"You're free to leave," Susie tells me.

It's surreal. I can really leave. Yet I stay a few more weeks in hospital while final arrangements are made. In July we receive a report in response to the complaint I made through Consumer Affairs. It's lengthy and technical and after hearing all the detail my family and I are hoping that the lessons learned from my case will guide better practice for patients in the future and most importantly help all the disciplines to work better together and get patients released from hospital as soon as is realistically possible.

The Report of the Investigation provides closure to the burning questions that remained unanswered for so long. A sense of calm comes over me. After all the waiting, suddenly I don't want to rush. I want it to be right. I want it to be safe.

"Everything's in place at home, Tricia," Dad assures me. "Mam has nurses and carers organised. We've bought everything you're going to need."

"Thank you."

"It's up to you to decide your release date. You're quite the celebrity now. Susie has been fielding calls from the media. They're all interested in hearing your story."

I look at the calendar for the first time since 2008 and choose my date to rejoin family life in the Ingle household.

*

On the 5th August 2011, after 1,069 days in hospital, I say goodbye to Room Number 6 and leave the Mid-Western Regional Hospital.

The ward nurses are quiet today. I've hardly seen them. Everything is packed up, most of it already taken home.

Mam, Dad, Melissa and Kiera arrived at 7.30 a.m. this morning. They were excited. I was excited.

Room Number 6 looks forlorn, the drab walls bare of photos, the shower room no longer holding my suitcases of clothes.

One last look around. I can't help smiling at the sweet bowl. Even on this last day, it hasn't emptied. Dad kept it replenished right to the end.

Mam knocks on the HDU door to say goodbye. But nobody answers.

"I'll let the nurses know we're taking you, Tricia," Melissa says. "We have to tell them. We can't just disappear!"

I try not to care when she tells us they're too busy to come out and say goodbye. I've spent two years and three months in HDU and nine months in ICU of this hospital. I don't want to be here a moment longer.

As we head along the corridor toward the front door, I'm surprised and thrilled to see hospital workers lining up to say their farewells. Porters, shop staff, the HDU kitchen lady – they've all come to wish me well.

"Best of luck, Tricia!" they call as I pass by. "Don't forget about us!"

How can I ever forget these people? I've practically lived with them for three years. I've certainly relied on their kindness to get me through some of the toughest days and nights.

Fr. Coffey and Rose had made a point of saying their goodbyes early this morning. They've been tremendous support, their regular visits keeping me going. They might not have had the answers I was looking for but they were terrific listeners. Getting my complaints off my chest to such competent listeners was a great relief at times. I told them this earlier today.

"Who's going to buy all our teddies now?" the lady who runs the shop teases, leaving the line to give me a hug. "Sales will plummet!"

A ward sister from another unit also takes a moment to wish me luck.

Some people shake my hand; others share a kind word. They all smile as I pass them by. They all know how long I've waited for this day. They all know I'm getting my wish and going home at last.

Just inside the exit doors, the girls put the brakes on my wheelchair. Kiera and Melissa come either side of me and help me into a standing position. It takes a few moments to balance right but I get there without fuss. I can't believe how far I've come since those first dizzying attempts with 'Tilting Tom'!

The car park attendant and health care assistants hurry over and join in the farewells.

I place my feet firmly on the ground and we move a little away from my wheelchair. I stand tall, supported by my sisters, savouring the cheering and clapping of family and friends.

The excitement outside the hospital drowns out the silence inside HDU and Room Number 6.

I take a few moments to smile for the waiting photographers before leaving the confines of hospital to go home with my family.

Finally, I Am Free!

Chapter 39

Patricia Ingle
August 2011
Murroe, Co. Limerick
Home at last …

Looking back on those three years, I will never understand why the hospital stood in the way of letting me home. Life since August 2011 has had numerous challenges but I'm constantly improving and reaching new goals.

I have started over a new life where I have to relearn everything. But I'm doing it. I'm getting there. I'm making continual progress. I feel I've been born again. I feel I've received a second chance.

Ironically, the hospital's letter of apology was posted on the day of my release from Room Number 6. An unusual and bittersweet parting gift, considering the silence from the HDU staff on my important day.

> *5th August 2011*
> *Office of the Area Manager,*
> *Health Service Executive*
> *Limerick*

> *Dear Patricia,*
> *In accordance with the terms of agreement reached with you and your solicitors in June, I set out below an apology from the Mid-Western Regional Hospital and the HSE.*
> *The Mid-Western Regional Hospital, its clinicians and staff regret the events that have given rise to Patricia Ingle's current disabilities and hereby acknowledge the very difficult time that Patricia had since September 2008. The Hospital is delighted that Patricia's claim has been resolved to her satisfaction and would like to wish Patricia and her family the very best for the future.*

*The Hospital and the HSE recognise that since the time
of Patricia's readmission in January 2009 it has not always
been possible to afford to Patricia the kind of care that it
and Patricia and her family would have wished for and the
Hospital and the HSE sincerely regret this. The Hospital and
the HSE look forward to continuing their relationship with
Patricia in the future, using their very best endeavours to
assist Patricia and her family in relation to her care in any
and every way possible.*

Yours sincerely,

Area Manager, HSE Mid-West

*

It took me a few days to realise that my return home was permanent. Waking up in my own room brought a smile to my face every morning. I felt so happy surrounded by family. There were no restrictions. I could see my niece anytime I wanted. I didn't have to watch my family leave every night or tearlessly cry myself to sleep when I lay there alone. Remembering the heaviness and sorrow I felt inside on those long lonely nights, it was far worse than any tears I could have shed.

In those initial days at home in Murroe all I wanted to do was embrace the happiness I was feeling. Having a nurse and care assistant in the house all of the time meant I felt safe. But it also took a bit of getting used to – not only for me but for my parents and sisters too.

Privacy was a thing of the past – for all of us.

*

Because I had missed out on critical neuro-rehabilitation, there was little time wasted in putting a plan in place to book me into the Oxford Centre for Enablement as a matter of urgency. Naturally I understood how important the rehabilitation was. I had great hopes for the improvements it would make but I was sad to leave home so soon after settling in.

Still, I wasn't going to miss out on any chance of improvement. But neither was I going to leave for Oxford without having my homecoming party first. Planning this occasion kept me going during those last difficult months in hospital. I decided on a huge Hollywood-themed fancy dress party. I'd been longing to dress up as Cinderella, wear a beautiful gown and have my hair set in curls. It's easy to guess why I chose Cinderella. I wanted to defy the fairytale when the clock chimed midnight. I no longer had to leave the ball. I no longer had to return to the hospital. I no longer had to be separated from my family. I no longer had to be treated differently.

With my sisters' help, we made lists and got on with the party planning. Online shopping was a lifesaver and gave me the freedom to pick out every accessory I could think of without the worry of getting around the shops. Shopping from the comfort of home protected me from people staring and asking questions. What it didn't protect me from was overspending! The choice online is endless. The postman and couriers made a beeline to my house, the online stores getting to recognise my name!

The party date was set for Saturday 14th August. With my sisters' help, I sent out 200 invitations to friends, family, neighbours, the Liverpool Club my parents were involved in, and anyone who had given us support over those difficult three years.

As the day came closer, we started to panic. We had enough food for 200 people. What would we do if nobody arrived? What if the party was a disaster? Was it a silly idea to have it in the first place?

But we needn't have worried. We had a full house. The atmosphere was electric and the decorations and novelties I had ordered online looked fantastic. Everyone dressed up, some of our guests going to great effort with their costumes.

Dad dressed up as a gangster, complete with gun. Kiera loved being Audrey Hepburn for the evening and Melissa copied an outfit from Sense and Sensibility. I couldn't believe it when Mam dressed as a surgeon – I thought we'd seen enough of hospitals. But she was the real thing in her scrubs, a stethoscope hanging around her neck and clog shoes on her feet.

As people arrived, it was great fun trying to recognise them behind the make-up and headgear. I was thrilled and amused to see Grace arriving as Pocahontas and her husband dressed as Shaun the Sheep. My aunt came as Captain Hook and another friend hadn't been able to decide on a specific fancy dress so she wrapped a white sheet around her and wore a McDonald's crown on her head. Improvisation at its best!

It was a fantastic night. I presented those with the most imaginative costumes an 'Oscar' trophy for their efforts! Sitting in my satin gown, I really felt special that evening. It was a huge success and made up for all the miserable birthdays and Christmases I'd had in hospital, the parties and celebrations I'd felt I'd missed out on. There was a big cheer when the guys lined up to give me a kiss, some going back to the end of the queue and stealing a second one!

Our local pub set up a full bar in the living room. There were gazebos along the back garden and staff from the pub served beer on the night. One of them even dressed up as Prince Charming and was teased for the evening about getting down on one knee. He couldn't look me in the eye, however, when he found my 'slipper' and went to slip it on my foot.

The party continued until six in the morning. I couldn't keep my eyes open beyond 3.00 a.m. Even then I was reluctant to let the nurses take me to my bedroom and get me settled for what was left of the night. I wanted the party atmosphere to continue forever.

Taking a last look around before being wheeled to my room, the colourful scene in our living room reminded me of the parade in Euro Disney. Mam and Dad, the gangster and surgeon, were laughing with their friends as though they hadn't a care in the world. I went to sleep with a big smile on my face that night, too weary for disturbing dreams, too happy to wonder about the obstacles I still had to overcome.

In the clean-up the next morning, Mam found Harry Potter's glasses in the midst of the mess! And despite the magic of the evening before, there wasn't a trace of a wizard weaving spells in our home. This was our reality now. Setting new targets and achieving goals. I had achieved one of my first – to throw a party of a lifetime and let everyone know I was back where I belonged – home.

It was time to plan for what came next.

Chapter 40

Patricia Ingle
August 2011
Oxford Centre for Enablement
Hard work begins …

On August 22nd 2011, I left for Oxford for a period of intensive rehabilitation therapy. Mam, Dad and two nurse travelled with me. Packing for this trip (and every trip since) was more difficult than moving house for Mam. The list of requirements was endless – bottles of oxygen, my PEG feeding machine complete with cartons of food and water, spare tubing, suction machine, nebuliser, an enormous bag filled with medical materials, towels, clothes, hycin patches to limit saliva, medication for blood pressure and pain, shoes, make-up – anything we thought we'd need.

The first few weeks in the Enablement Centre were difficult. I was homesick and unsettled. And exhausted! The therapy was non-stop during the day. But I got to know other people and this helped me settle in.

Most of the patients were older than me but they were very nice and I found it easy to talk to them. Every day I worked hard on physiotherapy, occupational therapy and psychological therapy. Any wonder I was shattered every evening!

I took my therapy very seriously while I was there, determined to improve in whatever way I could, no matter how small. I had waited long enough to get there. I wasn't going to waste it.

The doctors in Oxford assessed me from head to toe – my health, my ability, my treatment. They reduced a lot of my medication, gradually changing it and monitoring my reactions. I couldn't have been happier. I was never a fan of tablets so the more I can get rid of the better. And it'll save money as some of my medication is extremely expensive. Dad was scared I wouldn't manage without them. The pharmacist made sure they had them in stock to be on the safe side, and maybe to put Dad's mind at ease. Though they left me on a minimum dosage, they promised to review this on a future visit.

I'd been having stomach injections to avoid blood clotting every single day since I became ill. The needle hurt! And it proved I still had some feeling, despite not having a sense of touch. But Oxford didn't see a need for these injections anymore and they discontinued them. Dad and I were particularly delighted! He had been the worst at giving me injections. Neither of us will miss the fuss it caused.

Every day was busy. The physiotherapy was intensive but effective. I did everything they asked and knew I'd be able to continue a lot of the exercises when I went home. I was on my feet a lot more, taking more and more steps with assistance and continually beating my own record.

Sometimes I was lucky and was only scheduled for a half day's therapy. On those days, Mam and Dad took me somewhere nice as a break from the hospital. The feeling of freedom is still a novelty.

Kiera and Melissa visited a lot of weekends while I was there. Layla came with them and everyone in Lane Fox got to know my family. The first weekend they came over was Kiera's birthday and, with the help of my therapist, I baked her a huge cookie and wrote 'Happy Birthday' in icing sugar.

It was exciting to see the girls and have something to look forward to after a week of working hard. We travelled a lot to places outside of Oxford.

On a really hot day in October when the temperatures soared to 30 degrees, Dad drove us to a zoo.

"Your skin is burning, Tricia," Mam warned, stopping to apply more sun cream.

My skin had changed texture from years indoors. It took a few months to return to normal but eventually it started to tan again and I looked healthy.

Layla celebrated her first birthday while I was in Oxford. Melissa brought her over so I could be part of her first celebrations. I was thrilled not to miss out on this special birthday.

And before Christmas that year, Melissa shared some other good news. I was about to be an aunt again. As with Layla, I was the first to know and the news brought a new target to mind. With two little ones to enjoy, I needed to be physically and mentally strong to make sure my niece and the new arrival would see their Aunt Tricia full of life and fun, the same as I always was.

The opportunities to accomplish small things in Oxford were phenomenal. The staff saw challenges as little blips, their positive attitude contagious. Nothing was off the agenda. If there was a chance a particular exercise or gadget could help me, it was introduced to my care.

Part of my therapy included using a computer so I bought a brand-new laptop to practise on. But I found the keyboard very difficult. I needed to use both hands together. My left side has more power than my right. It has become the dominant side. Using my right hand or leg requires a lot of work. The laptop wasn't a great success but I did use it to Skype Kiera and Melissa. At least it was useful for something!

But giving up on the laptop wasn't the end. I had got an iPad as a present when I was in Room Number 6 but never bothered much with it. I tried it again while I was in Oxford and realised it was easier to use than the laptop. I could see exactly what my hands were doing but I could also see the letters appearing on screen at the same time. I can focus on the iPad screen. It's unlike any other computer screen I've tried.

My iPad has expanded my life. I write, play games, go online, listen to music, watch music videos, purchase items, download things, email, read stories, research and go on social meda. Two months after arriving in Oxford, on 5th October 2011, I posted my first Facebook message. Being able to communicate with the outside world and be part of the online community felt liberating.

I got to experience so many new things in Oxford. It's unbelievable the work being done for people with brain injuries in the Enablement Centre. I can't help feeling a little cheated that I didn't get a chance to come here much earlier in my illness. I saw amazing things happen for other people – one person walked when she was told she wouldn't, others were being assessed to discover misdiagnosis and once their treatement was corrected, they were on a far better road to recovery.

I had plenty of adventures there, probably the most exciting when I got to use a power wheelchair for the first time. The therapists had a really fun system in place to help the newbies learn to drive. And safe too. Before they would let me off on my own, I had to do my driving test, going in and out between cones. It reminded me of driving my green VW Polo, stalling and starting and stalling and starting.

Dad took a video. I know they didn't expect me to manage it. Mam was holding the ventilator and running after the chair while I drove up and down the corridors and around the hospital. Poor Mam and her bad back, not to mention the staff jumping out of the way when I was approaching! I picked it up so fast that they asked if I had done it before.

It was great sport and gave me a sense of independence and a thrill to be doing something for myself. The sense of achievement I felt mastering the driving technique kept me going for weeks.

In total, I spent six months in Oxford, coming home for a break at Christmas and then returning for more rehab in the New Year.

I was surprised – and delighted – when the doctor said I could come home permanently on the 25th March, 2012. I had expected to be there longer but thankfully my hard work with the therapists paid off and soon I was back in Murroe and doing so much better than before. To celebrate being home and the success in Oxford, we all went into the garden where I released 13 paper lanterns into the sky. Together we watched them flying high in the sky above!

For some reason Grandad entered my mind as the lanterns floated towards the clouds, in particular the dream where he stood in front of me telling me it would all be okay. Whether it's a myth or not, I'm beginning to see what he's seeing. It will take time and a lot of hard work but I can see a future. I think he's right. It will all be okay.

Chapter 41

Patricia Ingle
March 2012
Murroe, Co Limerick
Road to improvement …

Mam wasted no time in organising physiotherapy, occupational therapy and speech therapy, making sure that the progress I made in Oxford continued. In the beginning I found therapy sessions exceptionally tiring but I've gradually built up stamina and can manage a lot more exercises and routines without it exhausting me.

I have speech therapy and physiotherapy four times every week. I have occupational therapy for two hours on a Saturday. This has continued right up to the present day. Therapy has done wonders for my confidence. And my posture! My physiotherapists work diligently with me, assisting me to stand with less and less support. My balance has improved greatly! The number of steps I take continues to increase. I take satisfaction in counting each one and if I'm disheartened I remind myself that I've progressed a long way from the initial excitement of just shaking my head. I'm determined to keep working hard in the hopes that one day I will be able to walk independently again.

Though I'm still reliant on the speaking valve to speak aloud, my speech is faster and easier to understand. And I can wear the speaking valve for longer periods. Every week I'm improving. Every week I measure the difference, recording it and working to surpass it. It's motivating to see the changes on my wall chart. I'm lucky the people working with me take a real interest in helping me take back more and more of my independence. They continually encourage me and show me how to accomplish something new. The exercises are often difficult but the rewards are invaluable.

*

Since 2011, we've seen a lot of nursing staff and care assistants come and go for one reason or another. It's difficult to find staff at times. Because they are with me constantly, they have to be people I can connect to and feel comfortable with. Working in a home environment is probably unusual and a little isolating for nurses and it's understandable that it doesn't always work out. Some of the girls working with us left to go to Australia, others to take up jobs elsewhere. I missed them when they left. We had become friends and every departure made me feel I was being left behind.

Hiring new staff is upsetting for all of us but for me in particular as I have to start all over again getting to know them and learning to trust them. But I give everyone a chance. My nurses and carers are a huge part of my life, more like friends and companions than staff. I'm very lucky to have my sisters as part of my care team. Kiera and Melissa are trained as carers and from the time I left hospital they've worked with me on a fulltime basis. It's comforting having them with me. They know my likes and dislikes better than anyone! And they are brilliant at arranging surprises for me, like the time in February 2013 when we went to Darren Shan's book-signing in the Crescent Book Shop in the Crescent Shopping Centre, Limerick.

My all-time favourite author was, and still is, Darren Shan. I loved nothing more than immersing myself into his fantasy world before I got sick. While I was in hospital, Mam, Melissa and Kiera bought every Darren Shan book that was published. We had always been encouraged to read when we were younger. Though reading is difficult for me now, I'm thrilled to have all of his books on my shelves and I'm hoping one day to get to a point where I enjoy reading books again.

It was really exciting to meet the author in person. The people working in the shop couldn't have been kinder and made me feel very special when Darren presented me with a special T-shirt with a logo of his latest book cover. All the other fans queuing that day were very disappointed when they didn't receive a T-shirt like mine! There were plenty of photographs throughout the course of the afternoon and once again I received special media attention.

*

We've had our photographs taken for newspapers and television many times since the courtcase, with publicity being part of the consequence of going public with my case. In the same way we approached the media after the case, we greeted them pleasantly on every occasion and were just ourselves. My sisters were as excited as I was when we were interviewed on live TV and Radio in our own home. Working with the researchers and producers was very interesting. My family helped me tell the reporters my story but they made sure I got a chance to speak too.

TV3's Ireland AM had me on their show, not once but twice! Anna Daly and her team came to our house with their TV crew and she was so easy to chat with that we forgot we were being filmed for TV! The entire TV crew were lovely and made the experience really enjoyable for us.

RTÉ's Miriam O'Callaghan also paid us a visit to record an interview with me for radio. Her show is obviously very popular as loads of people got in touch to congratulate us after the interview was aired. The sound guy travelling with her was really nice. He and the rest of the crew were delighted when I presented them with handmade chocolate and gifts I had bought them in Glenstal Abbey. Coincidentally we have bumped into the sound guy a few times in Limerick since. He always makes time to chat and see how we're doing.

The media interest in my case lived on long after the courtcase and our family were featured on numerous occasions. Thankfully Susie managed the majority of enquiries for us. She advised us to 'pick and stick' with specific journalists and presenters. As usual her advice was invaluable and I went to a lot of trouble to get her a special gift as a thank-you and a memory of our close bond while she represented us. I chose a bronze statue of the Children of Lir. It sits in a prominent place in the reception area of Cantillons Solicitors, the inscription 'Thank you for lifting me from the water and setting me free' a permanent reminder that their successful investigation set me free.

*

What the media are mostly interested in is how I spend my days and whether I'm still improving. And I'm happy to report that my life is busy and, yes, I am making huge progress. Unfortunately, it hasn't been all plain sailing since I've come home and I've had a few serious infections, the worst of these happening when we were on our way to a seminar in Dublin in 2014.

Dad wanted to attend a seminar in the University of Limerick to learn a little more about tracheas. At first he was told it was for medical people only but then he made further enquiries through the ward sister in Ward 2C MWRH where I attend regularly to have my trachea changed. She was very kind and understanding and arranged for me to be invited so Dad could go as my companion. The ENT specialist from Limerick who has been extremely kind to us over the years welcomed me to the seminar and apologised to Dad for any confusion.

Dad watched and learned while they used a sheep's windpipe sourced from a local abattoir to demonstrate changing a trachea. The ward sister gave a lecture and Dad found it very informative.

The following year they arranged to hold a similar seminar in the Royal College in Dublin. I was invited along and they were going to do a trachea change on me as part of the lecture.

We went to Dublin, stayed in a hotel the night before, and were looking forward to the event. But the following morning I felt off. The ward sister from 2C MWRH was also in the Royal College and came over to the hotel to check on me when Dad phoned her. She brought two doctors with her. They examined me and recommended I return home because, unfortunately, I had pneumonia. The doctors arranged a prescription with our local chemist in Limerick.

We set off on our long journey home but five miles from Dublin I took a really bad turn. My NIPPY machine was working but I was too weak to take in the oxygen. Dad stopped the van to help. My nurse did resuscitation and Dad was assisting while Mam was on the phone. The nurse was scared but remained calm.

I was exhausted. I became unresponsive. Dad sat beside me. My oxygen levels were very concerning. Dad only had two small bottles of oxygen with us. He had thought would be enough. He had no choice but bring me to the nearest hospital.

Relying on Sat Nav we were directed to St Vincent's Hospital. They were expecting us but we got stuck in traffic jams. Dad drove through red lights, fuming when a Garda car ignored him beeping for attention. Eventually we arrived. He ran in to get help. A nurse came out with oxygen and my private nurse was behind me bagging me, trying to do the job of a ventilator while we waited for emergency oxyen.

Lucky I got help in time. I dread to think what might have happened otherwise.

Inside the hospital, they got me back on a ventilator in the resuss room. My lungs were clogged but apparently (they told me afterwards) I was responding.

A lady doctor explained I was really sick and very far from out of the woods, one of my blood counts triple what it should be.

"You've been doing so well, Tricia. Your immunity, youth and good health have hidden the normal telltale signs of this sneaky infection. It has suddenly overwhelmed you. A more vulnerable person would have displayed signs far sooner."

Each time they suctioned me, all that was coming out was blood. This scared Mam when she was in charge of suctioning. The container was pure red.

I was put in a room by myself. I continued to lose blood, far too much blood. The doctors mentioned transfusion but thankfully it didn't come to that. Very slowly I improved. On the fifth day they started doing physio on me. The next day I was sitting in my chair looking up and down the hallway, eager to prove I was well enough to return home.

I watched as a storm lifted the roof off the Boathouse, remembering years before when I went rowing there with my Rowing Club. My aunt sent a message to let us know the storm had hit Limerick too. And just like that Christmas Eve when I came home for an overnight stay, the power went off for quite a few hours. As usual, Mam went into organising mode and decided she'd book us into a hotel in Limerick if things hadn't improved by the time we got home. Electricity is as important a requirement for me as my ventilator. Thankfully by the time we got home the storm had eased and the power was restored. We were saved the trouble of staying in a hotel and were very relieved to be back safely in Murroe.

*

Despite being told by the doctors that the signs of that infection weren't visible and nothing was missed, the whole ordeal set Dad back worrying again. It shattered his confidence when we were travelling anywhere and made him nervous in case I took ill again. No fault lay with anyone but it highlighted risks all over again. But eventually we upgraded the van so we can now carry bigger bottles of oxygen and there's less fear of running out. We can store more gear too – the bigger the car, the more we bring. And I love to shop!

A few weeks after the infection I had X-rays taken in MWRH. There was fluid in my lungs from the pneumonia so I had to go into hospital again and have 3 litres of fluid drained. The doctor was called in to do it under local anesthetic. The fluid came flying out. It was sore. I wasn't able to sit back on the chair. The nurse expected the morphine would put me asleep but, the very minute the procedure was finished, I was wide awake asking to be put out on a chair. It did take a lot out of me though and I was prone to infection for a while afterwards.

Around this time I started holding multidisciplinary meetings at home. I lead the meeting and have an agenda ready, usually detailing my progress as well as setting new goals around what I can achieve. My family, my therapists and the nurse and care assistant on duty on that day all attend and we assess how far I've come since the last meeting, and decide on new targets and work out a plan on how I can hope to meet these targets. The meetings are focused and it's good to have everybody involved in my care in the same conversation at least once a month.

*

I've been back to the Lane Fox Unit in St. Thomas' Hospital for assessments on a few occasions, sometimes as part of my court interim review. Unlike my jaunt on a plane the first time, we take the ferry to Pembroke and make the five-hour drive to St. Thomas'. Dad never risks being too far away from a hospital and uses the Sat Nav Help button to locate the nearest hospital no matter where we are – just in case.

I get such a warm welcome from the Lane Fox staff and they always have everything ready for me when we arrive. One nurse was finished her duty on one occasion but waited until I arrived so she could greet me personally. Each time I visit, they're amazed at the improvement since my first trip in 2009. On these visits they do a little physio and speech therapy but concentrate mostly on assessing and monitoring my ventilation. They run tests on me awake and sleeping, regulating settings and monitoring my reaction to the change. It gets a little boring after a few days but I'm usually allowed out for a while to break the monotony. Generally, they adjust my ventilator settings to allow me take more breaths myself and also make it easier to use the speaking valve for longer. Unfortunately, the infection I got in Dublin meant these settings had to be reversed temporarily until I built up immunity and was better able to fight infection.

St. Thomas' Hospital is huge. It has its own shopping centre with two large shops, a number of restaurants, a beauty parlour, cinema, libraries and computers. It even has an open area for bands to play and promote themselves. A nurse told us it's one of the wealthiest hospitals in UK as it's across from Westminster and politicians go there when they're ill. I'm not one bit surprised, it really is a fabulous facility and I always feel better leaving here.

I returned to Lane Fox in 2015 for another repiratory assessment and time off my ventilator. I enjoyed this trip despite it being a medical one. My nurses and care assistant had come with me. While we were there, they received training and competency testing. Having such a good relationship with my nurses and care assistant makes this trip to Lane Fox a little like a trip away with friends – except for my parents being there!

During the day I had my own staff with me as well as Lane Fox's. I was a little nervous sleeping in the unit by myself the first night, anxious in case the

Lane Fox nurses wouldn't understand me if I needed help. Without a voice, it's scary if something happens and I need to get somebody's attention. But the staff were understanding. They tried an emergency call button to see if I could use it but unfortunately not. They reassured me there was nothing to worry about, that they'd be monitoring me very closely throughout the night.

Early the first morning, the girls brought me to get my hair cut in the hospital's hair salon and we bought some books from a bookstall on the way there – even though I don't read. My shopping addiction remains very much alive and I couldn't resist buying colouring books for Melissa's children. There's so much to do around St. Thomas', the relaxing atmosphere by the River Thames something we enjoy as often as possible. There's even an aquariam fifteen minutes away with some very interesting crocodiles!

The trip was a mixture of therapy and having fun, although the OT put me through my paces. They observed my care assistants working with me and suggested I could be doing a little more for myself. On my most recent visit, they suggested to my nurse and care assistant that they should start letting me take off my clothes at bedtime and brushing my own hair. I will take this advice and work on her suggestions. But it isn't as easy as it might sound.

We had one day left before getting the ferry and Dad took us to Longleat Safari Park. My love of animals remains as strong as ever. As Dad drove through the park, we saw rhinos and monkeys, tigers and cheetahs walking very close to the traffic. A lion was practically beside our van as he crossed the road in front of us. The monkeys were hilarious, climbing on top of the van and scampering over the roof and down the other side. Apparently they also have a tendency to pull off wing mirrors but thankfully ours survived!

As some of the areas weren't wheelchair friendly, we took a ramble around the haunted house instead, laughing at Dad when he insisted he'd seen a ghost!

We slept for most of the ferry trip home, exhausted but contented after our latest trip to Lane Fox.

*

My health continues to improve but I'm still not immune to infection. I find infections so annoying. The bad ones usually see me back in hospital as I need to be treated in a special resuss unit in A&E in MWRH. At times it's difficult to get a bed. There are only four in the unit. If I'm showing signs of infection, Mam phones the hospital and talks to the staff, asking them to let us know when a bed is available and, providing it's safe to do so, I stay at home until they ring.

I don't think I will ever like hospitals. Then I'm sure very few people do. I avoid them as much as possible and other than the emergency visits, I visit MWRH every month to have my trachea changed in Ward 2C, the ward I was almost moved to when the hospital were contemplating putting me in a nursing home! But now I have good experiences when I attend, apart from the procedure itself which isn't painful as such but is uncomfortable.

The staff are lovely to deal with and little things have definitely improved, even something as simple as moving the Patient Welfare Office to a prominent location instead of hidden away like the complaints room in the Carlsberg TV advertisement! We have good banter and I always leave there laughing at one of their parting jokes – such a different experience to the day I left Room Number 6.

My superpubic catheter is also changed monthly and this is both uncomfortable and painful! It's not something I look forward to. Mam and Dad leave it until the last minute to tell me this is happening. They also make sure I'm given paracetomol. And this helps to make it bearable when the kind community nurse comes to change it.

My PEG hasn't been changed as yet but it's closely monitored. Once it starts to show signs of perishing, it will need changing. After the initial change, it will need to be repeated every three months. No doubt this will also be uncomfortable and painful. Still it's nothing to what I've been through already.

Chapter 42

Patricia Ingle
June 2016
Home sweet home
A day in the life …

We are a more relaxed household now than when I came home from hospital first. Naturally, my parents – Dad in particular – were nervous at first. He jumped every few minutes to see to everything. The responsibility was stressful for him. He was always the first to rush to me and barely gave any of the others a chance to do something for me.

I wanted to be treated the same as my sisters as much as possible. I didn't want it to be any different for me. I hated being overprotected. At one point I wrote him a letter to try and explain I needed a little space. I understand he felt responsible but I needed him to know he could be a little claustrophobic at times.

*

Prior to September 2008, Mam and Dad had a good social life. They were Liverpool supporters and went out to watch the matches in the local pub as well as travelling to Liverpool to attend games at least twice every year. They had great friends. They had fun. They were free. They had a good life.

They were members of the Limerick Liverpool Fan Club and organised trips, tickets, flights and ferries. When they got there they'd often arrange a 'meet and greet' event with an ex-player or a trip to the Melwood training ground. Melissa was secretary. Dad was assistant treasurer. And I helped out with the arrangements sometimes.

When I got ill, all of that stopped and since then they've barely had time to watch the matches on TV!

"Forget me, just go out and enjoy yourselves!" I told them.

"It's not always possible, Tricia, particularly when the staff are new. And sometimes, when it is possible, by the time the evening arrives we don't have the energy."

It's unfair their lives have changed with mine but our house isn't designed for our needs. We don't have enough rooms to allow for staff quarters or separate living areas for us to enjoy in the evenings. But I have plans to build a purpose-designed house and privacy is a key priority in every aspect of the architect's drawings.

*

How I pass the day varies, depending on therapist appointments and the schedules I have to keep, but my care plan is as routine as clockwork.

I wake at 7.30 a.m. without fail. I have a clock that shines up on the ceiling so I can see the time. I hate being in bed after 8.00 a.m. and even if we're staying in a hotel and I can't see the time I'll still wake at the same time. The TV Music channel 703 comes on automatically. The room is always warm as the heating is on a timer – no need for Dad to climb into the attic!

The night staff work 9 p.m. to 9 a.m. and when I wake I receive a nebuliser through my trachea and Ensure nutrition through my PEG.

My care assistant and nurse wash and dress me while I'm lying down. When they wash my legs, I get a strange sensation and nearly kick my poor carers! Then I sit up and wash my face and brush my teeth myself. I need to be suctioned after this.

Dad is called to help get me out of bed. My care assistant hops on the bed to help me sit up while Dad helps swing out my legs.

I do my bit to help, but it's a team effort!

Then my nurse puts on my Swedish nose. This is a cap that's attached to my tracheostomy tube to help maintain humidity and ensure I'm not exposed to infection. Next I move from my bed to my chair. No more hoists or banana boards – I'm able to walk from one to the other with assistance. Once I'm in my chair, my jumper is put on and then my ventilator is reattached.

If I need my hair washed, it's done as soon as I get out of bed in the en suite bathroom. I have a manual chair for this. Dad helps get me into it and wheels me in. The nurse carries the NIPPY. The oxygen is also brought in and the suction machine is right outside the door just in case. I have the oximeter on my finger to monitor my oxygen levels in case they drop while I'm leaning backwards and Dad gets to work shampooing!

Once my hair is rinsed, I'm transferred into my wheelchair.

My blood pressure, pulse, temperature, heart rate and oxygen levels are all checked by my nurse when I'm sitting in my chair. Then my care assistant fixes my hair and applies my make-up. I like to have my eye make-up and eyebrows done. I usually fall asleep if I'm having my eyebrows plucked!

Once I'm ready, I move to the living room straight away. I hate being in the bedroom during the day.

Four days every week, I have therapy. Sometimes I have it at home. Other times I go to the clinics. It's nice to have a bit of variety.

Monday, Tuesday, Thursday and Friday are my days for physio and speech therapy and Saturday for occupational therapy.

At midday, I have a nebuliser and sometimes chill out with my iPad while the staff take their lunch break.

I spend the afternoons doing different things. But I'm always learning and trying something new. For a while I wrote regular pieces for a newsletter, keeping readers up to date on my progress. Having a deadline at the end of each week kept me very focused and gave me something definite to aim for.

I even went to college in 2013. I completed an eight-week course on intellectual disabilities in the University of Limerick and was really proud of this achievement. Unfortunately, there wasn't a graduation ceremony, but I worked so hard I believe I deserved a hat and gown after that performance!

I was also invited to present a power-point presentation to Speech & Language students, describing the various communication methods I've used, sharing my journey from those first attempts at blinking. I was so proud to deliver the entire presentation using my speaking valve. The Q&A session that followed was very interesting and enjoyable and I fully participated in the entire event!

If I'm home in the afternoons, I do some cooking a few times every week. I manage as much as I can myself – with my nurse or care assistant helping using hand-over-hand technique. On a really nice day, my nurse, care assistant and I will go out together for a walk. Murroe has lovely walks. We're spoilt for choice. On one of the first walks Siobhan took me on, we set out to go to the shop. The day was so nice I asked if we could keep going as far as Glenstal Abbey. Wanting to stay out in the fresh air, I asked if we could go to the secret gardens. We went around all of the gardens and the little graveyard where the monks are buried.

The hill on the way back was steep. Siobhan and my care assistant had to push my chair because the motor wasn't able for it. We'd been gone around three hours and Dad had already phoned to see if all was okay. At that point it was. But we had to swallow our pride and call him back when the battery of my chair died and Dad had to drive to the village to collect us.

Other than getting out for fresh air, I try different hobbies all the time. It keeps me occupied and is usually great therapy to help improve my movements. I have a creative streak and spend hours trying arts and crafts of different types. I've improved a lot with time and practice. I've made loom bands and knotted quilts. Leggo is my latest passion and I've made entire villages of Leggo. Mam is running out of shelf space at this stage.

Another important and regular part of my day is doing stands. I have to stand every 90 minutes. I get help from my nurse but even with this my posture and balance have improved enormously.

I hate if the stand interrupts what I'm doing and I hate when I'm reminded that I need to do it. To take a little bit of initiative I started using an alarm clock as a reminder. For some reason it doesn't annoy me half as much then!

I watch a bit of television in the evenings with my family. The Big Bang Theory and Impractical Jokers are my favourite shows. Other than that and the music channels, I'd rather be working on my iPad or on one of my latest hobby crazes. I'm always doing something. I don't like being idle.

Most nights I go to bed around 11 p.m. I plug out my iPad and my nurse and care assistant know that's my signal. I'm ready to go to bed. They pack up the emergency bag with suction machine, suction catheters, syringes, yellow bags, oximeter, monometer, tissues and so much more and take it to my bedroom. The bag is stocked up again every morning. The size of the bag has increased over the years and it has become a part of my entourage!

Mam usually comes into the bedroom for a chat. The care assistant helps pick out my clothes for the next day while my nurse organises emergency equipment to ensure it's at hand during the night. Once I've agreed on my clothes for the next day, I get into bed by doing a roto stand, edging myself out of the chair and putting my legs on a frame that has wheels. Then I hold onto the bars and stand and rotate back into the bed.

The care assistant helps me into the bed. Mam holds the circuit tubes and I'm switched from the day circuit to night circuit. I help as much as I can.

Mam says goodnight and brings my chair out to the living room and puts it on charge overnight. The NIPPY is also put on charge overnight.

My care assistant undresses and washes me. She usually has my blanket, nightie and socks warming on the heater so they're nice and cosy when she puts them on me. I get a full suction before I sleep. I like the bedrail to be up and I like the light off. Then I fall asleep very quickly.

I start out lying on my back but I'm turned on to my side every two hours. While I'm sleeping, the girls stock up on supplies.

Mostly my sleep is unbroken unless I need suctioning. I'm particularly vulnerable when I'm getting washed and dressed at bedtime and early in the morning. The build-up of phlegm and secretions overnight can move and cause a blockage or a plug to my airways. I'm fed through the night and switched to water at 5.00 a.m. and medication at 6.00 a.m. I receive all of this through the PEG. And at 7.30 a.m. a new day begins and the process starts all over again.

*

The way I am now and the amount of help I need is difficult at times. Mostly, I'm positive and upbeat and I always keep looking forward and working on ways to improve. But I do get occasional moments when I wish things were different. I wish I could walk to the kitchen like my family. They can just walk up and down. They take it for granted. I wish I could do that too but I need a lot of help. However, I have reached a walking record with my physiotherapist of 40 laps of the kitchen! Hard work and determination pays off – as well as the support of excellent therapists.

Whenever a negative thought enters my head, I push it away and focus on something happy, like my nieces and nephews. Melissa has four children now, Layla, Aoife, Noah and Oliver who arrived in June 2016. The children spend a lot of time in our house which is great as I get to watch them grow!

Before I was sick I loved babies and sometimes I get annoyed because I can't play with them properly. I can't interact like I should. Occasionally I feel left out and wonder how things would be if I hadn't got ill. Mam says I would be doing a lot of baby-sitting! But my nieces and nephew don't know any different. They don't judge me. They have grown up knowing me like this and they all love me just the way I am. They hug and kiss me and sit on my lap. Sometimes they come over and hold my hand for no reason.

They understand some of the medical terms being used every day, like 'the cuff is down' and 'the cuff is up' so they are learning to understand about the speaking valve. They like when the cuff is down so I can speak. Layla always did my exercises with me. When they have colds or infections, they know they can't kiss or hug me. Instead we do 'knuckles' until the infection has passed.

Layla teases me sometimes. "What did you say, Tricia?" she asks over and over to torment me, knowing what I'd have said but just pretending not to hear so I'll repeat it.

The little ones love me following them up and down in my wheelchair. My new power-chair is different to my last one and raises me to eye level if I want. This is very useful if I want to look somebody in the eye!

When Melissa asked me to be godmother for her second daughter, Aoife, I was over the moon and so proud to be offered such a treasured responsibility.

Chapter 43

Patricia Ingle
July 2016
Murroe
All work and no play …

Having something to look forward to keeps me going, keeps me working to improve and keeps life fun. I love concerts and shows and since I've come home I have been to loads of events, mostly in Dublin's 3 Arena. Mam books the tickets through Ticketmaster, always ordering at least three so my nurse and care assistant accompany me to the event while Mam and Dad usually stay back in the hotel. Luckily they enjoy similar acts to me so it's fun for them too. My account with Ticketmaster is extremely active, barely a month passing when I'm not at an event. They should be offering me discount at this stage!

To mention a few, I've been to see Hilary Duff, Christina Aguilera (twice), Kelly Clarkson (twice), the Meteor Awards, Pussycat Dolls, Shane Ward, Westlife, Amy Winehouse (RIP), The Script, One Republic, Ant and Dec, Disney on Ice (loads of times), Walking with Dinosaurs and lots more!

The U2 concert was limited to two tickets per person but Mam went to great lengths to get three, finally contacting the 3 Arena and explaining that because I'm in a wheelchair I don't even take a seat. They agreed to release the third ticket if I could provide medical documentation to prove I need two people with me at all times. And of course Dad had an email ready for them in no time at all! All this trouble and I wasn't a particular fan of U2. But Dad is a huge fan. And out of kindness and sympathy for him, my care assistant gave him her ticket on the night and let him go in place of her. So for the sake of U2, Dad was my care assistant for the evening! And I have to admit I'm slowly converting to being a fan after the fun Siobhan, Dad and I had that night.

We stay in the same hotels when we're travelling to concerts and shows. It's such a relaxing experience now in comparision to that stressful trip to Dublin for the courtcase. And the hotel staff want to know what gig I'm going to when Mam rings to book the rooms. This familiarity adds to our trips away and in a way the hotel is a bit like a home from home. The number of staff travelling with us varies. If we're staying for more than one night, we could need four people working with me to cover the day and night shifts. But nothing is a problem for the hotel staff and they can't do enough to make our stay enjoyable. They accommodate us with the most suitable rooms and whatever else we need.

Choosing the right hotel makes such a difference when we're away. And a good location with plenty to see and do as well as more shopping keeps us entertained! Any wonder I'm always planning another trip? They're such fun.

2015 was the first time I started to have overnight trips away with my nurse and care assistant but without my parents. One of my sisters was always there either as a friend or on duty.

*

My 27th birthday party on 6th September 2015 was the perfect excuse for a weekend in Galway with a select few friends, nurses and carers. But no parents. This was a first for me to be away without Mam and Dad and a first for them to have a night at home without me. It was exciting. And a little frightening. For everybody.

I know my parents have a fear of letting me go. They've been by my side for over seven years. They've seen a time when I didn't want them to be in the other room and now I wouldn't even be in the same province! But they pushed their concerns aside for my sake and got involved in the preparations.

The hotel room was filled with balloons and streamers when we arrived. As usual Mam had gone to huge effort and she knows how much I love novelties. The hotel had left a lovely birthday card and chocolates on my bed.

At the greyhound track that night, we had a brilliant laugh, particularly when Siobhan knelt on a chair to get my emergency bag and the chair keeled over and she was upended!

Not one of the girls got up to help – we were too busy laughing.

It might sound innocent but for me being out in a group of girls just having a laugh before going back to the hotel and chatting in the room for hours was bordering on normal 27-year-old behaviour. I was very happy with that.

My birthday was a great success the next day. We fitted in as much as we could.

I'm proud of the new goals I achieved on that trip. I walked a little with help, a lot more difficult out in a public area than in the safety of the kitchen with my physiotherapist! I stood for most of our photos. I need far less assistance now when I'm standing, just a gentle support to help me balance. At the cinema, I put my physiotherapy practice to very good use and climbed the steps into the seating area to avoid having to sit in the wheelchair area. It took a while and a lot of effort and energy but it was well worth it. I felt like a normal person, in a normal seat, watching a movie with my friends, instead of being stuck right in front of the screen in my wheelchair. Cinema managers are probably unaware of how uncomfortable and unsuitable some of the wheelchair viewing areas can be!

*

My birthday dinner was a brilliant end to the evening. Mark, our friendly waiter, was even flirting with me when he followed Melissa and Kiera out with the cake and a huge bundle of birthday cards. The cake took my breath away – literally – which is very difficult for someone who has a ventilator doing their breathing! Mam knows how much I adore VW Camper Vans. The cake was an exact replica. It was magnificent. A chandelier of candles blazed on top. The girls gathered around me and sang 'Happy Birthday', the whole restaurant applauding when they'd finished.

Kiera sent Mam a photo to let her see the big grin on my face! She was thrilled her surprise was such a success, and sang 'Happy Birthday' down the phone!

I visualised Mam and Dad with their feet up, enjoying the rarity of having the house to themselves. I hope one day will get to follow their own travel dreams and see the places like Niagra Falls they'd been planning before September 2008.

I looked around the table at my sisters and friends, watching as they tucked into their food and laughed at the silliest jokes.

Not being able to share the meal or cake didn't bother me in the slightest. I didn't feel excluded. I felt lucky. And I still do. I'm lucky to be alive to celebrate another birthday, each party more fun than the year before. I have a great team in my life. With their help anything is possible.

As I waited for them to finish dessert that evening, I thought about where I'd like to go next. I knew I was ready to travel with just nurses and carers – and without family for the first time since 2008. I was ready to spread my wings like the Children of Lir. Killarney came to mind. We could take the ferry from Kilrush and see the sights and maybe do some shopping … the views are amazing there in summer … and maybe the trips after that would be to Belfast or Waterford.

But one of my dreams is to get the supports I need to take a long-haul flight and revisit Florida. I would love to have the holiday I missed out on when I got ill. I'm aware it's a complicated trip to organise, but I'm confident that in time I'll find my way back to International Drive and remember the person I used to be.

The Upside Down House would make the perfect first stop after my journey through an Upside Down Life for the past number of years.

*

It feels so good to have choices; it feels so good to be free.

A Family Trip To Killarney – Annette, Pat, Melissa, Tricia and Kiera

A Night Out With My Sisters – Melissa, Tricia and Kiera

Swimming With Dolphins in Florida – Tricia And Kiera

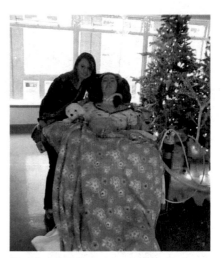

Christmas 2008 – seriously ill in Cork University Hospital

Life goes on in Room Number 6

Personalising Room Number 6

A Family Occasion from Room Number 6

I Am Free – leaving MWRH, 5th Aug 2011

Family time back home

Cinderella stays at the ball

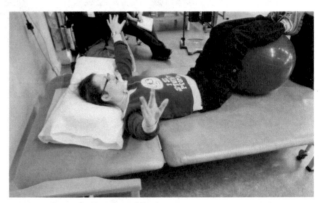

Working hard in Oxford

My first Facebook post since I got ill

Susie presenting me with my settlement cheque and letter of apology

My gift to Susie –
The Children of Lir

'Thank you for lifting me from the water and setting me free'

Presentation to Speech & Language students in University of Limerick

Epilogue

Patricia Ingle
July 2016
Home sweet home
Back to the Future …

Moving to Murroe from Room Number 6 was a gradual settling-in experience, starting with day trips, my eventual overnight on Christmas Eve 2010, and finally moving home in August 2011. It was quite some time before I started to take in my surroundings – apart from a beautiful tree, perfectly shaped, in the field at the top of our road. On one of those first visits home, it caught my eye and seemed to reach out and welcome me.

In recent weeks, after numerous disappointments in securing a plot of land over the last few years, I closed the sale on a field at the top of our road where the beautiful tree, perfectly shaped, sits centre-stage.

New goals, new targets, new beginnings are all waiting for me.

The architect is in discussion with my occupational therapist. They're deciding room sizes, storage space, a kitchen to cater for my improving culinary skills, huge walk-(or drive!)-in-wardrobes, automated controls, a staff room, family rooms, accessibility, privacy, a therapy room, a garden with raised flower beds and so much more.

*

I continue to accomplish what doctors considered impossible and one day in the future, I dream and hope that I will:

communicate in a more satisfactory manner than mouthing or a speaking valve,

work with animals,

eat and drink normally instead of using a PEG,

live independently of my parents,

travel to numerous destinations,

find my Prince Charming, fall in love and honeymoon in Hawaii …

But for now, I'm busy on my iPad planning my new home and researching everything I'll need for the two adorabale Golden Labradors that will be joining our family as soon as I get the keys to the door ...

I Am Free.

Acknowledgments

I would like to thank my parents, Patrick and Annette, and my sisters, Melissa and Kiera, who stayed at my bedside from morning till night for three long years, helping me through a very tough time.

My advocate, Grace Moore, became my independent voice and champion. Sincere thanks, Grace.

I want to thank my legal team, Ernest Cantillon Solicitor, Susie Elliott Solicitor, and Mary Barry Legal Assistant, together with my Barristers, Dermot Gleeson SC, Liam Reidy SC, Oonah McCrann SC, Alan Keating BL and our Engineer, Tony O Keeffe, who worked very hard on my behalf and are responsible for getting me home and giving me this chance to live a normal life.

To my friends who stayed with me through thick and thin, thank you.

I am happy at home now and comfortably moving on.

I Am Free.